WORKING WITH INTERFAITH COUPLES:

A Jewish Perspective

A Guide for Facilitators

Prepared by the
COMMISSION ON REFORM JEWISH OUTREACH
of the Union of American Hebrew Congregations
and the Central Conference of American Rabbis

Spring 1992

Revised Edition of
"TIMES AND SEASONS:
A JEWISH PERSPECTIVE FOR
INTERMARRIED COUPLES"
A Guide for Facilitators

Sources for Guide

The following authors and publications have graciously permitted the Union of American Hebrew Congregations to include their works and reprint them in this Guide:

Charlotte Anker, "We are the Children You Warned our Parents About," from *Moment Magazine,* February 1991.

Rabbi Michael J. Cook, "The Start of the Rift," from *Keeping Posted,* December 1973.

Daniel Goleman, "Family Rituals May Promote Better Emotional Adjustment," from the *New York Times*, March 11, 1992.

Susan Greenberg, "Intermarriage: A Sunday School Teacher's Perspective," 1992.

Annadee Hockman, "Slow Rise: Braiding a Tradition," from *Ms. Magazine,* January/February 1992.

Paula Hyman, "Shoah Guide: Background to the Catastrophe," WNET/Thirteen Publishing Department, Educational Broadcasting Corporation, 1987.

Primo Levi, "Shema," from *Primo Levi: Collected Poems,* translated by Ruth Feldman and Brian Swann, Massachusetts: Faber and Faber, 1988.

Egon Mayer, "All in the Jewish Family," adapted from "Is the Jewish Family Dying?" from *Keeping Posted,* April 1978.

Ronald Osborne, "Marriage of Christians and Jews," from *Plumbline*, Vol. 13, issue 3, September 1985.

Esther Perel, "Ethnocultural Factors in Intermarried Couples," from *Journal of Jewish Communal Service,* Vol. 66, no.3, Kendall Park, New Jersey: Conference of Jewish Communal Service, Spring 1990.

Judy Petsonk, "Crossover," from *Hadassah Magazine,* December 1991.

Adrienne Rich, "XVI," from *Your Native Land, Your Life,* New York: W.W. Norton, 1986.

Rabbi Harold Schulweis, "The Hyphen between the Cross and the Star: Mixed Marriage," from *In God's Mirror: Reflections and Essays,* New Jersey: KTAV Publishing, 1990.

Dr. Ron Wolfson, "Confronting the December Dilemmas," from *The Art of Jewish Living: Hannukah,* Federation of Jewish Men's Clubs and University of Judaism, New York, 1990.

הוּא הָיָה אוֹמֵר: מַרְבֶּה תוֹרָה, מַרְבֶּה חַיִּים; מַרְבֶּה עֵצָה, מַרְבֶּה תְבוּנָה

Hillel: ...the more Torah, the more life;
the more counsel, the more understanding....

This book is dedicated to

Audre and Bernard Rapoport

whose vision of Outreach
has provided counsel and understanding
to so many
and enhanced the life of Torah

Acknowledgements

UAHC-CCAR Commission on Reform Jewish Outreach
Harris Gilbert, *Chairperson*
Rabbi Leslie Gutterman, *Co-Chairperson*
Elizabeth Linkon, *Vice-Chairperson*
Pamela Waechter, *Vice-Chairperson*
Dru Greenwood, *Director and Executive Editor*
Sherri Alper, *Editor*
Rabbi Renni Altman, Director, *Task Force on the Unaffiliated*

Regional Outreach Staff
Canadian Council, Jessie Caryll
Great Lakes Council/Chicago Federation, Mimi Dunitz
Mid-Atlantic Council, Elizabeth Farquhar
Midwest Council, Marsha Luhrs
New Jersey-West Hudson Valley Council, Kathryn Kahn
New York Federation of Reform Synagogues, Ellyn Geller
Northeast Council, Paula Brody
Northeast Lakes Council, Nancy Gad-Harf
Northern California Council/Pacific Northwest Council, Linda Walker
Pacific Southwest Council, Arlene Chernow
Pennsylvania Council/Philadelphia Federation, Linda Steigman
Southeast Council/South Florida Federation, Rabbi Rachel Hertzman
Southwest Council, Deborah Stein

Administrative Staff: Mickey Finn
Typists: Mickey Finn, Meryl Resnicoff
Cover Design: Helayne Friedland

***

We express our gratitude to all those whose insights, skill and knowledge have enriched our work with interfaith couples and whose efforts have made this new version of *Times and Seasons* possible. In particular we wish to thank those whose work appears in these pages:

Debora Weinberg Antonoff
Arlene Sarah Chernow
Mimi Dunitz
Sharon Forman
Nancy Gad-Harf
Sheila Pearl
Esther Perel
Linda Steigman

Special thanks to:

Arlene Chernow, whose insights into couples with children have given depth to many aspects of this guide.

Sharon Forman, Outreach Intern for 1991-92, who helped in myriad ways to prepare the final manuscript and whose talent for "quotations and questions" is evident here.

Lydia Kukoff, whose vision helped shape our work and this book.

Finally, we thank all facilitators—past, present and future—for reaching out, and all couples who have participated in these interfaith programs and who have taught us so much.

1992 Commission on Reform Jewish Outreach

Executive Committee

David Belin
Carol Beyer
Robert Jayson
Janet Kahn
Myra Ostroff

Colleen Rabin
Henry Seiff
Jay Stein
Jerry Tilles
Paul Uhlmann, Jr.

Joan Wachstein

Commission

Patricia Anixter
Gerald Bass
Rabbi Lee Bycel
Harriet Carson
Rabbi Paul Citrin
Dr. Norman Cohen
William Daniel
Rabbi Harry Danziger
Sue Eckstein
Rabbi Kenneth Ehrlich
Dianne Friedman
Rabbi David Gelfand
Toni Golbus
Ernest Grunebaum
Lois Gutman
Susan Halpert
Joan Harf
Rabbi Steven Hart
Ron Herrmann
Isabelle Horne
Richard Imershein
Lee Kahn-Goldfarb
Fern Kamen
Roger Karlebach
Robert W. Kohn

Mary Lynn Kotz
Jack W. Kuhn, Sr.
Marilyn Kustoff
Roslyn Lando
Madeleine Lebedow
Dr. Richard Lewis
Stanley Loeb
Terri Michelson
Rabbi Eugene Mihaly
Rabbi Frank Muller
Theodore H. Pailet
Judy Picus
Beverly Raker
Constance Reiter
Anita Rosenberg
Rabbi Jeffrey Salkin
David W. Sampliner
Beverly Shafran
David Silverman
Cantor Raymond Smolover
Ernest Stern
Ella Stoch
David Toomim
Rabbi David Wolfman

Ex-Officio

Rabbi Howard Bogot
Rabbi Joseph Glaser
Rabbi Walter Jacob
Mel Merians

Rabbi Arthur Nemitoff
Rabbi Alexander Schindler
Rabbi Daniel Syme
Rabbi Mark Winer

WORKING WITH INTERFAITH COUPLES: A GUIDE FOR FACILITATORS

Table of Contents

CHAPTER 1

INTRODUCTION

INTRODUCTION

In 1983, the Commission on Reform Jewish Outreach piloted "Times and Seasons", the first organized effort by the Reform Movement to reach out to unaffiliated intermarried couples in an effort to draw them nearer to Judaism. Since that time, groups for interfaith couples have been sponsored in virtually every region of the country. The format of the groups has varied from the original eight-week model to programs of various lengths. The topics covered have also varied, addressing the needs of participants and reflecting the expertise of individual facilitators.

USING THE FACILITATOR'S GUIDE

This updated manual is based upon the first decade of experience with interfaith couples' programs. It provides information on single session programs, "December Dilemma" programs, programs for couples with children, a regular "drop-in" model, multi-session support groups, and special programs for affiliated couples.

It is recommended that you read through the entire manual and review each model before deciding which alternative will work best for you. You will find material in each section that will be useful to you regardless of which alternative you choose.

DEFINING THE POPULATION

The programs outlined in this manual are intended for use with interfaith couples at any stage of a serious relationship. In some cases, this will mean that couples in the early stages of their relationship will choose to attend in order to determine whether or not they have a future together. Other couples will be engaged to be married, and will choose to attend when issues related to planning their wedding arise. Some participants may be newly married and interested in decision-making in regard to newly-formed families. In all cases, one partner is Jewish, the other is not.

- **Isn't one partner Jewish and the other Christian?**

  Not necessarily. "Christian" is a very specific term, connoting a particular belief system and commitment. Some partners are of other, non-Christian backgrounds (Hindu or Buddhist, for example). Others are "unchurched" — not committed to any particular religious belief system. Interfaith relationships are not necessarily between a Jew and a Christian, but rather between a Jew and someone whose background is not Jewish.

- **Who should attend?**

  All couples are welcome to attend the single-session model, drop-in sessions, or December Dilemma programs. Couples who have not made a decision about their religious orientation or who would like to explore Judaism are appropriate for all programs outlined in this manual, and make up the population for the multi-session model. Couples who have made a decision to raise their children exclusively as Christians (or any religion other than Judaism) are *not* appropriate for the multi-session model, since the focus of that program is the exploration of Judaism as an option. It is important to remember that the drop-in sessions and the multi-session model are intended for couples only: parents, no matter how well-intentioned, should not be permitted to attend.

Parents (or anyone else interested in issues related to intermarriage) are welcome to attend the single session program.

Terminology is often confusing. All programs in this manual are intended for *interfaith couples,* with one Jewish partner and one non-Jewish partner. Couples in which one partner is a Jew-by-Birth and the other is a Jew-by-Choice (a "conversionary" couple) are considered Jewish, and hence are not appropriate for these programs. While they may have issues in common with interfaith couples (family concerns, etc.), they have already chosen a Jewish identity for their family.

- **Are all couples affiliated with a synagogue?**

  Most couples are not affiliated. They may be college students or young people launching their careers. In other instances, depending upon their ages and the affiliation patterns in your community, they may well be temple members.

- **In the interest of fairness, are both the Jewish and non-Jewish perspectives represented?**

  No. Sponsored by the Reform Jewish community, these programs address interfaith relationships from a *Jewish* perspective. Facilitators are not expected to be experts in other religions, nor should clergy from other religions be invited to provide "equal time."

OUR GOALS IN WORKING WITH INTERFAITH COUPLES

The goals for the interfaith couples programming of Reform Jewish Outreach are as follows:

1. To convey the message that the Reform Jewish community welcomes interfaith couples and invites them to make Jewish choices for their families.

2. To provide an opportunity for participants to explore the impact of religious tradition on their lives in order to make informed decisions about their future.

3. To enable participants to consider how they will relate to their families of origin in regard to religious observance and tradition.

4. To include education about Judaism to facilitate participants' decision-making about religious practice and childrearing.

5. To convey the philosophy of the program that states that it is important for children to be raised with a singular religious identity.

Clearly, the extent to which each goal is met will vary depending upon the program chosen and the skills of the facilitator. Note that all goals are related to religious clarity and the decisions that follow. Benefits to couples for participation in the series include the following:

- *Validation and Clarification:* Participants have an opportunity to share common experiences, feelings, and perspectives about one another's cultural and religious differences.

- *The Need for Knowledge:* Participants discover the need for further exploration and study about one another's heritages beyond what can be accomplished during the programs outlined in this guide.

- *Recognition that Conversion is Not an Instant Solution:* Non-Jewish partners have the support of the group and the facilitator in not feeling pressured to convert to Judaism.

- *Exploration of Individual Needs in Decision Making:* The programs often raise questions rather than provide answers. While there is much to be learned by identifying with other participants, couples ultimately realize that they must seek solutions that reflect who they are as individuals within the broader context of family and community.

• *More Effective Communication:* With the assistance of a trained facilitator, participants communicate more effectively about emotionally-laden issues in a safe group setting. The skills learned become a part of their relationship.

• *Reform Judaism as a Positive, Welcoming Option:* Participants become aware of Reform Judaism's open door to interfaith couples and their children, and begin to learn about the richness of Judaism as both a religion and a culture.

A Note About Jewish Choices

Decisions to establish a Jewish home, raise children as Jews, affiliate with a synagogue, or convert to Judaism can be and have often proved to be a long-term result of participation in these programs. However, making such commitments is an individual and extended process. Facilitators can take pride in providing participants with a positive experience of the warmth of Reform Judaism that may serve as a first step.

Because participants frequently come with fear of a "hidden agenda", it is important for the facilitator to acknowledge fears and to stress that the goals of the program do not include conversion. Both Jewish and non-Jewish participants often need to be reassured that there will be no coercion or manipulation. Although conversion is certainly not discouraged (and is of course welcomed by the Jewish community,) it is not a goal of *this* program.

ROLE OF THE FACILITATOR

Regardless of which format you choose, the role of the facilitator for interfaith couples' programs is complex and challenging. While there are no magic formulas to guarantee success, experience during the first decade of programming for this population suggests that the most effective facilitators are the following:

1. Rabbis and Jewish educators with strong group skills.
2. Mental health professionals with excellent group skills, a strong Jewish background, and positive feelings about Judaism.
3. Co-facilitators from the above categories who demonstrate mutual respect and communicate well with each other.

All programming for interfaith couples presented in this manual is:

Supportive	It promotes a safe atmosphere in which couples can begin to address potentially problematic issues.
Educational	Each program strives to teach couples new ways to approach sensitive issues and to create a forum in which couples can learn both from the facilitator(s) and from their peers.
Jewish	These programs have been created by the Commission on Reform Jewish Outreach and are sponsored by synagogues and by the Union of American Hebrew Congregations. They present a Jewish perspective for interfaith couples and provide information about Judaism and the contemporary Reform community. The facilitators are teachers and models of Judaism.

A Word About Co-Facilitation

Co-facilitation provides an opportunity for another perspective, insurance if you're having an "off" night, and doubles the expertise available to your participants. In order for co-leadership to be successful, however, the facilitators must have mutual respect and an open and trusting relationship.

To maximize your effectiveness as co-facilitators, take twenty minutes following each session for feedback and planning. Was the session successful? Did it meet your objectives? Were the concerns of participants adequately addressed? Did the two of you work together effectively? What new ideas were generated for future sessions? What do you need to do to prepare for next time?

The Central Challenge: Owning the Jewish Perspective

The programs described in this manual are not therapy groups. They are **Reform Jewish Outreach** programs. Each program includes significant Jewish content and constant reference to the Jewish community. The groups are conducted under the auspices of a Jewish organization, and are held in a Jewish setting.

What does this mean in terms of the role of the facilitator? Simply put, it means that facilitators are role models, and as such should be positive, knowledgeable Jews. Taking a specifically Jewish perspective is sometimes difficult for mental health professionals who have been trained to be clinically neutral. The following "Do's and Don'ts" will help clarify this issue:

DO

1. Provide background on Outreach and on the contemporary Reform community. (Use "What Is Reform Jewish Outreach?" in Appendix C and "Outreach Statistics At-a-Glance" in Appendix A).

2. Use the phrase "a Jewish perspective for interfaith couples" or similar language in your publicity.

3. Make reference where appropriate to your own Jewish involvement and commitment.

4. Use the setting of the group to advantage: synagogue tours, use of the library, a Jewish art exhibit in the building are all opportunities for familiarization with Judaism.

5. Provide accurate information about Judaism.

6. Be aware of your own feelings about intermarriage. Know your own biases, fears, and convictions before you begin your program.

7. Assure both partners that *all* concerns and viewpoints are encouraged in the group. The group will lose its value if they are inhibited. (This will mean that in your role as facilitator you will need to hear and attend to many statements that are likely to make you feel uncomfortable).

DON'T

1. Don't provide a constant authoritarian perspective. You do not have to respond to *every* statement or *mis*statement.

2. Don't engage in debates. You are not the embodiment of the Jewish establishment whose task it is to show group members the error of their ways.

3. Don't answer direct questions about relationship issues ("Do you think we should go to

her mother's for Christmas?"). Do answer questions related to Jewish content ("Can we have a bris if Mary hasn't converted?").

4. Don't be afraid to say "I don't know, but I'll find out the answer for you."

It is not always easy to find the delicate balance between being an advocate for Judaism and playing the role of the neutral facilitator. Providing a Jewish perspective simply means that you are a Jewish resource and role model. It does not mean that you cannot fully understand couples' dilemmas and empathize with their pain.

A decade of experience with these programs has indicated that facilitators who are mental health professionals need to be especially careful in monitoring the Jewish *content* of these programs. Rabbis and other Jewish professionals are advised to be sure to attend to group *process*. See the Bibliography for suggested readings in both areas.

The role of the facilitator will differ according to which program format you choose. Refer to the descriptions of each format for further information about the facilitator's role.

Resources for the Facilitator

1. If you are a mental health professional, rabbis and other Jewish professionals can be valuable resources for you, and vice versa.

2. Your regional Outreach coordinator has had extensive experience with programs for interfaith couples and knows your local Jewish community and its resources well. She can be a most valuableresource for you. Her name, address and phone number can be found in the back of this guide.

3. Particularly if you are conducting a multi-session group, you may find it valuable to debrief after some of the sessions with another facilitator. For names and addresses of other facilitators in your area, contact your regional Outreach coordinator, listed in Appendix D.

4. If you have never done programming of this kind before, there is another resource that may be especially helpful. "Intermarriage: When Love Meets Tradition" is a videotape of an actual multi-session series for interfaith couples. It will familiarize you with the issues, the dilemmas, and the strategies of couples grappling with the issues that you will encounter in your programming. It may be ordered from: Direct Cinema Ltd., P.O. Box 69799, Los Angeles, CA 90069, or call (213)652-8000.

CHAPTER 2

OVERVIEW OF ISSUES FOR INTERFAITH COUPLES

OVERVIEW OF ISSUES FOR INTERFAITH COUPLES

Each program outlined in this resource is both supportive and educational. While the agendas of all programs include concerns and issues raised by participants, each program provides a unique opportunity to educate participants about Judaism and Jewish perspectives on intermarriage as well. Any program that is exclusively educational in nature will be ineffective if the concerns brought by participants are not addressed. Likewise, a program that addresses only psychological and family issues will inevitably grind to a halt if the context of those issues — Judaism — is not clearly represented.

In general, interfaith couples come to these programs with three levels of concerns:

- *Childrearing* (How will we raise the children? What holidays will we celebrate? Can we have two religions in our home? If we choose one religion, how can the heritage of my partner be incorporated in our home? etc.).

- *Family and Friends* (How can we make everyone happy? If we choose Judaism, what will happen to celebrations with non-Jewish relatives? How can we make a decision for our selves, despite pressure from our parents? etc.).

- *Religious Identity* (What do I believe? What are my emotional ties to the religion of my childhood? What religious values are important to me to preserve? etc.).

While many couples would rank these three categories according to their importance in the order described above, for the purposes of the programs outlined in this manual, the order must be reversed. Couples cannot make clear decisions regarding childrearing until they have clarified feelings about their religious traditions. Similarly, understanding the meaning of religion to them personally will empower participants to deal effectively with family and friends. The order of presentation, then, is: religious identity, family and friends, and childrearing.

In Chapter 4 you will find a variety of group exercises designed to promote discussion and clarification of the three categories outlined above. It is suggested that you take time to read through all of them in order to have a full sense of the complexities involved.

The following are common concerns related to each of the three categories.

RELIGIOUS IDENTITY

Questions often include:

"I'm not a 'religious' person. But my kids just have to be Jewish."

"I've never been a religious person. I doubt having children will change me."

"I could see not having my religion be the main one in our home. But who will I be? I stand to lose a lot."

"I've never been a very active Jew. I don't think I have the right to say I want our home to be Jewish."

"I don't think organized religion of any kind is necessary. Religions just divide people. We believe the same things anyway."

"I think of myself as a spiritual person, not a religious person. I'm not sure 'community' really matters to me."

"Should we talk about conversion?"

Many couples who attend these programs have never had the opportunity to consider fully their feelings and ties to their religious tradition. It is difficult for most of us to think clearly about religious feelings. The issue often arises most urgently during crisis or at specific points in the life cycle — a marriage, a death, etc., and few of us have the luxury of a "safe," supportive environment in which to discuss feelings honestly. In addition, feelings about religious tradition are inseparable, for the most part, from relationships with families and our childhood memories.

Like young adults in general, many interfaith couples are not clear about the personal meaning of religion. What holidays *are* important to them? What religious values do they hope to pass on to their children? What early memories are special? How has their religion helped them to cope with a problem in the past?

It is important for the facilitator to normalize the uncertainty of participants. Feelings about religion are complex, and no one is expected to be fully clear. An interfaith relationship, however, *demands* clarity and honesty from both partners, and your program will be successful only if participants have an opportunity to consider their religious values and share them with their partner and the group.

The educational component of these programs is especially important in relation to this category. Facilitators should be prepared to provide information about the following:

- Why religion? (See Quotations and Questions for Discussion, Chapter 5).
- The meaning of Jesus to both Jews and Christians

  (see "Judaism and Christianity: The Parting of the Ways" in Appendix A).
- The "asymmetry" of Judaism and Christianity (see "Marriage of Christians and Jews," Appendix A).
- The Holocaust and its impact on the Jewish psyche (see Quotations and Questions for Discussion, Chapter 5).
- The meaning of Israel to the Jewish people (see Quotations and Questions for Discussion, Chapter 5).
- The Reform Movement's position on intermarriage and related officiation issues (see Appendix A and "The Hyphen Between the Cross and the Star," Chapter 5).
- Reform Jewish Outreach (see Appendix C).

FAMILY AND FRIENDS

Here are some common concerns:

"How do we talk to our families about religion? It's such a touchy issue."

"It seems we're encountering a lot of prejudice from Jews. I think there's a real desire to break us up."

"How can we make a decision that is just ours? We're getting a lot of pressure from both sides."

"What should we do about the holidays? My family has always been together."

"My family is really upset. It makes me feel like I've deliberately hurt them."

"We're in love. We'll work it out, if people will just give us a break."

"I don't know if we'll affiliate anywhere. Our 'community' is our friends. We don't need anyone telling us they disapprove of   how we're living our lives."

"Where will we be in ten years? I keep wondering...."

Experience has shown that much discussion in programs for interfaith couples is devoted to the pressures created by families and friends. Many couples express the desire to find a solution to their dilemma that will make everyone happy (having both a rabbi and a priest officiate at the wedding is an example). It is important for the facilitator not to accept participants' solutions at face value. Questions such as "Will co-officiation really be acceptable to your family?" will encourage participants to think critically. It is often useful, as well, to ask one partner about the *other's* family: "Is Linda right about what her mother really wants?" etc.

Facilitators should stress that family attitudes and behaviors can change over time. Participants should be encouraged to build strong relationships with families and friends, regardless of which religious option is chosen ultimately.

It is important that facilitators create a "safe" environment in the group which will enable the non-Jewish partner to feel comfortable raising concerns. Discussion sometimes focuses on the reactivity of the Jewish family to intermarriage. Be sure that all participants have the opportunity to talk about their family concerns.

Educational opportunities related to this topic include:

- an explanation of the Jewish attitude toward family and the concept of *l'dor v'dor* (see "All in the ^Jewish Family," in Appendix A).

- intermarriage in the context of family and friends (see "Intermarriage in Context" in Appendix A).

CHILDREARING

Questions that will be raised in relation to this topic include:

"Should we expose our children to both religions and let them choose when they are old enough?"

"Should we practice no religion?"

"What holidays should we celebrate in our home and why?"

"If we choose one religion, won't one partner 'lose?'"

"What proof is there that two religions in the home are damaging to children?"

"I know people from mixed marriages and they turned out just fine."

"I can't even think of religion and children now. Neither one is a part of my life."

"How should we raise the children?"

"Will we do a bris or baptism? What do they mean?"

"The rabbi and the priest both want guarantees about which religion we'll choose for our children before they'll agree to marry us. It feels like religious coercion."

"Will our feelings change later, when we really do have children?"

"How do you prevent children from being confused if the parents are different religions?"

Many couples assume that if they can come to a decision regarding how to raise the children, they will have accomplished all they need. Again, it is important to avoid extended discussions of childrearing until, in the facilitator's view, the issues of religious identity and family and friends have been addressed fully. Note that this does not mean that there will always be a linear progression from religious identity to family and friends to childrearing. Often the topics will overlap. The skilled facilitator, however, will not permit participants to focus on "solutions" until they are amply grounded in both self-awareness and an understanding of the related Jewish issues.

Participants must be encouraged to voice their wishes for their children and their strategies for dealing with the challenges ahead. Couples will often resist choosing one religious tradition and may come up with a number of strategies, including: raising children equally in both religious traditions and allowing them to choose; raising a boy in the father's religion and the girl in the mother's; raising the first child in one religion, the second in the other, etc.

Facilitators can be helpful in posing the following questions:

- Is it possible to be simultaneously included in and excluded from the Jewish people?
- Will children be accepted by peers and families if they are "both?"
- Is it possible to be both Jewish and Christian?
- Are couples' strategies reflective of what's best for the children or easiest for the parents?
- How old is "old enough" to choose between mother and father?

  Jewish educational issues related to this category include:

- Patrilineal descent and who is a Jew (see Appendix A).
- Information on the Jewish life cycle and customs (see Bibliography).
- Information on holidays, the December Dilemma, etc. (see December Dilemma articles in Chapter 5 and Bibliography).
- Choosing one religion (See "Crossover", "Mixed Marriage Soup", "Adult Children of Intermarriage Speak," and "Intermarriage: A Sunday School Teacher's Perspective" in Chapter 5).

As a facilitator, you will find that no group is like the last. Couples' perspectives, coping strategies, agendas, and flexibility will vary from group to group.

A Word About the Search for a Perfect Answer

Experience has shown that some couples will attend programs in a search for a solution in which neither of them has to give up anything. While these couples discuss concerns related to religious identity, family and friends, and childrearing, they are struggling with the reality that they are in a difficult situation for which there is no simple solution.

For many couples this struggle is the first step toward being ready to begin a dialogue, but it is a step often fraught with disappointment, sadness, frustration, and anger. As part of the process, the facilitator must constantly give couples support for participating in the program, for facing difficult issues, and for dealing with the problems now instead of later.

In their search for solutions, couples have been known to say:

"Surely in a city as large as Los Angeles, there must be a church or temple that offers both perspectives." (Judaism and Christianity).

"We thought that we would split it down the middle like everything else."

"We are looking for a class that will teach us how to do both."

Often couples who are in the process of this search think that if they talk to enough people, read the right books or just keep looking, they will find the magic solution that has eluded them thus far. It is helpful to enable them to distinguish between the search that they have been pursuing and the kind of growth and hope that can come from facing the issues openly and honestly.

CHAPTER 3

PROGRAM MODELS

I. The Single Session Model

The single-session program is the model of choice for a setting in which no previous programming has been done for interfaith couples or when a recruiting model for longer, on-going programs for couples is appropriate. It provides a vehicle for raising relevant issues in the congregation or the community, requires no screening or commitment to an on-going group, and is relatively simple to plan.

What can one evening accomplish? It can present an overview of the issues for consideration; it can educate participants (and, through careful publicity, the larger community) about Reform Judaism and its commitment to Outreach; it can introduce those present to rabbinic and Outreach expertise and caring; it can encourage both interfaith couples and Jewish parents of interfaith couples to attend other programs designed to address their needs further.

For ideas on recruiting and publicity, refer to Chapter 6 of this manual.

The Format

The total time needed for the program will depend on your own agenda and the number of participants. Generally, an hour and a half to two hours is sufficient.

The program begins with an introduction by the facilitator(s) which includes the following:

1. An introduction of the facilitator, including his/her background and credentials for presenting the program.
2. Acknowledgement and/or thanks to the sponsor or host of the program.
3. A brief review of the content of the program, including acknowledgement that in a single-session program it will not be possible to address all the individual concerns of those attending.
4. A statement of reassurance that there are resources for addressing the needs of participants within the Reform Jewish community.

Depending on the number of people attending, continue by asking participants to introduce themselves to one another and to make a brief statement about why they came. This will help participants to feel comfortable and will provide the facilitator with important information. However this is not recommended for groups larger than sixteen since it takes too much time from the program itself.

The Agenda

The programmatic objective of the single-session model is to present an overview of the issues for interfaith couples. The model will enable anyone who attends to leave with the following:

1. A basic understanding of why intermarriage is of such concern to the Jewish community.
2. Knowledge of Reform Jewish Outreach and its impact on a changing community.
3. A clearer sense of the central concerns of interfaith couples in relation to their religious traditions, their families, and the Jewish community.
4. Information about resources available to them for further explanation and exploration.

It is recommended that the facilitator deliver a brief "mini-lecture" encompassing the above information. (For specific help with content, see Chapter 2 and Appendices A, B and C.) If the program is co-facilitated by a rabbi and a group worker, the above issues can be divided into two brief presentations, depending on the expertise and interest of each. Regardless of whether there are one or two facilitators, the formal presentation should be kept relatively brief (under 20 minutes is recommended).

Ample time should be left for questions and answers and discussion. Sometimes couples and parents attend these sessions wanting their individual views to be vindicated or to air grievances. Remember that this is primarily an information session, and be sure to adhere to the "Do's and Don'ts" for facilitators in Chapter 1. Your program will be most successful if you keep the tone general and informational in nature so that the needs of the larger group are met.

In closing your single-session program, it is important to let participants know where to turn next. Flyers for upcoming interfaith couples groups and parents of interfaith couples groups, the name and telephone number of the Outreach coordinator in your area, and information about how to reach the facilitator(s) are all important. Consider providing a handout for participants to take home at the end of the program. Offering participants something to read and talk about will give your program extra mileage even after it is over. Consider adding "For further information about Outreach or programming for interfaith couples, contact (name and telephone number of facilitators or regional Outreach coordinator)" on the last page of anything you hand out. For ideas regarding possible handouts, consult Chapter 5 of this manual.

Refreshments are an important addition to any program. They will set a warm, relaxing tone and encourage participants to interact informally. You may choose to serve simple refreshments at the beginning or at the conclusion of your program.

II. A December Dilemma Program

For nearly all interfaith couples, December is the time of year when making decisions about religious traditions becomes most problematic. A season traditionally associated with warmth, joy, and belonging suddenly becomes a metaphor for compromise and sacrifice. Memories of family celebrations and childhood combine to make decision-making in the present even more complex.

Many couples believe that if only they can solve the "December Dilemma," their future will be secure. Nearly all programming for interfaith couples (especially programs just before or during the holiday season) includes some aspect of this issue. Facilitators may choose to do a separate single-session program called "The December Dilemma" or may incorporate elements discussed in this section into an on-going group such as a synagogue-based or a multi-session support group.

The goal of December Dilemma workshops is to enable couples to clarify and articulate their feelings about the holidays in order to help them begin to consider the impact of decision-making. This is no simple task, since many couples would rather not deal with potentially problematic issues in order to keep peace in their relationship. It is not realistic to assume that couples will come away from such an evening with mutually agreed upon solutions to their "dilemma." In fact, they will probably leave with a heightened sense of the complexity of the issues at hand. It is, therefore, especially important to provide participants with resources for follow-up: the name and phone number of an Outreach coordinator or rabbi who can help, other programs such as the multi-session support group, a synagogue group that meets on a regular basis, etc.

> Note: A December Dilemma workshop is not a "Chanukah How To" program. Be sure you are clear in your publicity so that participants will not be mistaken about the agenda. You and your group may choose to schedule a "Chanukah How To" session separately.

You may choose one of several formats for this program:

1. A mini-lecture by the facilitator, followed by discussion. Breaking into small groups may help participants talk about their own situations in response to the remarks of the facilitator.

2. It is often easier for participants to begin talking about someone else's dilemma rather than their own. It's less risky, less self-disclosing, and is a useful format for groups that have not had a chance to develop cohesion. Choosing an exercise or scenario from Chapter 4 as a starting point will inevitably lead to the discussion of personal issues.

With Chanukah and Christmas as symbols for Judaism and Christianity, the questions couples ask take on a special urgency: they are looking for answers that will make the holidays joyous and everyone happy. Typical questions include:

• Should we celebrate both holidays in our home or just one?

• Should we have a Christmas tree, especially if it makes the Jewish partner uncomfortable?

• Should we decide not to celebrate either holiday, since one of us will be uncomfortable no matter how hard we try?

• How can we deal with our parents' expectations at this time of year?

• How will our decisions affect our children?

There are two key elements that are crucial for the facilitator to understand in order for this program to be successful:

FROM THE JEWISH PARTNER'S PERSPECTIVE, Christmas may symbolize oppressive commercialism and the persecution of the Jewish people. It serves as a powerful reminder that Jews are not members of the majority culture. Christmas trees are often seen as symbols of a Christian household. Chanukah may be viewed in a variety of ways: as a holiday with an especially relevant message about being a minority, as a holiday whose observance is joyous and beautiful in its own right, or as a means of "compensating" for the cultural preoccupation with Christmas.

FROM THE NON-JEWISH PARTNER'S PERSPECTIVE, Christmas may be a central religious holiday. In any case, it is symbolic of warmth and family unity. Discord at this time of year is especially upsetting. Childhood Christmas memories are powerful and the need to be with family may become especially pressing. Most non-Jews know very little about Chanukah and its meaning.

Facilitators must be aware of these issues in order to help participants understand each other's complex reactions to the holiday season and the power of its symbols.

OPTION I: Lecture and Discussion

To prepare your lecture, which should be no longer that 15 minutes, refer to Chapter 5, December Dilemma Materials, for ideas.

The following points are especially important to include:

1. The feelings of many Jews at Christmas time are a reflection of an especially strong annual reminder that Jews are a minority and, especially at Christmas, do not share in mainstream culture. Participants should be reminded that the story of Chanukah is a story about being different.

2. There is a tendency to believe in "the ideal family" at holiday time. All around us the media is focused on how ideal families celebrate the holidays. Remember that television doesn't show the argument that preceded the warm fireplace scene and doesn't let you know that one of those adorable children is planning to run away later that evening! (This is a wonderful opportunity for the facilitator to inject humor and lighten the mood).

3. There is a strong pull back toward families of origin for the holidays. The real dilemma may be: "How can we be with both our families and make decisions that will make everyone happy?"

4. Decision-making in the present is tied to memories of holidays past. Those memories remain a part of who we are, no matter what decisions we make.

5. Despite the secularization of Christmas, Christmas symbols are Christian symbols. Briefly talk about the meaning of a tree, a wreath, etc.

6. Acknowledge that the dilemma is difficult when there are (or will be) children involved. Participants must first clarify what the holidays mean to them before considering what values, traditions, and celebrations they want to pass on to their children.

After the facilitator has finished, the following discussion questions may open up the topic. Remember that small groups may encourage participants to be more open.

- What aspects of Christmas and Chanukah are most important to you? Give examples.

- How do you feel during the month of December? Try to identify the cause of these feelings.

- Think of one thing that you haven't shared with your partner about your feelings about the holidays. Why haven't you talked about it? Can you talk about it tonight? Why/Why not?

- How does it feel to be part of a minority group?

- Is Christmas a religious holiday or has it become a national holiday? Can't all Americans, regardless of background, join in the celebration?

- Should Jewish children sing Christmas carols?

- What are your family's holiday traditions? Which ones do you currently share?

- How might parents respond to children's desire to celebrate Christmas and to bring objects related to Christmas into the home? What is the impact on Jewish children of having a tree and receiving Christmas gifts?

OPTION II: Exercises and Discussion

Many facilitators have found that the easiest format for December Dilemma programming is to use an exercise as a discussion starter. Participants will quickly move from the exercise or scenario at hand to a discussion of their own concerns.

The following exercises in Chapter 4 are especially appropriate for this program:

- The Holiday Dinner Table
- The Tree Scenario
- Choosing Family Symbols
- Exploring and Negotiating Differences

Finally, at the close of any December Dilemma program it is important to congratulate participants for their willingness to confront difficult issues. While there are no quick and easy answers, note that it is precisely through discussions such as this that solutions may come. In closing, let participants know about resources available to them and distribute handouts. (See December Dilemma Materials in Chapter 5.)

III. The Drop-In Model

The Drop-In Model does not require an on-going commitment from couples. It is most effectively co-facilitated by a rabbi and a knowledgeable group leader; and each session is topic oriented. It may be used either in a stable community — a suburban area or small city, for example, where membership is relatively consistent — or in a more transient setting, perhaps an urban environment where couples are apt to be present for a time because of jobs or college before moving on. Either way, participants are free to attend for a period of time and to return to the group if the need arises.

Consistency

Perhaps the most important ingredient for success of the Drop-In Model is consistency. If maximum participation is to be encouraged, couples must know that the group will take place on a monthly basis at a familiar place with the same facilitators. While these "givens" are consistent, group composition may or may not be. The format enables couples to attend on an as-needed basis.

Because the group is open-ended in nature, publicity becomes an on-going challenge. Press releases and flyers with a consistent and distinctive logo should be distributed on a regular basis to encourage new participants to attend and to remind couples who have attended in the past of the group's existence. Regular publicity also serves to highlight new topics for discussion and keeps Outreach in the news.

Setting and Timing

The Drop-In Center should be a place where interfaith couples can go on a regular basis to talk about issues that concern them with others who will understand. Think carefully in choosing the location of your sessions. The groups are best sponsored by a synagogue in order to promote a level of comfort and positive associations with Reform Judaism. Choose a room that will be consistently available: the Temple library, the rabbi's study, or a youth lounge. Be certain that you will have regular access, privacy, and comfortable furniture.

It is recommended that you plan monthly meetings of an hour and a half to two hours. If your program is to be successful on a long-term basis, it is crucial that you choose a time when couples will be available to attend regularly. The following times have worked well in various settings: a weekday evening (one group called itself "First Wednesdays" because it met on the first Wednesday of each month); a Sunday morning or Sunday evening with baby-sitting provided; a weekday lunch or 5:30 group, planned around work schedules. For best results, let your group decide. Providing coffee and a snack will help participants to feel welcomed and comfortable.

The Topics

The topic for each session is a collaborative decision. Often the facilitator will have a sense of what will be an enticing offering – "The December Dilemma" in late fall or a session devoted to extended family concerns as wedding season approaches, for example. More often than not, the couples themselves will generate ideas to be addressed. Suggested topics may include any of the following:

- The December Dilemma
- When There Are Children
- Yours, Mine, and Ours: Dealing With Families
- Stereotypes: Jewish and Gentile
- When a Jew and a Christian Marry
- Interfaith Relationships: Are Our Differences Only Religious?
- The High Holy Days: Conflicts and Opportunities
- The Hows and Whys of Jewish Weddings
- The Passover Seder and the Last Supper
- Talking About God
- Reconsidering Our Pasts: Religion in Context
- Jesus: Jewish and Christian Perspectives
- Religious Identity Development and Children

Consider other creative possibilities as well: Show a videotape of the "thirtysomething" episode on the bris (check with your regional Outreach coordinator if you can't locate a copy) and follow it with discussion, popcorn, and soda. Invite a panel of interfaith couples to reflect on their own decision-making processes and lead a discussion. The possibilities are endless.

Regardless of what topic or format you choose, be sure that you are prepared with brief opening remarks or a brief "mini-lecture" about the topic at hand. Remember that couples attend because they want to talk, and handouts are always welcome.

IV. Synagogue Groups

Non-affiliated vs. Affiliated Groups: Understanding the Differences

Experience has shown that synagogue groups made up of affiliated couples are somewhat different in perspective and content from groups comprised of couples who are not affiliated with a synagogue. Affiliated groups tend to be composed of couples who are already intermarried, often with children. Some are dealing with issues related to second marriages and newly-blended families. Unaffiliated groups, on the other hand, are usually made up of couples considering marriage, newly engaged, or recently married. While the two groups express similar concerns, it is important for the facilitator to understand the differences in focus.

The theme of an unaffiliated group is decision-making: "Can we...?" "What will it mean if...?" Members of this group are often just beginning to grapple with the fact that they have a problem in what is seen otherwise as a perfect relationship. Participants often note that they can talk about anything *except* religion. They are beginning to be aware that although they feel they are fine by themselves, they anticipate that problems will appear when they have children. They often do not understand the depth of their feelings about their religion and have difficulty understanding those of their partner. Discussion of children and their needs is intellectual and theoretical. Most often, couples are hoping for a resolution that will not cause either partner to give up anything. They may hope that a solution to their dilemma exists that will make both families happy and their own problems insignificant.

One facilitator who has worked with numerous affiliated groups reported that affiliated couples often begin their discussion with a huge sigh, a loving smile to their partner, and the statement, "This is more difficult than we had imagined...." Couples in these groups are most often concerned with the day-to-day realities of being intermarried: negotiating religious involvement, talking with their children and parents, and creating a balance between individual needs and family unity. Facilitators should not assume that the fact that participants have joined a temple means that they have necessarily processed or resolved their religious conflicts or that they practice Judaism exclusively in their home.

Synagogue Groups

Synagogue groups usually follow one of the following program models:

- Topic-centered discussions
- Monthly discussion groups
- Shorter versions of the multi-session model

Topic-Centered Discussions

Topic-centered discussions are usually a safe and comfortable way to introduce the concept of programming for interfaith couples to a congregation. The topics and dates are usually chosen by the temple's Outreach committee and rabbi. Most often, the rabbi leads the discussions and facilitates the programs, while the committee or temple staff takes responsibility for the logistics: publicity, refreshments, arranging a meeting place, etc.

The number of sessions offered during the year varies from three to ten. The format of each evening is generally a combination of "gentle teaching" and discussion. The opening presentation by the rabbi or facilitator usually lasts about twenty minutes. The goals of the presentation are the following:

1. To enable participants to gain insight into Jewish practice, theology, and perspectives on various issues.

2. To communicate to participants that the temple values both partners and understands their struggles.

3. To create a safe atmosphere in which no question is too simple.

4. To enable partners to explore differences in their religious backgrounds and upbringing.

Typical topics for a congregation's first year of topic-centered discussion groups may include:

- Welcome to the High Holy Days

- The December Dilemma

- A Passover Workshop

Topics to be addressed later in the series or during a subsequent year of programming may include:

- Jewish Theology: Concepts of God

- Jewish Lifecycle Events

- Israel

- Jewish Peoplehood

- Synagogue Geography: A Hands-on Exploration of the Bimah

This kind of programming is non-threatening since it is externally focused. Couples do not expect to come to talk about their own concerns, but rather to learn about Judaism. They should be encouraged to attend together, so that both partners have the same basic information to facilitate their decision-making. (A divorced, non-Jewish parent raising the children as Jews is the exception). The facilitator should be sensitive to the fact that one partner who attends alone repeatedly may be in need of extra support.

It is advisable to plan for a year at a time. Consider printing a flyer that lists all discussion groups and information about Outreach. Examples may be found in Chapter 6. Be sure to include a brief statement or letter of welcome from the rabbi and/or congregational president. Each session should again be publicized in the temple bulletin. Once you have developed a core mailing list, it may be advisable to send reminders prior to each session.

Monthly Discussion Groups

Monthly discussion groups differ from the topic-centered program in that they are more personally focused, providing more of an opportunity for introspection than the teaching model outlined above. Facilitated by a rabbi or mental health professional with strong Jewish knowledge, they usually include topics like the following:

- Holidays: Yours, Mine and Ours?

- Intermarriage as a Family Affair: Talking with Our Parents

- Intermarriage and Children

The group decides the agenda for the next session at the end of each program. Monthly announcements in the temple bulletin and/or reminders sent out to the core mailing list are important in keeping the group viable. The rabbi or temple administrator should be asked periodically for additional names for the mailing list. As with all programs, it is recommended that participants sit in a circle to encourage discussion and interaction.

It is important for monthly groups to meet regularly at the same time (the first Monday night of each month at 7:30 for example). Couples may attend regularly or periodically.

> • *Note:* In many congregations, the lines between the topic-centered discussion model and the monthly discussion groups will be blurred. It is important to remember that nothing is written in stone, and that each congregations's program will be different. Variations may include using the topic-centered discussions as a magnet for attracting a core of couples to the monthly program or adapting the Multi-Session Model to a monthly discussion group format. Consider adapting any of the models to sub-groups within your congregation: nursery school parents, religious school parents, as a Sisterhood/Mens' Club series, etc.

In whatever format you use, remember that these groups are designed to meet specific needs that couples have. The groups strive to address issues pertinent to their interfaith relationship and to welcome them to explore Judaism for their family. The programs are *not* intended to separate interfaith couples from the congregation, and, therefore, should not devolve into independent, on-going groups or *havurot*.

V. Intermarried Couples With Children

Because childrearing is often the primary concern of intermarried couples, couples with children may attend a program on childrearing more readily than they will attend other programs. Groups of intermarried couples with children have been very successful in some regions.

Couples who attend these programs may be affiliated with a synagogue or active in other ways in the Jewish community. They have (or are soon expecting) children. The facilitator should not assume that they practice Judaism in their home or that they have made a decision to raise their children exclusively as Jews. Participants come from a wide variety of backgrounds. Some are well-integrated in their synagogues and attend to talk about day-to-day matters with other intermarried families. Others are just beginning to realize that they need to deal more directly with the religious issues that exist in their families. Some are in conflict with a spouse or extended family member. It is critical for other than a single-session program that the facilitator have a sense of where on the spectrum the individuals in the group fall.

A program for interfaith couples with children can be adapted easily from other programs in this resource. It begins with opportunities for parents to clarify their own feelings about their religious background, the role of religion in their lives, and their relationship with their families before moving on to childrearing issues. Like the other programs, it also provides an opportunity for participants to develop further understanding in regard to their partner's newly-clarified feelings about religion. (Be sure to read the description of the Multi-Session Model which follows for a description of this process). The final agenda — childrearing and communication with children about religion — focuses specifically on enabling participants more easily to discuss religion with one another and with their children, and to make realistic decisions about religion in the home.

Programs for intermarried couples with children have been successful in the following formats:

- a one-day conference/retreat open to the community with child-care provided
- an adaptation of the multi-session model
- a single-session program for synagogue-affiliated participants held during religious school

Two titles to consider are: "Parenting and Religion: Answering Our Children's Questions" and "The Intermarried Family: Ourselves, Our Spouses, Our Children."

The following areas are of special importance in programming for interfaith couples with children.

Religious Identity

• In the material that has been written by adult children of intermarried parents, two issues emerge:

1. Both as children and even now as adults, children of interfaith couples want to know

who they are religiously. They describe the experience of participating in two religions and feeling as if they belonged to neither.

2. The other concern often voiced has to do with feelings of loyalty and betrayal of parents. "How will my mother feel if I choose to be...?" or "I would like to consider myself..., but it would hurt my father."

While the writers clearly are speaking of their own experience, they raise important issues. The facilitator should raise these issues and ask participants for reactions. Do they see these as pitfalls for their own families? How will they avoid them?

Refer to the Multi-Session Model for an in-depth discussion of this issue. You may find additional material in *The Intermarriage Handbook* and *Mixed Blessings* (see Bibliography in Appendix B.) "Adult Children of Intermarriage Speak: Questions for Discussion" (Chapter 5) can be used to begin discussion.

Extended Families

Holidays and relationships with family members from both sides seem to be especially problematic for many intermarried families. Participants will be anxious to discuss their own holiday dilemmas and how they have handled them. The goals of decision-making are relatively simple:

1. To insure that participants have carefully considered their feelings about religion and their own religious identity. (This is a long and complex process, and will not be achieved in a single-session program).

2. To enable participants to find ways to insure that their children love and respect both sides of the extended family.

3. To help couples find ways of communicating clearly about religion with both their children and their parents.

Decision-making in relation to holiday celebrations can be especially difficult. The facilitator can help bring structure to the way in which a family deals with holidays by pointing out:

• The difference between celebrating a holiday in your home and helping friends and family celebrate their holiday.

• The benefit of being as clear as possible about decisions regarding religion in the home.

• The need to communicate clearly those decisions and expectations to the extended family.

• The importance of sharing holidays to whatever extent possible with both families.

• The fact that a set of decisions made by one couple may not be appropriate for another.

Family members vary greatly in their reactions to intermarriage. Experiences range from parents being fully supportive of a couple's decisions, to making errors unintentionally, to willfully telling grandchildren things that go against the couple's wishes.

Children's Questions

Children have been described as little scientists, asking the same questions over and over again. The "experiment" is to see if the answer to a question will be the same each time.

How will parents respond to questions that children ask repeatedly? They may think that the child is testing their patience; they may think that the child is hoping for another answer; they may become concerned about his/her memory. The child, in fact, is looking for a sense of security. (If I ask my Mom the color of the sky, I want to know that it will always be blue).

It is not always easy to know what a child needs on any particular day. While thinking about children's questions or comments, it is important for parents to consider the *context* of the questions by understanding the following issues:

- How old is the child? Every parent knows the example of a child asking "Where did I come from?" The parent gets out the books on reproduction with all of the drawings, etc. and finally realizes that the child merely wanted to know which city the family lived in when he/she was born.

- What do you think the child is looking for? Information? Help in sorting out a feeling? Time to talk to you?

- Is the question stemming from an incident that might be of special interest to the child like a lesson that captured his/her imagination, or from a comment of a teacher, friend or relative that was disturbing?

- What does the question or comment trigger for the parent? Would the parent react differently if the subject matter were different?

With these thoughts in mind, ask participants to consider some of the kinds of questions children ask, especially as they relate to religious identity:

"I have blond hair; Daddy has blond hair. Why do you have brown hair, Mommy?"

What is the child asking? What are his/her concerns? How would you deal with the issues of difference that he/she is raising?

Ask participants to reconsider the same kind of question, this time with specific Jewish content:

"How come Mommy is Jewish and I'm Jewish, but Daddy isn't?"

Does this kind of question feel different to a parent? Why? What is comfortable or uncomfortable about it? What is this child trying to figure out?

These two examples will bring forward a wide variety of situations and stories from parents. Ask what questions they have had from their children that they didn't know how to answer. The stories will range from children's questions about God to Easter baskets. The goal is to reassure parents that they can handle their children's questions about religious identity and to demonstrate through the group ways of responding. Parents often fear the questions that will trigger their own unresolved issues. Support their desire to encourage their children to talk to them directly, even if the discussions may be somewhat uncomfortable.

Asking parents to consider the following questions will provide them with the basic tools they need to begin to respond appropriately and to be effective parents.

- What is the child *really* asking?
- What does the child need?
- Why does this question make me uncomfortable?
- What do I need to do to resolve this issue for myself?

A final note to facilitators:

It is especially easy to fall into the trap of focusing on childrearing issues *before* considering religious identity and relationships with families of origin when the group is focused on children. Beware of providing band-aid solutions before the underlying issues are addressed.

VI. The Multi-Session Model

The multi-session model is a support/education format which provides couples with an opportunity to consider issues related to intermarriage in depth and over time with others who share similar concerns. Some brief questions and answers will help to explain the model:

Why is it called a "support/education" model?

The groups have two important components. They offer support by enabling interfaith couples to meet with others who share a common experience and who may have similar concerns. Through creating a relaxed and comfortable atmosphere, the facilitator sets the stage for productive problem solving, reduced isolation, and potential growth. Yet while the supportive component is crucial to a successful group, education is equally important. Sponsored by the Reform Jewish community, these groups offer opportunities for education at every juncture. Couples want information about Judaism, especially in relation to other religions, and about Jewish attitudes towards intermarriage. It is often the knowledge gained from participation in such groups that enables couples to make productive decisions regarding their religious lives.

How are these groups different from the Introduction to Judaism classes offered by the Union of American Hebrew Congregations and Reform congregations?

The primary goal of the Introduction to Judaism classes is to provide participants with a broad, basic understanding of Judaism and Jewish history and culture. The interfaith couples groups, on the other hand, focus primarily on the couples' decisions about the role of religion in their lives. This process is informed by educational issues that arise within the context of the group. Introduction to Judaism classes have an educational agenda, with a clearly developed curriculum to be covered. While couples' groups also have an educational component, the experience is that of a discussion group which often has a personal and family focus.

What is the recommended size of couples groups?

Six to eight couples is ideal. It is recommended that you not begin a group with fewer than five couples.

What is the format?

The group meets weekly for six to eight weeks. Experience has shown that it may be difficult to get couples to commit themselves to attend an eight-week group. Groups originally planned for six sessions often opt to extend to eight. Eight sessions are recommended in order to accomplish the goals outlined here and to extend the experience over time. The sessions are two hours each. Regardless of the length of the series, the conclusion of the group is followed by a Shabbat dinner, which all participants and the facilitator(s) plan and attend together. The Shabbat dinner provides a warm Jewish experience and the opportunity to assess the group experience from the distance of a few weeks.

Who attends these groups?

Interfaith couples (not necessarily intermarried couples) ranging in age from their mid-twenties to late thirties generally make up the population of the groups. Their religious backgrounds and current levels of religious commitment vary greatly. Remember that

PROGRAM MODELS • 37

these groups are for interfaith couples, not conversionary couples (in which one partner has already converted to Judaism). Although there may be some similar concerns, in a conversionary couple both partners are Jews.

Do the groups meet in the couples' homes?

The groups meet in synagogues for several reasons. The facilitator has no control over the environment in members' homes. Crying babies and ringing telephones will inevitably impede group process. Meeting in a temple helps couples to become comfortable with the building and its symbols, and becomes a metaphor for the willingness of the Reform community to reach out to interfaith couples. Be sure to choose a location in the synagogue where the group will have privacy and be free from interruptions. A youth lounge or library often works well if there is comfortable furniture available. Try to choose a time when other activities will be taking place and the synagogue seems attractively busy.

A Word About Titles

"Times and Seasons" has been the name most commonly used for the multi-session model, and the materials (flyers, forms, etc.) that you will find in Chapter 6 on logistics use that title. Feedback from many facilitators has indicated that that particular title is not clear enough. Potential participants may not know at a quick glance that these groups are for them. You might consider another name for your group that is more specific:

"Opening Doors: A Liberal Jewish Perspective on Intermarriage" or "The Interfaith Couples Connection: A Jewish Perspective."

If you have an established program that is well known in your community, however, stick with your current title.

Screening

The multi-session model requires that you screen participants beforehand to insure that they are appropriate candidates for your group. Ultimately, careful screening will make your job as facilitator much easier and the group experience most productive for participants.

Screening has a number of purposes:

1. To determine that couples are appropriate for the group. (Interfaith couples with or without children who will be, in your best judgment, receptive to the experience of the group).
2. To determine that both partners are interested in attending and are willing to commit themselves to all of the sessions. (Partners are not permitted to attend alone except in the case of an unforeseen emergency).
3. To clarify couples' expectations and answer questions about the purpose and goals of the group.
4. To socialize participants to the group experience. (Explaining group format, size, what to expect, etc.).
5. To screen out couples who are not appropriate for the group.

Screening is best done in person. It will provide the most accurate sense of prospective participants and will give them an opportunity to get to know you and become comfortable. If a personal meeting is not possible for some reason, telephone screening is second best. Be sure you talk with *both* partners.

Screening individuals out because they are not a good fit for your group need not be seen as rejection. Be sure to explain that the group's focus will be different from what they need right now and that, in your judgment, their needs will best be met in other ways (a referral to counseling, an appointment with a rabbi, a meeting with the Outreach Coordinator, enrollment in an Introduction to Judaism class, etc.).

Agenda Setting and Car Talk

The couples themselves play an active role in setting the agenda for the group and for raising concerns for discussion. During the first session they will have an opportunity, with the guidance of the facilitator, to brainstorm a list of questions and topics. This list will be useful to you in planning sessions and choosing exercises to meet the group's needs.

"Car Talk" provides another mechanism through which couples can process what occurred in each session, thereby keeping the group in their minds beyond the limits of the actual meeting time. On the way home each week, participants are asked to talk with one another about what was discussed in the group that evening. At the beginning of each session, the facilitator asks participants to share Car Talk with the group. This insures a carry-over between sessions, reviews issues, and enables participants to personalize the topic at hand.

The Model

The multi-session model addresses the three central concerns of interfaith couples: religious identity, relationships with family and friends, and childrearing. The progression of topics has been carefully designed to address the issues in the sequence recommended. While you may want to make changes in the content, exercises, or approach you choose for each session, *the order of the topics themselves should be maintained.*

Session I: Introduction, Expectations and Concerns; Reconsidering Religious Backgrounds

Session II: What Does My Religion Mean To Me?

Session III: Considering Religious Differences

Session IV: Relating to Families and Friends

Session V: Choosing a Faith for Our Family

Session VI: Transmitting a Faith

Session VII: The Jewish Community

Session VIII: Closure; Reviewing the Group Experience

A Word About Using Exercises

Exercises can serve as discussion-starters (to help participants achieve a new level of awareness). You will find exercises in Chapter 4 for each of the three areas of concern commonly raised by interfaith couples: religious identity, relating to family and friends, and childrearing. See the descriptions of each session for specific suggestions for appropriate exercises.

A PROGRAM TO INTRODUCE THE MULTI-SESSION MODEL

It is sometimes difficult to get couples to commit themselves to attend a long-term program about which they know very little. In some areas, facilitators have found that inviting prospective participants to an "introductory session" serves several purposes:

- It may replace the necessity for screening, since the facilitator will have an opportunity to talk with potential participants personally.

- It makes the facilitator known to participants and "safe."

- It provides information about the content and goals of the series.

A program to introduce the multi-session model should include the following components:

- The facilitator(s) introduce themselves and explain their background and qualifications.

- Couples are asked to introduce themselves briefly and explain why they came.

- The facilitator(s) explain Outreach, the Reform Movement's commitment to interfaith couples, and the fact that couples often have difficulty in talking about issues related to intermarriage.

- A description of the multi-session series, including:

    Logistics: Time, dates, number of sessions, Shabbat dinner.

    Sponsorship: Who is sponsoring the program, and why it is "a Jewish perspective" on interfaith relationships.

    Format: There is an educational component, but the series is generally for discussion with others who share similar concerns.

    Agenda: Group members will help to set the agenda and topics for discussion. (Be prepared with a list of commonly-discussed topics).

    Conversion: Conversion of the non-Jewish partner is *not* a goal of the program, although Judaism warmly welcomes anyone who chooses to become Jewish.

Usually after this initial presentation, group members are anxious to jump in with questions and comments. General guidelines for discussion include:

Acknowledging Fears

Encourage couples to share their concerns about the group. Non-Jewish partners will be relieved to know that conversion is not the agenda, but they still may not know what is expected of them. Both partners are often fearful of raising issues that will result in discord. Reassure couples that they will not be "forced" to discuss anything they are not ready to discuss. There may be times when they will choose simply to listen and learn from others. You will be there to hear their concerns at every juncture.

Applauding Their Willingness to Consider Participation

All couples need encouragement and praise for their willingness to grapple with issues most would rather avoid. It is often helpful to say that no matter what they decide about the group, they have taken the first step toward their future.

Understanding Process

Be certain to let participants know that the group is scheduled over time for a reason. There is "process" time—an opportunity to hear what is being said, to reflect on it, to talk about it, and to consider the implications of decisions they will make. Nothing will be rushed. They will have input into the agenda.

Be sure to provide your phone number on a handout to each *participant* (not each couple). Within a week after the program, call each partner to let him/her know of your continuing availability. Encourage group participation, but promise to be available regardless of their decision about the group.

It is useful to distribute flyers and registration forms at the conclusion of the presentation, with specific instructions about how to register.

THE OUTLINE OF SESSIONS

While all sessions that follow are considered important in order to accomplish the goals of the program, facilitators leading six-week groups should consider using the outlines for sessions I, II, III, IV, V, and VIII. Read through the materials for all sessions. You may choose to combine some elements from sessions VI and VII.

Note: a Shabbat dinner concludes all groups, regardless of the number of sessions.

Session I: **INTRODUCTIONS, EXPECTATIONS AND CONCERNS; RECONSIDERING RELIGIOUS BACKGROUNDS**

Objectives:

1. To introduce participants to one another and begin the group in a warm, supportive environment.

2. To explain to participants how the group is representative of the Outreach effort of Reform Judaism.

3. To clarify goals, dispel fears, and discuss participants' expectations regarding the group experience.

Preparation:

1. Arrange chairs in a circle.

2. Set up coffee and refreshments.

3. Prepare name tags in large block letters written with a dark, felt-tipped pen. (Names should be legible at a distance).

4. Bring copies of the schedule of sessions with titles and dates.

5. Bring index cards and pens for participants.

Welcome:

1. Greet participants and ask each person to put on a name tag.

2. When everyone is present, formally welcome group members and ask them to go around the circle and introduce themselves. To begin, you might ask participants to state their name, what they do "in real life" (student, profession, etc.), and why they decided to attend the group. Be sure to introduce yourself in a similar manner. (Going first may break the ice).

3. Give a brief background sketch about the sponsorship of the program. It will be important to:

- Define *Reform* Judaism as a liberal branch of Judaism with over 850 congregations throughout North America.

- Explain that Outreach, now more than a decade old, is the Reform movement's program which provides education, referrals, and support for interfaith couples, those with no religious preference seeking information about Judaism, individuals considering conversion or Jews-by-Choice, and anyone with concerns regarding any of these topics. (See "What Is Reform Jewish Outreach?" in Appendix C).

• Explain the sponsorship of the group (synagogue or other Jewish institution, a regional UAHC Outreach program, etc.).

Introduction to the Series:

Include the following points in your remarks:

1. The series is designed to clarify important issues faced by interfaith couples at all stages of their relationships. Participants who are exploring the implications of intermarriage, those who are engaged, and those already intermarried will benefit equally.

2. The series is sponsored by Reform Jewish Outreach and offers a Jewish perspective on interfaith relationships. That is why there is no minister or priest co-facilitating the group.

3. There will be absolutely no attempt to convert the non-Jewish partner. The program will, however, encourage participants to consider creating a Jewish home and raising their children as Jews.

4. Group members will help set discussion topics within the outline provided. (It is often helpful to provide participants with a list of the session topics in the order listed above with the date of each session next to it). Briefly go over the sessions and the Shabbat dinner (which will be planned at a later date).

5. The major topics for the series are: religious identity; relating to family and friends; and childrearing. They will be considered in that order, since they build on one another. Parents can't decide what role religion should have in their children's lives until they are clear about its role in their own lives.

6. Information will be provided about Jewish customs and beliefs when appropriate. Those in the group who are not Jewish are still connected to the Jewish people through marriage or impending marriage, and it will be important to understand the Jewish community.

7. The group will focus on issues that may be complicated and anxiety-provoking, often ignored by couples because they threaten the status quo. Experience has shown repeatedly over the past ten years that attention to these issues early in a relationship is crucial so that both partners are clear about the role of religion in the choices they will make.

8. Note that all group members share an experience that everyone in the group understands on a very personal level: loving someone of a different religious background. Although each family and relationship is unique, they will find many similar experiences and concerns.

9. No clear-cut solutions or outcomes should be expected from participation in the group. Rather, it is hoped that the experience will stimulate continued conversation between partners.

10. Briefly go over group "rules": commitment of both partners to attend all sessions; necessity for timely arrival; smoking or non-smoking; confidentiality (group members are not to discuss other group members or anything that is talked about during the sessions with "outsiders." Let participants know that this is not because you anticipate any great revelations or secrets; it is merely insurance to help everyone feel comfortable in talking freely).

Personal Experiences:

Begin by explaining that the effectiveness of the series depends on participants' willingness to share backgrounds, attitudes, and feelings. *All* participants are encouraged to express their opinions and to question. It is important for all members to feel comfortable saying what is really on their minds. Everyone will benefit from the experiences, dilemmas, and perspectives of others.

Ask participants briefly to introduce themselves "religiously" to the others. What is their family background? Religious involvement? Significant religious experiences? What was their religious life like as a child, a teenager, a college student, now? It is often useful to ask if participants knew all of this about their partners. Were they surprised by anything? Comment on similarities in participants' introductions.

This is usually a good point to break for refreshments. When the group reconvenes, explain that you'd like to move on from religious backgrounds to the present. Ask participants to talk about: 1) how they met, and 2) what they fell in love with about their partner. This is usually lighthearted, and begins the group on a very positive note.

Setting the Group Agenda:

Pass out the schedule of sessions. Explain to the group that this is the order of topics for the series, but you would like their input to determine the agenda more specifically. Ask them to write down on the note card specific concerns, issues, questions, or problems that they would like to address during the sessions. It is important to note that these are anonymous and that all concerns are legitimate. Collect the cards randomly to insure anonymity.

You will use these lists as a guide in your planning. They will help you in selecting handouts, choosing group exercises, and planning discussions. Be sure to refer to the lists during the series to remind participants that you have taken their input seriously and want to respond to their particular concerns.

Closure:

1. Explain Car Talk. Each week on the way home, participants should talk with one another about what was discussed in the group during that session. Car Talk will serve as the opening of the following week's session and will insure continuity. Participants will be asked to share relevant parts of their Car Talk with the group next week.

2. If you have time, ask a volunteer to try to remember each person's name (with name tags removed). This is a light-hearted way to reinforce familiarity with each others' names.

3. Ask for a volunteer to bring refreshments to the next session. (Most synagogues will provide coffee and cups).

Session II: WHAT DOES MY RELIGION MEAN TO ME?

Objectives:

1. To enable participants to begin to clarify what their religious backgrounds mean to them.

2. To enable participants to have a clearer understanding of the role of religion in their partner's life.

3. To encourage participants to learn more about their partner's religious background.

Preparation:

1. Use name tags again.

2. Facilitator should read the article "Marriage of Christians and Jews" in advance of the session.

3. Bring copies of a roster of participants' names, home addresses and telephone numbers to hand out. Be sure to include yourself on the list.

4. Bring copies of the list of questions compiled by the group last week.

5. Check for any materials needed for the exercise you choose.

6. Bring handouts.

Car Talk:

Remind the group that Car Talk is intended to provide continuity between sessions and to provide a mechanism for attending to any unfinished business from the previous session. Ask the group what they talked about on the way home last week. What issues arose? Were there any special concerns? Ask for volunteers to report on Car Talk.

> *Note:* Car Talk can be productive and interesting or rambling and unfocused. Discussion should be kept short. Keep in mind that the order of issues to be addressed are: religious identity, family and friends, and childrearing. If childrearing concerns are raised during Car Talk, acknowledge that it is an important issue and that it will be addressed as the group progresses. Be sure that Car Talk discussions are kept short.

What Does My Religion Mean to Me?

The following exercises in Chapter 4 are recommended for this session. Review all of them before selecting the one best for your group.

> Choosing Family Symbols
>
> The Holiday Dinner Table
>
> Tracing Your Spiritual Journey
>
> Ethnic Ambivalence
>
> The Meaning of Ritual

"Why Religion?" (Chapter 5)

Follow the directions as they appear. At the conclusion, ask the group what the experience of the exercise was like. Were they surprised by anything that came up? By any responses from their partner?

Opportunities for Jewish Learning:

Explain to the group that all of what comes up in relation to personal issues is an important opportunity for learning about Judaism and how it may be different from other religions. You will provide relevant information and handouts at each session. Elicit and write down any questions that the group has about Jewish beliefs, rituals, customs, and holidays. Encourage participants to feel free to ask about anything that is on their minds. It may be important to encourage Jewish partners as well to ask about Judaism. Let everyone know there is no such thing as a dumb question. Explain that you will use the list to help you in your planning.

Judaism as a Civilization:

Use "Judaism as a Civilization I: Stereotypes" or "Judaism as a Civilization II: Participatory Mini-Lecture" to clarify one of the differences between Judaism and Christianity that is often most puzzling for interfaith couples. Refer to notes on "Judaism as a Civilization" for additional information.

Handouts:

1. "When a Jew and Christian Marry" (Chapter 5)

2. "Judaism and Christianity: The Parting of the Ways" and "The Hyphen Between the Cross and the Star" (Chapter 5)

3. *The Jewish Home* by Rabbi Daniel Syme, UAHC Press (available in both book and pamphlet form). It is recommended that this book be made available to group participants.

Closure:

Make handouts available. Participants should read 1 and 2 for next week. *The Jewish Home* is intended to be read at leisure and used as a reference.

Remind the group about Car Talk and invite someone to bring refreshments for the next session.

Session III: CONSIDERING RELIGIOUS DIFFERENCES

Objectives:

1. To enable participants to become more aware of religious differences.

2. To clarify the Jewish community's concerns about intermarriage, especially as it relates to the future of Judaism.

Preparation:

1. Review handouts from last week. Bring copies of this week's handouts.

2. Prepare mini-lecture as described below.

3. Review recommended exercises and bring appropriate materials.

Begin by reviewing Car Talk from last week. Then move on to the following "mini lecture."

"The Jewish Community's Response to Intermarriage"

Explain to the group that in order for the experience of the group to be most useful to them, it will be important to understand the Jewish community's perspective on intermarriage, which reflects some of the most painful aspects of Jewish history and is based on very realistic contemporary concerns about demographics and the future of Judaism. For help in preparing your remarks, refer to items included in the Bibliography and to the following articles in Appendix A:

> Outreach Statistics At-a-Glance
>
> All in the ∧Jewish Family

1. Begin by asking participants what kinds of reactions they have had to their relationship and their intermarriage. Have they felt welcomed? Congratulated? Greeted with open arms? Regarded judgmentally? Have the reactions been overt or covert? Has anyone talked with them about intermarriage? Have they noticed differences in the reactions of Jews and non-Jews to intermarriage?

2. Explain the minority status of Jews. There are now fewer than 6 million Jews (the number of Jews who perished in the Holocaust) in the United States. With an intermarriage rate of approximately 50%, there are some very real concerns about whether there will be a Jewish community in a generation or two. (You can note that most non-Jews are not concerned that in another generation there will be no Protestants, etc.).

3. Explain the concept of *l'dor v'dor* (from generation to generation). Jews believe that spiritual immortality comes from passing down Judaism from one generation to another. They see themselves as links in a chain. To break the chain cuts off not only all future generations, but also all that came before.

4. The legacy of the Holocaust still shapes how Jews view the world. The Holocaust was a trauma of great proportion remembered by all Jews, whether or not they personally lost relatives. The Holocaust forces Jews to remember a long history of anti-Semitism, much of which

was fostered by the Church. (Only in 1965 did the Vatican formally exonerate Jews from the charge of killing Jesus). The Holocaust reminds Jews that they are separate and different. (See "In the Shadow of the Holocaust," Chapter 5).

5. Someone in the group may ask (or you can note that people sometimes wonder) if it isn't time to forget the Holocaust. Explain that to remember is to keep alive the memory of the 6 million Jews who died only because they were Jewish, and remembering the Shoah helps to prevent history from repeating itself.

6. The ashes of the Holocaust gave birth to the State of Israel. Without question, the world granted Israel its existence out of sympathy for the annihilation of millions of Jews. For most Jews, Israel is a tremendous source of pride and symbolizes commitment to the future. (See "Jews and Israel" in Chapter 5).

7. By marrying a Jew, a non-Jew becomes connected to the tragedy of the Holocaust and the promise of Israel. Because the Jewish past and the Jewish future are such important concerns, intermarriage is related to the entirety of Jewish experience.

8. Questions/discussion.

Break

Considering Religious Differences:

When the group reconvenes, explain that the topic at hand is considering how religious differences play themselves out in their relationship. You have two options:

1. Lead a discussion of religious differences they have encountered in their relationship to date. Discussion questions might include:

- How do you decide what to do for holidays?
- What areas of your religious tradition are important to you?
- What is the most important thing you want your partner to know about you religiously?

Generate your own list of questions beforehand based on your knowledge of your group. OR

2. You may choose to use Exploring and Negotiating Differences (see Chapter 4).

Lead the group through the exercise and, as always, ask for feedback at the end.

Opportunities for Jewish Learning:

The information about the Holocaust, Israel, and the Jewish perspective on intermarriage make up the didactic portion of this session.

Handouts:

"Jews and Israel" in Chapter 5.

"Learning to Negotiate" from *The Intermarriage Handbook.*

Closure:

1. Remind participants about Car Talk and refreshments.

2. Tell the group that next week we will shift the focus to consider religion in the context of families, friends, and community. Ask them to think during the week about issues that have come up in relation to the topic or encounters (both positive and negative) that have already occurred. Next week's discussion will be enriched if there are particular examples for discussion.

Session IV: RELATING TO FAMILY AND FRIENDS

Objectives:

1. To enable participants to understand that their relationship does not exist in a vacuum, but rather within the broader context of family and friends.

2. To encourage participants to anticipate problems in regard to religion and to consider adaptive strategies for building healthy relationships with their families and friends.

Preparation:

1. Review exercises and Intermarriage in Context (Appendix A) for possible use.

2. Read and prepare handouts listed below.

3. Review the group's list of agenda items from Session I to find examples needed below.

Begin by asking about last week's Car Talk before moving on to the topic at hand.

Intermarriage in Context:

Begin by explaining to the group that most people come to couples groups with concerns about how they will relate to their families, friends, and the broader community. You can note that this group is no different, and read some of the concerns they wrote down in Session I that are relevant. (You may choose to jot them on a large pad or blackboard so the list is visible to everyone throughout the discussion). Ask participants if there are any additional concerns they would like to add, now that they have had an opportunity (as assigned at the end of the last session) to think about the issue further. Add to the list any additional concerns raised.

Encourage discussion by noting common themes, by wondering why intermarriage sometimes may make relationships with families difficult, by remarking on any change in focus that has occurred between the original list from Session I and today's additions, etc.

Participants usually have much to talk about in this regard. Remember that your challenge is to keep the group focused on their relationships with family and friends based on their awareness of their own religious identity as discussed in previous sessions. Do not allow the group to jump ahead to childrearing issues.

During this session the issue of rabbinic officiation at intermarriage ceremonies is often raised.

Be prepared to:

1. Provide information on the CCAR's resolution regarding officiation (see "Some Thoughts on Officiation" in Appendix A).

2. Explain that no rabbi makes the decision to officiate or not without a great deal of soul-searching and introspection.

3. Relate the issue to Jewish history and the concern about the strength of Judaism and numbers of Jews in future generations.

4. Do not permit a debate about officiation to dominate the session.

You may choose to use an exercise from Chapter 4 for this session. Consider either:

From Generation to Generation

Herb and Mary: Baptism or Bris?

Opportunities for Jewish Learning:

This session's educational component includes information about rabbinic officiation, and a discussion on Jewish families and family values.

Handouts:

Articles on the Jewish family, particularly "All in the ˄Jewish Family" (Appendix A).

Refer students to sections on the Jewish life cyle in *The Jewish Home* and to the chapter on "Dealing With Parents" from *The Intermarriage Handbook.*

Closure:

1. Remind the group that you are now halfway through the series, and ask for feedback.

2. Ask participants to read "Rituals Surrounding the Birth of a Child" from *The Jewish Home,* which they already have, for next week.

3. Remind participants about Car Talk and ask for a volunteer to bring refreshments.

Session V: CHOOSING A FAITH FOR OUR FAMILY

Objectives:

1. To enable participants to use the awareness of their own religious identity and knowledge about their relationships with family, friends, and the Jewish community to consider religious choices available to them for childrearing.

2. To underscore the program's perspective that choosing one religion in the home is desirable.

3. To provide a forum for honest exchange between partners regarding their religious choices for their children.

Ask for feedback about last week's Car Talk before moving on to the topic for this session.

Preparation

1. Review exercises for possible use.

2. Read and prepare handouts.

Choosing a Family Faith

Begin by reminding participants that they have now had an opportunity to consider aspects of their own religious identity and that the group has spent time considering relationships with their families as well. With those areas as background, the topic now at hand is that of considering a single faith for their family.

Why a *single* faith? It is the perspective of the program that it is better for children to grow up with one religious identity. Couples are more likely to be able to understand this perspective if they come to it themselves. There is no "proof" that one religion is better than two that you can share with the group. The evening's discussion is intended to highlight the complexities of attempting other solutions.

Be prepared for the fact that couples will voice all kinds of strategies for avoiding choosing one religion. Allow group members to challenge one another. Among the strategies you will hear are:

- Raising the child equally in both religions and later allowing the child to choose.
- Raising a boy in the father's religion and a girl in the mother's.
- Raising the first child in one religion and the next in the other.
- Raising the child either Jewish or Christian depending upon the ethnic composition of the family's hometown or the proximity of specific family members.
- Finding a "compromise" religion that is neither partner's original religion, most commonly Unitarianism or The Society of Friends (Quakers).
- Deciding that there will be no religion in the home.

Some couples enter the program committed to raising their children as Jews, but are troubled by the implications of excluding the religion of the other parent. In such cases, be prepared to validate the concerns expressed, while also suggesting ways for the non-Jewish parent to maintain a sense of individual religious integrity while raising a child as a Jew.

What options are available to couples grappling with these concerns? One strategy is for the non-Jewish partner to celebrate holidays in the home of a parent or family member. In that way, the opportunity for connectedness is maintained without introducing non-Jewish symbols or celebrations into the Jewish home. Children can be told that, whereas we celebrate Chanukah because our home is Jewish, we can help celebrate Christmas at grandma or grandpa's because we like to be together as a family at such festive times.

When discussing the reasons for raising children in a single religious tradition, refer to the discussion of Judaism as a civilization. While it may be theoretically possible to teach the child by taking the best of each spouse's religion, Jewish civilization defies such a mixture, since the intertwining strands of religion, peoplehood, language, history, and ethnicity combine to make Judaism. Pose the following questions:

- Is it possible to be simultaneously included in and excluded from the Jewish people?
- Can a group member be accepted by other group members if he/she participated in another religious tradition? Can a person affirm Christ and be a Jew?
- Should the decision to raise a child in both religions be based upon what is best for the parents or what is best for the child?

Remind the group that the focal point of the discussion is to clarify each partner's religious attachment and priorities before making decisions about the child's religious identity. Gently persuade each person to evaluate his/her religious tradition and determine specifically what should be preserved and why.

Holiday Celebration:

Closely related to the discussion of childrearing is the question of holiday celebration. Couples face many decisions:

- What holidays should be celebrated and why?
- Should Christmas and Chanukah, Easter and Passover all be celebrated in the home?
- What religious symbols should be in the home year-round (mezuzah, cross, religious artwork, etc.)?

The program position is clear: Since we encourage couples to choose one religious tradition for the home, hopefully Judaism, we also encourage them to celebrate only Jewish holidays in the home.

Many couples might be willing to celebrate only Jewish holidays in the home with the exception of Christmas. Christmas is often synonymous with family togetherness, gift-giving, good times, and good food, and may represent all that is beautiful in the Christian partner's family upbringing. Because little religious or theological significance is ascribed to the observance, many couples decide to have a Christmas tree and celebrate the holiday as a secular occasion.

Group discussion should focus on clarifying participants' feelings about celebrating Christmas or Chanukah in the home and exploring their religious identification. Most Jewish parents will express ambivalence or opposition to having a tree, though some may find it acceptable and even desirable.

It is important to stress the critical role of religious symbols in the development of religious identity. Because religious symbols stand for a particular religion, they generate powerful feelings. One religion cannot appropriate the religious symbols of another without devaluing them.

Using Exercises and Guiding Discussion:

You may choose to use "As If...", the fill-in-the-blanks exercise as a discussion starter. It will very quickly plunge the group into the central dilemmas associated with religious decision-making. If you have more time available, consider using "The Meaning of Ritual" or "Choosing Family Symbols". If you would rather go directly to a general discussion, the following questions will be helpful as catalysts:

- What aspects of your religious heritage do you want to pass on to your children?
- Do you need to choose one religious identity for children?
- What are the difficulties you foresee in actively practicing two religions in one home?
- If you raise children in one religion, what exposure should the child have to the other?
- What is the parent whose religion is not chosen likely to experience?
- What birth rituals will you choose when a baby is born? What commitment is involved in participation in those rituals?

Opportunities for Jewish Learning:

This session offers an excellent opportunity to educate participants about what is involved in raising a child as a Jew. Be prepared to talk about the following: bris, Jewish baby-naming, Jewish religious school (and therefore synagogue affiliation, which is different from the way that one is a member of most churches), Bar/Bat Mitzvah, and confirmation. See the Bibliography for suggested readings.

Handouts:

"Adult Children of Intermarriage Speak"
Suggest additional chapters from *The Jewish Home*.

Closure:

1. Acknowledge that this evening's discussion may have raised some uncomfortable issues. Congratulate participants on their willingness to confront what is probably the most difficult dilemma for intermarried couples. Note that if tonight's discussion has been productive, most couples will not have made a definitive decision about the religious orientation of their family, but they will have a greater awareness of the complexities and the strong feelings involved.

2. Distribute handouts.

3. Remind participants about Car Talk and ask for a volunteer to bring refreshments next time.

Session VI: TRANSMITTING A FAITH

Objectives:

1. To enable participants to understand that religion in the home doesn't "just happen."

2. To help participants further clarify their feelings about the transmission of their religious values and to consider how that will or will not be accomplished in their home.

3. To provide information about specifics of Jewish family life.

Preparation:

1. Review and copy handouts.

2. Plan for Shabbat dinner so that arrangements can be coordinated with the group.

3. Review exercises for possible use.

Car Talk:

Ask participants about last week's Car Talk. Was it any different from previous times? Were issues more difficult to talk about? It is important to remind participants that the group didn't "create" areas of dissension. Rather, the issues have been there in their relationship all along. The group experience enables participants to recognize differences and address them realistically.

Transmitting a Faith:

An effective way to begin is to ask the group to recall aspects of their religious background or values that they want to pass on to their children (refer to last week's discussion). When several examples have been given, ask the group where they think those religious feelings or values came from. In other words, how did they get them? It will soon become clear that much of what participants identify as important to them was rooted in their own childhoods. What do they want to pass on to their children? How do they want to bring up their children differently from the way they were brought up religiously?

There are several exercises that may be especially useful. Consider:

From Generation to Generation

The Holiday Dinner Table

Choosing Family Symbols: Beyond the Christmas Tree

(If you have already used any of these, tie that experience into tonight's agenda and remind participants of the experience.)

During this evening's session be sure to bring the focus back to specifics. When someone says, "I want my children to know that they are Jews," ask *how* their children will know. Who will teach them what a Jew is? Where will that identity come from? When a participant says their children will have some religious education, ask for details. What kind? How much? How often? Where? Ask if partners have discussed it. Do they agree? If not, what stands in the way?

This session is an opportunity to consider the specifics of religious education, holiday celebration, and how participants anticipate sharing their religious life with their parents and extended family.

   • *Note:* It is important to reassure participants that choosing one religious faith for the home does not mean that the children will be cut off from the family of the partner whose religion is not chosen. Thus, *Jewish* children from a *Jewish* home can visit Christian grandparents' homes for their *grandparents'* holiday celebrations. As long as parents are clear that they are visiting relatives who celebrate different holidays, children will not be confused about their own religious identity.

Opportunities for Jewish Learning:

Like the theme of the previous session, the theme this evening is: the Jewish home, Jewish holidays, the Jewish life cycle. Be sure that you are knowledgeable about these areas. If there is a Jewish holiday about to happen, provide information about how a family might celebrate it and consider bringing in holiday foods for the group to share. Encourage participants to ask questions. If you haven't already done so, ask participants if they are interested in a tour of the synagogue next week.

Handouts:

Selections or articles relating to particular topics above. Refer to *The Jewish Home* or other items listed in the Bibliography, particularly *Raising Jewish Children in a Contemporary World* by Steven Carr Reuben.

Closure:

1. Be sure to acknowledge that all of this is hard work, and let participants know that they are not expected to have all the answers neatly packaged at the end of tonight's session.

2. Remind them that there are two sessions plus the Shabbat dinner left. Begin to plan various aspects of the Shabbat dinner. Be sure to allow time for couples to react to the fact that the series is drawing to a close.

Session VII: THE JEWISH COMMUNITY

Objectives:

1. To build on the previous sessions in helping participants to understand that their families will live and grow within the broader context of community.

2. To enable participants to have a basic understanding of the richness and complexity of the Jewish community and the notion of Judaism as a civilization. (see "Notes: Judaism as a Civilization" in Appendix A).

3. To provide couples with specific information regarding the Jewish community as it exists in their area.

4. To reaffirm that interfaith couples are welcome to participate in Reform synagogues and that Reform synagogues will provide support in raising Jewish children.

Preparation:

1. Prepare and copy handouts suggested below.

2. Prepare and copy specifics of the Shabbat dinner plans. Consider including favorite readings and recipes, besides the "who will do what" list and logistics.

Car Talk:

In asking about what was discussed in Car Talk last week, remember that the last two sessions are bound to have stirred up strong feelings and questions. It will be important to reassure participants that this is to be expected. They are making decisions for a lifetime, and there are no recipes for instant answers.

The Jewish Community:

It is often easiest to begin by reminding the group that you have frequently talked about the fact that part of the reason for having a group like this is precisely because people are part of a community: families do not live in a vacuum, but are instead part of a larger whole.

The following questions will be helpful in engendering a discussion of the meaning of community: Why do we talk about a "Jewish community" at all? Is there a Presbyterian community? A Methodist community?

The dictionary defines a community as:

1. A unified body of individuals. (Is this true of Judaism, given what they now know? Why? Why not?)

2. People with common interests living within a particular area. (Is this more appropriate? What about the notion of *k'lal yisrael,* the tie that binds Jews together all around the world?)

3. A group with common characteristics or interests. (Is this true of your Jewish community? What are the characteristics shared? The interests? Note that historically Jews have been a minority often persecuted by outsiders who labelled them with common characteristics or stereotypes.)

4. Persons with a common history, social, political, and economic interests.

While these may be objective definitions, real knowledge of what a community is may be more personal. What are examples of community that participants have experienced? (Note: Examples given may not all be Jewish. Be sure to include non-Jewish partners in the discussion.) Jewish examples may include: the phenomenon of "Jewish geography" — everybody knows everybody through somebody. Other examples may include participants' perceptions, both positive and negative: *tzedakah* and mutual responsibility, the experience of being a minority in a Christian culture, the perceived "clannishness" of Jews, the number of Jewish cultural institutions, and the "It's better to marry somebody Jewish" attitude within the Jewish community.

Other questions for discussion may include:

- Why do communities exist?
- Why do people need them?
- Does our relationship to community change as we grow older?
- How do you become a part of a new community?
- What has been the role of community in the lives of the families of participants?
- Why has the Jewish community traditionally been wary of "outsiders?" (Note: In the Reform High Holy Day prayer book, we ask forgiveness "for the sin of xenophobia... ." While our fear of strangers may have been adaptive historically, we are admonished not to hang on to prejudice.)
- Why has the synagogue traditionally been the center of the Jewish community?

If you would like to consider using an exercise for this session, consider "Judaism as a Civilization I: Stereotypes."

Opportunities for Jewish Learning:

Participants will leave this session with a much broader sense of the importance of community and the complexity of the Jewish community. Sometimes an effective discussion starter is to ask participants to brainstorm a list of all the Jewish organizations they know. (You'll find Jewish participants less knowledgeable than you'd expect). Be prepared with your own (exhaustive) list. Why does the Jewish community support all of these diverse community services — hospital, home for the aged, Hebrew Free Loan Society, Burial Society, etc.?

Distribute copies of the blessing for Torah from the weekday service (*Gates of Prayer,* CCAR, pp.52-53). How do Jews console the bereaved, rejoice with the bride and groom, visit the sick? These acts of mutual responsibility are an important aspect of community that are reflected in the institutions of the Jewish community.

This session is a good opportunity to talk about the diversity within the Jewish community. Be sure you can provide a brief explanation of the difference between Reform, Reconstructionist, Conservative and Orthodox Judaism.

Handouts:

1. A list of Jewish organizations and resources in your community, with addresses and phone numbers. Include synagogues, bookstores, organizations, etc. If the synagogue or UAHC region offers an Introduction to Judaism course, be sure to include information about it.

2. A list of Jewish periodicals that may be of special interest to your group (a local Jewish newspaper, *Tikkun, Moment, Sh'ma, Reform Judaism,* etc.) Include subscription information. (See list at end of Bibliography, Appendix B.)

A synagogue library or local Jewish Federation will be especially helpful in your preparation.

Closure:

1. Note that next week is the last session before the Shabbat dinner. Next week members will:
   • Finalize Shabbat dinner plans
   • Attend to unfinished business of the group
   • Consider "Where do we go from here?"
   • Fill out evaluations of the group experience

Session VIII: CLOSURE

Objectives:

1. To attend to any lingering concerns of participants that the group has not adequately considered.

2. To enable participants to discuss what the experience of the past weeks has meant to them.

3. To provide a forum to consider future get-togethers or programs.

4. To provide both verbal and written feedback to the facilitator for evaluation of the program.

Preparation:

1. Bring any final plans for Shabbat dinner, including copies of Shabbat blessings with transliteration and translation so that couples may familiarize themselves with what will happen beforehand. Refer participants to *The Jewish Home* as well.

2. Bring copies of the evaluation form (see Chapter 6) and pens.

Car Talk:

Car Talk during this last session can lead productively to the accomplishment of the objectives listed above. What is on participants' minds as the group ends? What will they miss? What have they learned about themselves? About each other? About their families and communities? About Judaism?

Many couples are unwilling to have the group end completely, and discussion may include consideration of future plans: a monthly gathering in members' homes; a Chanukah party, a Shabbat dinner. Be sure that the group doesn't jump to planning for the future without fully considering what this group has meant to them.

You will need to be clear about your own feelings and your role in the future. You may want to share your own feelings of loss as the group ends, your fondness for participants, your interest in their future. Emphasize that you will no longer be the facilitator, but that members have the skill to continue on their own. You may want to volunteer yourself as a resource and a link to the Jewish community. Remind participants as well that Reform rabbis and congregations are ready to serve as resources for them.

Finally, be sure to thank group members for participating and for their willingness to confront difficult issues. While they will not leave the group with all the answers they were seeking, they are leaving with a fuller understanding of themselves and each other in relation to Judaism.

Closure:

1. Attend to any leftover details about the Shabbat dinner. Encourage couples to bring their own candlesticks and kiddish cups if they wish.

2. Distribute evaluations for participants to complete and hand in *before* they leave this session.

CHAPTER 4

EXERCISES

Chapter 4: EXERCISES

The exercises included in this section have been selected for their relevance to the topics for discussion outlined in this guide and for their success in use with various groups. You may use the following guide for suggestions in finding an appropriate exercise for various topics:

For an exercise on:	*Consider using*
Understanding Judaism	Judaism as a Civilization I: Stereotypes Judaism as a Civilization II: Participatory Mini-Lecture
Religious Identity	The Holiday Dinner Table Tracing Your Spiritual Journey Ethnic Ambivalence Exploring and Negotiating Differences The Meaning of Ritual As If... Choosing Family Symbols The Tree Scenario
Family and Friends	The Holiday Dinner Table Exploring and Negotiating Differences Mary and Herb: Baptism or Bris From Generation to Generation Choosing Family Symbols
Childrearing	Mary and Herb: Baptism or Bris From Generation to Generation As If... The Holiday Dinner Table Choosing Family Symbols: Beyond the Christmas Tree

THE HOLIDAY DINNER TABLE

Objective: To provide participants with increased clarity regarding the personal meaning of religious holidays and traditions.

Materials: Pencils and paper

Time Required: 30 minutes

Instructions: Ask each person to write a brief description of a typical holiday dinner that took place when he/she was a child. (Encourage participants simply to make notes about what they want to say, rather than taking time to write it all our longhand.) Each participant will then describe the scene to his/her partner.

The dinner table is a universal center of family gathering that evokes memories of family members, interactions, moods and family rituals. By identifying and articulating the specifics of their own backgrounds, participants can acknowledge feelings of loss, as well as choose to recreate experiences that they value.

Note to facilitator: You might use some of the following questions to trigger memories for the group.

What is the holiday? Where is the table? Who is there with you? Does each person have a special seat or a certain task? Who heads the table? How does it change when the leader dies? Remember what is discussed. What rituals are performed, or what prayers are said? What is your role? How do you feel? If you had to use one word to describe the meaning of that scene, what would it be?

Ask participants to expand their awareness and to remember back to the days preceding the event. What was the mood of the house? What preparations were made? What did your parents do? What were the children doing? Is there a special holiday one year that stands out in your mind? Why was it special? How did you feel about it at the time? What are you feeling now, remembering?

When participants have finished describing their scene to their partners, reconvene the group and discuss the exercise. Suggested questions: Was anyone surprised by anything their partner described? Was anyone surprised by their partners reaction to the scene they described? What kinds of feelings were evoked in doing this exercise with their partner? What value does this exercise have for them as part of an interfaith couple?

Adapted from an exercise by Esther Perel, a family therapist specializing in work with interfaith couples.

TRACING YOUR SPIRITUAL JOURNEY: A TIME LINE

Objective: To enable participants to become aware of their own history of religious experience and expression.

Materials: Pencils and paper

Time Required: 20-30 minutes

Instructions: Ask participants to draw a long horizontal line on a piece of paper. At one end they are asked to write the age at which they were at their earliest memory, at the other end their current age. Along the line they should note religious events and/or realizations and the ages at which they occurred. Ask them to clearly label each point, and to consider where their "spiritual time line" is going. Finally ask them to project the line into the future. What additions might they note there?

Ask a volunteer to share highlights of his/her Time Line with the group as a way of starting discussion. Did others record similar events or realizations? Are there differences in content and themes in men and women or Jews and non-Jews in the group? Was it hard to project into the future? Why/why not? What feelings, memories, or concerns were evoked in doing this exercise? Why do they matter in relation to being a part of an interfaith relationship?

Adapted from an exercise by Judy Petsonk and Jim Remsen.

ETHNIC AMBIVALENCE

Objective: To provide participants with clarity and an opportunity for discussion regarding ambivalence toward their own ethnic group.

Materials: Copies of this exercise (see next page) and pencils

Time Required: 20-30 minutes

Instructions: Ask participants to begin by filling in the blanks in the following exercise with the name of their own ethnic group (Italian, WASP, Jew, etc.). They should then briefly answer each question. When everyone is finished, ask for volunteers to share their answers with the group. Discuss. Was anyone surprised by their partner's responses? Did they know their partners felt this way?

Ask participants to share any specific experiences they can remember that are related to the content of this exercise. How did that experience shape their perspective on their ethnic background? Is it possible both to hate and love your ethnic background? Note answers that might seem contradictory. (Example: "I dislike it when people say that all Irish are heavy drinkers" and "I love the Irish people and their joyful celebrations.")

What does ethnic ambivalence mean in terms of your relationship with your partner? Is it realistic to think that this ambivalence will be resolved?

Ethnic Ambivalence

First place the name of your religious and/or ethnic group in the blanks. Then answer the questions.

1. What do you love or appreciate about being a _____ ?

2. What's difficult for you about being a _____ ?

3. What do you dislike about other _____ s?

About _____ men?

About _____ women?

4. What do you never again want to hear anyone say about your group?

EXPLORING AND NEGOTIATING DIFFERENCES

Objective: To provide an opportunity for participants to consider what religious compromises they have made for the sake of their relationship.

Materials: Paper and pencils

Time Required: 30-40 minutes

Instructions: Exploring and negotiating differences is a normal part of life, particularly as a new couple is formed or as a family faces life changes, such as the birth of a new baby. Although this process can be stressful, acknowledgement of feelings and open communication can relieve some of the tension and enable couples to search for satisfactory solutions.

In this context, ask participants to consider any religious experiences or religious holidays they have shared, recalling the specifics of the event (when? with whom? where? etc.) Then ask each partner to list any issues that arose and how they were handled. Were compromises involved? Out of respect for their partner, did they change anything they normally would have done (attending midnight mass, saying a Hebrew blessing, etc.). Finally, ask participants to note the feelings they associate with what they have written. When this is completed, ask them to share their recollections and what they have written with their partner.

Finally, reconvene the group and ask for feedback on the experience. Were the incidents they chose the same as their partners'? Were their recollections the same? Were they surprised about anything that they learned about themselves? About their partner?

In some groups, couples will see negotiating differences as making compromises. Use the opportunity to explore whether or not these mean the same thing. What does compromise mean in relation to religious observances and celebrations? Does compromise necessarily mean losing something that may be important to them? Ask for examples of compromises they haven't been willing or able to make. What have such compromises meant in terms of their relationship?

Be sure to note at the end that this exercise usually stirs up feelings that remain unexpressed. Encourage participants to continue discussing feelings or concerns that arose with one other.

Adapted from an exercise by Esther Perel

THE MEANING OF RITUAL

Objective: To provide participants with increased clarity regarding the personal meaning of religious holidays and traditions.

Materials: Pencils and paper

Time Required: 30-45 minutes

Instructions: Ask participants to begin by making a list of religious or cultural holiday celebrations in their home when they were children. Ask them to note positive feelings they associate with the holidays they have listed (excitement, fun, security, warmth, etc.). They should then note any negative feelings associated with the holidays (loneliness, exclusion, tension, disappointment, etc.). Finally, they should also write down any religious experiences or feelings they would have wanted more of in their family of origin. Did different holidays have different feelings associated with them? Why/why not?

> Questions to trigger a response might include: What were the messages they received from their family about their religion and culture? About their ethnic group and other ethnic groups? Who communicated these messages to them? Who were the strongest influences in terms of restriction or support?

Ask participants to take a moment to underscore or circle the feelings in their list of most importance to them. What were the most important positive aspects? What negative feelings were especially uncomfortable? What aspects of their family's approach to holidays are most important? Least important?

Once participants have considered what has been important for them in relation to holiday celebrations, ask them to write a brief paragraph about what kind of religious experience they would like their children to have and how they would like their home to be religiously for all family members.

Finally, instruct partners to compare their lists. How are they similar? What is different? What steps can they take to meet their needs as they anticipate holiday celebrations? How can their partner help? Have they identified any potential areas of disagreement? Discuss.

Note to the facilitator: Beware of instant solutions! This exercise is aimed at highlighting needs, not solving problems. It is always helpful to remind participants that the first step toward decision-making in intermarriage is a clear sense of each other's memories, feelings, and hopes for their future.

Adapted from an exercise by Esther Perel.

JUDAISM AS A CIVILIZATION I: STEREOTYPES

Objective: To promote an understanding of Judaism as a civilization as well as a religion.

Materials: Blackboard and chalk or large pad and markers

Time Required: 20 minutes

Instructions: At the top of the board or pad, write "Jew" on one side and "Christian" on the other. Ask participants to call out stereotypes, first of Jews, then of Christians, and list them below each heading. Typically, "Jew" will trigger many more stereotypes than "Christian."

The facilitator poses the question, "What's going on here?" Someone in the group usually observes that "it would have been different if you had said "Irish Catholic" or "Quaker", etc. This opens the door for discussion of Judaism as a culture/ethnicity as well as a religion.

Go back to the list under "Jew" and note how different Jewish stereotypes can be classified (religious, cultural, historical, educational, economic, etc.) Note how the list under "Jew" encompasses so many aspects of life. It's difficult to separate the religious aspects of being Jewish from the cultural. (This is a point that many people who haven't been exposed to Judaism don't necessarily understand.) Conclude by asking participants what they learned from this exercise. What is the relevance of these issues to interfaith relationships?

Adapted from an exercise by Linda Steigman.

JUDAISM AS A CIVILIZATION II: PARTICIPATORY MINI-LECTURE

Objective: To promote an understanding of Judaism as a civilization as well as a religion.

Materials: Blackboard and chalk or large pad and markers

Time Required: 20 minutes

Instructions: In American life, Judaism and Christianity are usually characterized as two great religions, with distinctive beliefs and practices to be sure, but essentially religions. This equation is simplistic, however, and can lead to misunderstanding in an interfaith relationship. Mordecai Kaplan, the founder of Reconstructionist Judaism, saw Judaism as a civilization.

Draw a large circle on the blackboard or pad. This large pie is a civilization. Ask participants to list the various components of a civilization and write them in different pieces of the pie. (Language, law, cuisine, religion, land, history, ethnicity, literature, music, traditions might be mentioned).

Point out that Judaism encompasses all of these and that Jews relate to all of the components. An individual Jew (mark with a dot on the pie) might feel most strongly connected to Judaism through Jewish history or peoplehood, for example, but he or she still bears a relation (sometimes negative) to the other aspects of Jewish civilization. Individual Jews may also change over time in their relationship to various aspects of Judaism—for instance becoming more attached to Israel after a visit or more involved religiously after the birth of a child.

By virtue of connection with a Jew through marriage or relationship, non-Jewish partners also are related to this civilization. But the point of connection is often through the religious piece of the pie, (mark with another dot) particularly if the couple is considering raising Jewish children or the person is considering conversion to Judaism.

It might be helpful as well to point out that in American culture the single word "Jew" covers both religion and ethnicity, while two words are needed for others: Irish Catholic, WASP, Greek Orthodox, etc.

Ask for questions and reactions.

(Refer to "Notes: Judaism as a Civilization" in Appendix A.)

Adapted from an exercise by Sheila Pearl.

MARY AND HERB: BAPTISM OR BRIS?

Objective: To broaden participants' understanding of the difficulty of problems that may be encountered in an intermarriage, and to provide tools for con sidering solutions.

Materials: Copies of this exercise (see next page) and pencils

Time Required: 30 minutes

Instructions: Divide into groups of four. (Partners should not be together.) Distribute copies of the exercise and ask participants to discuss it and to complete it as a group. Reassemble the large group and ask each subgroup to report what they discussed. Be sure to provide feedback and ample discussion time for each question.

Conclude by asking couples what issues this exercise brought up for them. While Mary and Herb's situation may seem exaggerated, the feelings of couples and parents may be similar. Does the exercise trigger any concerns about their decision making in relation to their families?

Adapted from an exercise by Sherri Alper.

MARY AND HERB: BAPTISM OR BRIS?

Mary and Herb Kushner have just had their first child, a boy. They had never discussed birth rituals previously, feeling that they would make the necessary decisions when the time came. Now that their son is born, they are aware of very strong feelings on the part of both sets of parents. Herb's parents are concentration camp survivors who lost their families in the Holocaust. They are very excited about the bris (ritual circumcision) that they are sure will be held for their new grandson. Mary's father, Edward O'Brian, is dying of cancer. He has been a good Catholic all his life, and he has expressed a strong desire to have his grandson baptized.

Please discuss this situation with your group, considering the following:

1. What are the feelings of each person above? (When in doubt, imagine!)

2. What should Mary and Herb do? (Your group should come up with one "best" solution.)

3. List three funny solutions. (Be outrageous.)

4. What might Mary and Herb have done to prevent this dilemma?

FROM GENERATION TO GENERATION

Objective: To enable participants to think intergenerationally about the meaning of religion and to clarify their own religious values. To enable participants to think about continuity and change in the religious lives of their families.

Materials: Paper and pencils

Time Required: 45-60 minutes

Instructions: Divide the group into dyads. (Individuals should not do this with their partner.) Ask the group to talk with the partner with whom they are paired about:

1. The religious behavior of their grandparents
2. The religious behavior of their parents
3. Their own religious behavior
4. What they imagine the religious behavior of their children will be like.

Be sure to let the group know that we are not only talking about Jewish religious behavior and encourage them to define "religion" broadly. They should not limit themselves to descriptions of ritual observance, but should consider spirituality as well.

Allow twenty minutes to one half hour for this part of the exercise. Interrupt after ten minutes to remind participants to be sure that each partner has an opportunity to speak and that they move along to cover all four topics.

If a group is small and you are using this as an exercise to promote group cohesion, you can ask each partner to summarize briefly his/her partner's remarks to the group. If you plan to do this, be sure to let participants know beforehand that their remarks will be summarized for the group.

Pass out paper and pens and ask each person to write a brief paragraph summarizing any new insights or describing what he/she learned from the exercise.

Group discussion can follow if you have time. You might ask trigger questions such as:

- Can you be religious without being ritualistic?
- What did you learn about increasing or decreasing levels of religious commitment in past generations of your family?
- Were you surprised by anything you learned?
- Was any part of this exercise particularly difficult? Why?

Adapted from an exercise by Sherri Alper.

AS IF...

Objective: To provide participants with an opportunity to hear their partner's feelings about religion and childrearing.

Materials: Copies of the exercise and pencils.

Time required: 20 - 30 minutes

Instructions: Give each participant a copy of the exercise. Emphasize that they are filling out the exercise "as if" they were their partner. When complete, ask partners to exchange sheets. Discuss.

 What was the experience of pretending to be your partner like?

 Were you surprised at what you knew or didn't know about your partner's perspective?

 Were some questions more difficult than others?

Conclude the discussion by asking participants to trade sheets with their partner to take home. They should think about their partner's responses and continue to discuss these issues.

Adapted from an exercise by Sheila Pearl.

"As If..."

Please answer the following questions and respond to following scenarios *as if you were your partner:*

1. My first child has just been born. It's a boy. The first thought on my mind is to _____

_____

I would like to give him the name _____

because _____

2. When my children become 13 years old, I would like to have them celebrate by _____

_____; and when they turn 16, I would like them to have a

_____.

3. It is most important to me that my children learn the values of _____,

_____and _____.

4. I look forward to celebrating special holidays with my children. Two of my favorite holidays
   are _____

   and_____

5. We decided to raise our children as Christians, but also to celebrate the Jewish holidays.
   The way I would describe my feelings about my children receiving a Christian religious education is: _____

   _____

   _____

6. We decided to raise our children as Jews, and decided not to celebrate any Christian holiday
   in our home. During the Christmas holiday season, in order to give our children's
   Christian family an opportunity to be together, I would feel most comfortable doing the following: _____

   _____

7. My partner and I have discussed affiliation with a church or temple—or both. What I would
   feel most comfortable doing is: _____

   _____

8. My partner and I decided to raise our children as Jews. I think the most important aspect of
   being Jewish is _____

   _____

9. My partner and I decided that our children will not be raised in my religion. My greatest difficulty with this decision is: _____

_____

_____

My partner could help me with this problem by: _____

_____

What I feel saddest about, in not sharing my own heritage/religion with my children is

_____

10. In giving my children a religious education and identity which is different from mine, my greatest fear would be: _____

_____

11. In general , I would describe my greatest fear about these issues to be _____

_____

CHOOSING FAMILY SYMBOLS: BEYOND THE CHRISTMAS TREE

Objectives: To enable participants to consider the personal meaning of religious symbols; To explore ways in which religious symbols gain significance for individuals and families; To consider the role of religious symbols as carriers of identity.

Materials: A variety of Jewish and Christian religious symbols, such as a Chanukiah, dreidel, mezuzah, kiddush cup, small Torah scroll, a cross and/or crucifix, a small Christmas tree, etc. It may also be helpful to include a religious symbol, such as a totem pole or Egyptian ankh (key of life), that has no special significance for participants. The objects should be attractive ones.

Time Required: 45-50 minutes

Instructions: Begin with an introduction. The Christmas tree often serves as a lightning rod for tensions in interfaith families. Is it a religious symbol? a secular decoration? a marker of a Christian home? Feelings often run high as couples discuss what is, after all, only a tree. The tree is basically an innocent, very concrete stand-in for complex issues of family identity.

Ask participants to pass around a variety of religious objects (see above). Instruct group members to hold on to the item if they have a particularly strong connection to it—either positive or negative—and to discuss their connection with that object. Participants may ask for an object that has already been discussed as each person takes a turn.

You might raise the following questions for discussion:

How did the object you chose become such a powerful religious symbol for you?

How did you learn about your religious symbols?

Why did the ankh or totem pole not evoke any response?

What value do religious symbols have in enhancing our lives?

Adapted from an exercise by Dru Greenwood

THE TREE SCENARIO

Objective: To enable participants to consider "to tree or not to tree" objectively; To enable participants to gain a perspective on the issues and strong feel ings associated with religious symbols and holiday observance.

Materials: None

Time Required: 30-45 minutes

Instructions: Distribute a copy of the brief scenario on the next page and ask participants to divide into groups to discuss the questions. Each group should choose a "reporter" to describe what took place in their group when everyone reconvenes.

After the small groups have had time for discussion, reconvene the larger group and ask for reports. Have couples in the group had similar experiences?

Alternatively, ask two participants (not partners) to role play the scenario. A Christian might play Hannah and vice versa. Ask other participants to step into the roles. Continue with the discusssion questions.

To Tree or Not to Tree?

Dick and Hannah Johnson have been married for nearly 10 months when the holiday season begins. They were married in a civil ceremony, and have not discussed religion or participated in any religious celebrations or activities since their marriage. Dick unexpectedly tells Hannah that he plans to buy a Christmas tree for their apartment, and he'd like her to help in choosing and decorating it, since in his family cutting the tree and decorating it were always warm family times. Hannah responds that she couldn't possibly consider having a tree in her home, and she is appalled at Dick's insensitivity.

Discussion questions:

1. What are the feelings of each partner?

2. Are the reactions of each partner expected? Unexpected?
   Over-reactions? Justifiable?

3. As a friend, what suggestions would you give them for solving their dilemma?

4. How could this confrontation have been avoided?

5. Is there a "right" and "wrong" in this scenario? Explain.

CHAPTER 5

THOUGHT STARTERS
AND RESOURCE
MATERIALS

QUOTATIONS AND QUESTIONS FOR DISCUSSION

The following exercises maybe useful in stimulating informed discussions on topics of relevance for interfaith couples. These exercises contain quotations by scholars and experts on topics such as: the role of religion in the contemporary world; the relationship between Jews and the land of Israel; the impact of the Holocaust on the consciousness of modern Jews; and the reactions of adult children of intermarriage to their religious upbringing. Discussion questions are provided for each topic. Due to time constraints, you may wish to select only certain quotations for discussion in your group.

CONTENTS

QUOTATIONS AND QUESTIONS FOR DISCUSSION

I. WHY RELIGION?

The following quotations about religion can be effective discussion starters for programs of various kinds. They can be especially useful when participants begin to reflect on the value of religion in their lives. For maximum effectiveness, distribute copies of the quote(s) you plan to use to participants and be prepared with questions for discussion.

1. Religion (that is Torah: the full tradition of Jewish thought about the meaning of life, our goals and obligations as humans and as Jews) is for me the language in which I think about questions like: what is my purpose on earth? What do I owe my family, my friends, my community, my country? What policies should I support as a citizen and as a Jew? What do I owe my... profession? And what should my daily priorities be? Some people would say I turn to religion for my values. I see it more as being embedded, grounded in ways of thinking about my life that come from Torah and that revolve around the challenge: what does God want of me, now? Or what can I do with the powers and raw material that God equipped me with to add to God's glory and give thanks for body and mind, parents, community, tradition, love and care that I've received throughout my life?

My religious tradition doesn't give me specific answers to these questions (or let us say, some of the answers it purports to give I cannot in honesty accept), but it sets me in the direction for thinking seriously about them.

> Esther K. Ticktin
> "Religion and Psychotherapy"
> *Sh'ma* 22/423 Dec. 13, 1991

Discussion Questions

What is the influence of your religious beliefs on your everyday activities? your business? your social and personal life?

How does your religion make an impact on those "non-religious" moments of your life?

What values (if any) have you internalized from your religion? What have your rejected?

What is the religious language in which you speak?

Do you wish to pass this language on to your children?

How does the analogy of religion being like a language work its way out in terms of raising your children as "bilingual?"

Although it is possible to know two languages fluently, is it possible to speak two languages at the same time? Do you accept this analogy?

2. We believe in God to save our universe from nothingness.

Miguel de Unamuno

Discussion Questions:

Is God a human invention?

Does it matter if God is a human invention?

How does this statement make you feel (sad, hyperintellectual, no response)?

Can a Christian accept this statement and still be a Christian?

Can a Jew accept this statement and still be a Jew?

Why do you think some people believe in God while others do not?

3. In *Fear and Trembling* Kierkegaard says that faith in God is not intellectual, for God is beyond reason, just as the understanding of the infinite is beyond the ability of the finite. We cannot comprehend God; we simply believe in God out of our need to believe. We cannot argue rationally to the existence of God, despite the opinions of some mighty philosophers. Kierkegaard writes that faith begins where thinking leaves off. I realized that I needed to believe in God in order to make sense of my small square mile of existence. So I acknowledged the need, and I freely willed to believe in a creative and providential principle called God.

James P. Farnham
from an article in Judaism, summer 1985

Discussion Questions:

Is belief in God anti-intellectual?

What are different approaches to believing in God?

What are different names for God in different religions?

Do you feel more comfortable with some names than with others (e.g. Lord, Eternal, Ruler, King, Yahweh, Jehovah)?

Do you believe in God?

How is your belief similar/different from your partner's?

4. Religion is the opiate of the masses.

Karl Marx

Discussion Questions:

How do you react to this statement?

Do you agree or disagree?

Is an opiate necessarily an evil thing?

What was Karl Marx's religious background?

How does religion affect one's politics?

5. In Judaism, it is the emphasis on action, righteous behavior that I find so attractive. The ... encouragement of questions concerning belief, God, and truth is such a welcome relief. One can be religious and question! Once I learned that Israel meant "to struggle with God," I felt my destiny at hand.

Lydia Kukoff
from *Choosing Judaism*, 1981

Discussion Questions:

What does the author mean by the statement, "to struggle with God?"

Is a religious struggle necessary in today's already complex society?

What are the benefits of struggling with a religion's history and beliefs?

Can a good Jew or Christian doubt?

6. And I said to myself: Admit it, Salman, the Story of Islam has a deeper meaning for you than any of the other grand narratives. Of course you're no mystic.... No supernaturalism, no literalist orthodoxies for you. But Islam doesn't have to mean blind faith. It can mean what it always meant in your family, a culture, a civilization, as openminded as your grandfather was, as delightedly disputatious as your father was.... Don't let the zealots make Muslim a terrifying word, I urged myself; remember when it meant family....

Salman Rushdie
(from a speech adapted from his essay entitled, "One Thousand Days in a Balloon," 1991)

Discussion Questions:

How much of a religion is belief, and how much is culture and tradition?

Is being a Moslem, Christian, Jew, Buddhist, etc. much more than belief?

What does it mean for a religion to be a civilization?

Is one's religion equivalent to one's ethnic affiliation?

How is it the same or different?

7.   Social scientists increasingly focus on the bonding of family as a key factor in the growth and development of positive relationships among people and in the development of important values such as morality, empathy, compassion, and justice. The strengthening of the family and the reinforcement of these values thus have both religious and societal significance, adding immeasurably to the social fabric of our nation.

David Belin
(from "What Judaism Offers for You: A Reform Perspective," 1991)

Discussion Questions:

Does religion contribute to the common good?

What gifts does religion offer society?

How does religion strengthen the family?

Can religion tear families apart? Why?

Do you think religion is psychologically healthy?

8. The truth, though, is that the tannenbaum (Christmas tree) has precious little to do with Christian celebration and a lot to do with the stubborn survival through the millenia of pagan rituals of winter light and rebirth. Indeed, Christmas itself was superimposed over the ancient festivals that celebrated the winter solstice....

In the third century, when sun cults like the Mithraic religion of Persia found their way to Rome, days in December were given over to celebrate the rebirth of Sol Invictus: The invincible sun. In all likelihood both Hanukkah (the Jewish festival of light and national redemption) and Christmas were designed to compete with the persistence of idolatrous sun worship.

Simon Schama
(from "Whose Tree Is It Anyway?" *New York Times*, December 1991)

Discussion Questions:

If all religions have their roots in paganism, why can we not adopt whatever symbols we want?

Why should/ shouldn't a Jew have a Christmas tree?

Aren't we all the same anyway?

What gives integrity and meaning to a symbol?

9. I cannot be religious without belonging to a particular religion any more than I can talk without using a particular language.

George Santayana

Discussion Questions:

Is religion like a language?

Can a person make up a religious language of his or her own?

What does it mean to be the only person speaking one's own made up language?

Can a person be spiritual without religion?

What is spirituality?

10. Judaism is a religion of time aiming at the sanctification of time. Unlike the space-minded man to whom time is unvaried, iterative, homogeneous, to whom all hours are alike, qualityless, empty shells, the Bible senses the diversified character of time. There are no two hours alike. Every hour is unique and the only one given at the moment, exclusive, and endlessly precious.

Judaism teaches us to be attached to holiness in time, to be attached to sacred events rather than to sacred places, to learn how to consecrate sanctuaries that emerge from the magnificent stream of a year. The Sabbaths are our great cathedrals....

Abraham Joshua Heschel
in *Judaism,* 1952

Discussion Questions:

What does "to sanctify time" mean?

Does time have any intrinsic meaning?

How do religions view time?

Are certain times more holy than others (independent of human reactions to them)?

Give some examples of religious celebrations that are tied to the seasons.

What religious observances are tied to the "seasons" of our lives?

11.   Religion is the vision of something which stands beyond, behind, and within the passing flux of immediate things; something which is real, and yet waiting to be realized; something which is a remote possibility, and yet the greatest of present facts; something that gives meaning to all that passes, and yet eludes apprehension; something whose possession is the final good, and yet is beyond all reach; something which is the ultimate ideal, and the hopeless quest.

Alfred North Whitehead
(from *Science and the Modern World*)

Discussion Questions:

How does religion give "meaning to all that passes?"

How can something which "eludes apprehension" give meaning to life?

How can one gain understanding of a religion?

Is it a "hopeless" but worthy quest?

12.   I am a Jew because the faith of Israel demands of me no abdication of the mind.

I am a Jew because the faith of Israel requires of me all the devotion of my heart.

I am a Jew because in every place where suffering weeps, the Jew weeps.

I am a Jew because at every time when despair cries out, the Jew hopes.

I am a Jew because the word of Israel is the oldest and the newest.

I am a Jew because the promise of Israel is the universal promise.

I am a Jew because, for Israel, the world is not completed: we are completing it.

I am a Jew because, for Israel, humanity is not created; we are creating it.

I am a Jew because Israel places humanity and its unity above the nations and above Israel itself.

I am a Jew because, above humanity, image of the divine Unity, Israel places the unity which is divine.

Adapted from Edmond Fleg
("Why I am a Jew," translated by Louise Waterman Wise, 1929)

Discussion Questions:

Why are you a Jew, a Christian, Moslem, etc.?

Write your own version of this statement.

What would your parents write in their version?

What would you like your children to write in theirs?

FAMILY RITUALS MAY PROMOTE BETTER EMOTIONAL ADJUSTMENT
By Daniel Goleman

The question "Who's coming to dinner?" has taken on new meaning for researchers who find that household rituals like gathering for meals are a hidden source of family strength.

Casting an anthropologist's eye on rituals of family life, the researchers find that when families preserve their rituals, their children fare better emotionally, even in the face of disruptive problems like alcoholism.

"If you grow up in a family with strong rituals, you're more likely to be resilient as an adult," said Dr. Steven J. Wolin, a psychiatrist at the Family Research Center at George Washington University who is a leader of the research on family rituals.

Use of Rituals in Therapy

This new understanding has led some therapists to help families establish rituals as a way to heal family tensions.

At the same time, there is growing evidence that such bedrock rituals as a nightly dinner are giving way as more children are raised in single-parent homes or by mothers and fathers with demanding jobs. As a result, psychologists are urging these families to create alternative rituals to fit their circumstances.

The family rituals that provide psychological sustenance range from daily routines like reading children a book at bedtime to traditions like going the same place for a vacation every year to celebrations like Thanksgiving and graduations to going to church or synagogue regularly. Some families have offbeat rituals, like an "unbirthday party," celebrated at time of year when no family member has a birthday.

While such rituals may have obvious value in expressing a family's religious beliefs or cultural legacy, the research interest is in their long-term psychological value. It is unclear whether family rituals are a sign of an already strong family or play a crucial role in adding strength to the family. The main evidence for the emotional benefits of these rituals comes from a series of studies of families in which one or both parents were alcoholics. The research was conducted by Dr. Wolin and Linda Bennett, an anthropologist now at Memphis State University.

In the families studied, dinner was often a matter of family members' helping themselves to food in the kitchen and then going off separately to eat.

But not always.

A member of one family described dinners as a time "to talk and laugh," adding, "The best part is getting into everybody's life, finding out what they're doing." In that family, the dinner ritual included ringing a bell to call everyone to the table and holding hands while saying grace.

In a major 1980 study of 25 families, the researchers found that given equivalent severity of alcoholism in a parent, those children who came from homes where family dinners and other rituals continued despite a parent's heavy drinking were less likely to become alcoholics or to marry alcoholics.

Another study by Dr. Bennett and Dr. Wolin involved 68 married men and women who had an alcoholic parent. In 24 of the 31 couples who were least deliberate in carrying through rituals like regular dinner time and holiday celebrations, there was an alcoholic. But among the 12 couples most protective of such rituals, there were only three alcoholics.

The choice of a spouse whose family had strong rituals was especially protective for sons of alcoholics who are at much greater risk than daughters of becoming alcoholics. Even when their own family's rituals had repeatedly been ruined by a heavy-drinking parent, such children seem to acquire a resilience by marrying into a family dedicated to preserving rituals. In fact, some of the children of alcoholics may be drawn to marry into such families.

"It's unclear," Dr. Wolin said, "whether the advantage comes from the rituals themselves or whether the rituals are a marker of some other healthy capacity in family life."

Part of the power of rituals like dinner time, Dr. Wolin and other researchers say, appears to be in offering children a sense of stability and security, dependable anchors despite chaos in other areas of family life.

They also teach children in the most rudimentary way the importance of making a plan and seeing it through, even when other temptations, like a tempting television show, come along. Such lessons may be particularly important in countering the development of problems like heavy drinking where impulse control is tested.

While earlier studies have focused on families with a severely disruptive force like an alcoholic parent, family rituals are proving to be beneficial for children in general.

In a study of 240 college students and 70 of their parents, the more meaningful they felt their family rituals to be, the more positive was the students' sense of themselves, and the better able they were to bear up under stresses of the freshman year.

"It's not just whether rituals are kept, but how family members feel about them that determines their effect," said Dr. Barbara Fiese, a psychologist at Syracuse University, who will publish the study later this year in the journal Family Process.

In this study, too, rituals were especially helpful for those students who had a parent who was a heavy drinker, Dr. Fiese found. In that group, those students whose families valued rituals had lower levels of anxiety and fewer signs of physical distress like headaches than did those students from families who also placed great value on rituals but had no such severe problems at home.

"If you have a chronic stress in the family, rituals take on a much more powerful effect," Dr. Fiese said.

Most families begin to establish their rituals while their children are preschoolers, setting up traditions around holidays like Christmas and Halloween. By the time the children are 4 or 5 years old, families are able to stabilize daily rituals like dinner time, bathtime and bedtime.

For children 5 to 7, Dr. Fiese finds, rituals are particularly important as a stabilizing force in life. "Their family's rituals give children a sense of security and how their family works together, which is crucial in their own sense of identity," Dr. Fiese said.

Yet, even as studies are proving the value of rituals, new data suggest they are under siege in an increasing number of families. The bellwether indicator of ritual life is the family dinner, and recent data suggest that dinner time is being missed by many American families.

Most people old enough to be parents remember family dinners as a mandatory nightly ritual, and 80 percent of Americans in a recent national poll said their families tried to eat together most nights. But a more detailed study in Seattle found that only a third of families with children sat down to eat together every night of the week. A third of the families managed to eat together four nights a week or fewer. And one in 10 families had dinner together twice a week at most.

The data, not yet published, were collected from a study of 400 families with at least one child. The families were selected to represent major demographic features of the nation as a whole, like the numbers of single-parent families.

While there are no precise comparative figures from earlier decades, researchers agree that family dinner is on the decline.

"With two parents likely to be working, the numbers of families who manage to eat together at night is decreasing," said Dr. Michael Lewis, a psychologist at the Robert Wood Johnson medical school in New Brunswick, N.J., who led the study of family dinners. In 55 percent of families, dinner is brief, lasting 20 minutes or less, Dr. Lewis found.

In another study of 50 families with a 3-year-old child, Dr. Lewis made videotapes of the family at dinner. Perhaps because of the effect of a 3-year-old on the orderliness of things, Dr. Lewis says he believes that "dinner is the single disaster as a family ritual, too rushed, too hassled, with parents' using it as a time to discipline and socialize their kids."

But imposing rigorous standards for rituals can backfire, he said. "Clinging to a fixed form of a ritual can kill the spirit behind it," he said. "When you have strong expectations that a ritual must be a particular way, for example, that every family member must be together for Thanksgiving, it can just build tension."

One woman in his study told him about family dinners in her childhood. "They always ate formally, with cloth napkins, crystal and a table cloth," she said. "At the start of dinner, the father would take off his belt and hang it from the chandelier to let the kids know he meant them to behave."

As the woman told her story, she started to cry. "She realized she was being too stern, demanding the same rigid obedience at the table from her kids," Dr. Lewis said.

Tension over family rituals can undermine their positive effect. In Dr. Fiese's study, when children felt their family rituals were far less important than did their parents, that was a sign that the child would have a more difficult time adjusting to college.

"Mothers seem to be carriers of most family rituals." Dr. Fiese said. "But you see mothers and children disagreeing about their value when students are feeling estranged from their families. Then, when the students are home, dinner time and holidays like Christmas become lightening rods for family tensions."

Even so, family therapists are finding rituals can be helpful to many families. "If there have been major changes in a family, like a divorce, both parents working, or a teen-ager having an after-school job, then a nightly family dinner may be impossible" said Dr. Janine Roberts, a family therapist at the University of Massachusetts, whose book "Ritual for Our Time" will be published this year by Harper Collins.

"People are returning to family rituals because the world is losing a sense of what's important, offering instead shallow beliefs and sound-bite values," Dr. Roberts said. "Family rituals help people affirm what their beliefs really are."

INNER SPACE
This article is reprinted by permission of Ms. Magazine in which it appeared in January/February 1992.

Slow Rise: Braiding a Tradition

By Anndee Hochman

It took me 28 years to realize that challah wouldn't rise by itself. I was waiting, the way women are taught to wait, for the perfect conditions. Waiting for a family that fit some recognizable template, for a partner to share my home, for a synagogue to reach out and enfold me in its Friday night Shabbes (Sabbath) ritual, for someone to assign me the task, for challah to spring spontaneously from the rightness of things.

I was behaving the way women are taught to behave, patient and passive, hoping for someone to endorse my idea, to invite me inside, to solicit my help, to say she was hungry and only challah would do.

This year I took the ritual into my own hands. I followed my partner's great-grandmother's recipe: six cups of flour, a toss of salt, make a well in the center, three eggs, half a cup of oil. When I'm finished, there are two braided loaves, brushed with eggs and freckled with poppy seeds, steaming when I pull off the first piece.

Before, I thought making challah from scratch was a cultural mystery owned by another generation; I was not quite deserving of induction into its secrets. My cousins and I, after all, grew up in typically assimilated late-twentieth-century Jewish homes. I didn't go to Hebrew School. I did not have a Bat Mitzvah. I know more French and Spanish than I do Yiddish. Was I Jewish enough to make challah?

The first time I made it by myself, the process was pure magic—the yeast burping alive in a bowl of warm water, the eggs and oil and flour suddenly smoothing together in a pale-yellow mass, the slow rise under a dish towel. Even the second time, the twelfth time, shreds of wonder remain. I push and prod the dough and think of my great-grandfather Samuel, in his Philadelphia bakery, tossing a few extra loaves into customers' bags.

But sometimes, I have to confess, it's a chore like any other chore. I mix the dough fast with my left hand, thinking about the deadline for my next article. I tear the dough roughly and wind it into quick, tight braids.

I do it anyway, because I am interested in the big picture, the persistence of a private ritual I've begun. I want that even more than I want to indulge my desire, on any particular afternoon, to make phone calls, or to take a walk and buy challah at the bakery. Sometimes in the course of measuring flour and pinching three strands of dough together, I feel my unruly thoughts slow down, my body settle into the routine like a carrying tide.

I look forward to interrupting my work on Friday afternoons, making the day different. I like Shabbes, observing the spasms of activity and quiet that make the world. The challah reminds me that while I am a writer, I am also a Jew, the great-granddaughter of a baker, and a human being who needs to rest once in a while.

I wish I could say I am making challah as my mother did before me, as my grandmother did before her. But it wouldn't be true. My mother's one botched attempt at making challah is the stuff of family legend (she and her cousin kept adding powdered sugar, instead of white flour). I'm not so much continuing a tradition as searching the cultural tapestry for a bright, textured thread and tugging it into my own life.

In that life, I sometimes eat challah alone. Sometimes I share it with my partner, housemates, or friends. I give one loaf to the neighbors across the street; I bring one to a dinner party. Sometimes we're busy and grab hunks of hot bread on our way out the door.

The challah is different each week, depending on the season in which the eggs were laid, the coarseness of the flour, the temperature of the house, the heat in my hands, the tightness of the braid, what I am thinking as I shape it. Each Friday night will be different from the

I took the ritual into my own hands. . . . Continuity does not mean sameness.

last, no matter how much I try to make it familiar. Continuity does not mean sameness.

When it is time to tear the bread and recite a blessing, I hesitate. "*Baruch Atah Adondai, Eloheinu Melech Haolam . . .*" ("Blessed Art Thou, King of the Universe"). The Hebrew words comfort me, their sounds ancient lullabies. But they clash with my sense of the universe, where power and reverence are diffused, a bit to each of us, a bit to the flounder and the Japanese maples, too. There is no king—nor queen, for that matter—in my prayers.

What I'd like to offer, whether anyone hears it or not, is a blessing of my own invention. I'd like to acknowledge the alchemy of tradition and imagination it takes for me to serve challah to my lover and friends 3,000 miles from the site of Samuel's bakery. I'd like to feel glad for a moment that there are still places on this earth where wheat can grow, and farmers can tend it.

The flour sits in the canister. The oven is warm enough for the dough to rise. The sun is three hours from setting. There is no reason to wait. **Ms**

Anndee Hochman is a free-lance writer living in Portland, Oregon. This essay is an excerpt from a book-in-progress, "Essential Outlaws: Women Exploring Kinship," to be published in 1993 by the Eighth Mountain Press, Portland, Oregon.

II. JEWS AND ISRAEL

Our Attachment to Israel

by Nancy Gad-Harf

As Jews, we are taught that three elements guide and inform our Judaism: God, Torah, and Israel. In this context, "Israel" is usually taken as a reference to *K'lal Yisrael,* the people of Israel or the Jewish people as a collectivity. It is that notion of *K'lal Yisrael,* the Jewish people, that helps to explain the attachment we modern American Reform Jews feel today to the state of Israel.

In a variety of experiential activities designed to focus on Jewish identity, the following question is sometimes asked: Do you consider yourself a Jewish American or an American Jew? The former, in theory, views him/herself as an American whose religious tradition and ethnic identity is bound to Judaism. The latter, again in theory, defines him/herself as one who is a Jew above all else, whose family happens to be living in America— a stop along the route of the wandering Jew. Both groups are loyal Jews and loyal Americans. The difference between the two, however, lies in where they place their Jewishness within the overall context of their lives and identities. As the Jewish community becomes more firmly entrenched in American society, as we become more assimilated into American culture, we as a community often tend to think of ourselves as Jewish Americans, one element in the rich mosaic of Americana. And now, when we think of Israel, we are inclined to think of a place— not of a people. We think of Israel as a miracle— the lone democracy amidst countries with long histories of totalitarian and oligarchic regimes, a blossoming landscape amidst a dry desert, a homeland created out of the ashes of the Holocaust.

This miracle of Israel has become a great source of pride for us as Jews. It is a place we think of as ours— ours to visit, ours to support financially and politically, and ours to protect.

Jewish "baby boomers" and their parents and grandparents tend to have an intense connection to the State of Israel, based upon an almost indescribable, unconditional love for and attachment to a place where many of them have yet to travel.

What explains this attachment, this fierce loyalty? These individuals witnessed the creation of Israel as well as its incredible survival in wars waged by its enemies. They witnessed the development of agricultural and technological innovations that have illuminated the world. They have witnessed Israel in some of its finest hours as it has struggled to become "a light unto the nations."

For the children of the "baby boomers," the great-grandchildren of Holocaust survivors, Israel looks a little less like a miracle and more like a nation run by mere, flawed human beings.

The challenge for us today is to teach the miracle of the Jewish state, including its problems, and to nurture among our young people and newcomers the connection between American Jewry and Israel that has defined our relationship for 43 years.

For the younger generation of American Jews and for those new to Judaism—whether through conversion or marriage, what they know about Israel tends to be what they read in newspapers or magazines or what they see on television. And a great deal of that is very grim. We watch the Israeli reaction to the intifada— without having an understanding for the underlying historical issues. We hear of the harsh reaction to the creation of Jewish settlements on the West Bank— without having accurate knowledge of either the Palestinian or Jewish perspective. We see the carnage of Sabra and Shatilla— without seeing the outrage of the Israeli public and its legal community's reaction to this destruction.

What our young and new Jews know about Israel is that it is a country mismanaged by an inept government in which the foreigner seems not to be treated well. It may appear to our young Jews that the leadership in Israel has forgotten that we, too, were once strangers in a strange land.

Our young people and newcomers also lack the need for the security that the notion of Israel offers to those of us who either lived through the Holocaust or have studied it. To consider that there would ever be a need for a "safe place for Jews to go" is inconceivable to them.

We need to consider Israel as a combination of the miraculous and the practical. It is, after all, a humanly conceived and executed political system, albeit a democratic one. It is a political system in which we American Jews have a vested interest and which we must support, but not uncritically. Indeed, because of our love for Israel, we have an obligation to help it. But we can neither expect its leadership to be perfect nor to meet more exacting standards than those applied to other world leaders.

Once we have accepted the practical, we must teach about the miraculous. For example, since 1985, Israel has rescued thousands of Jews from the Soviet Union and Ethiopia. Why? Because we as Jews are commanded to rescue the captive. With breathtaking political and diplomatic skill and great moral courage, Israel became the first country in history to bring blacks to its shores in freedom, not in the chains of slavery. Israel struggled valiantly to bring endangered Soviet Jews home to the land of Israel. Indeed, even as SCUD missiles landed in Tel Aviv during the Persian Gulf War, planes carrying Soviet Jews landed at Ben Gurion Airport.

The arrival home of these Jews has not been without political problems, ranging from questions of Jewish authenticity to homelessness. But what country on earth could absorb a similar proportion of its population without some difficulty? And what country on earth would try?

As we begin to explore Israel and its significance to us, then, we must do so by putting the issues within an historical context. We must understand the issues which led to the creation of Israel in order to be able to understand the current rage of the intifada and the conflict between Arab and Jew.

An historical context will also help us to understand the fundamental Jewish mission of the State of Israel, as understood and implemented by its leaders, working to preserve a very young democratic process.

A sense of history will also help us to understand the critical need for American Jewish support for Israel and the responsibility our community has to urge Israel to follow the right course. We must teach that we, even as Jews living in America, have the right and the obligation to express our concern as well as our support for Israel and its government's decisions.

Finally, a sense of history will help us to understand that our own survival as a people is inextricably linked to the survival of a strong, secure, democratic Israel.

The story of Israel should be an inspiration to all people, but especially to the Jewish community. For those coming of age or joining the Jewish people today, it may be hard to be inspired by Israeli politics and policy-making. Thus, it is imperative that we begin the story of the modern State of Israel with its birth and discuss its strengths and weaknesses realistically and honestly. At the same time, we must seize every opportunity to underscore the Jewishness of the Jewish State. Ultimately, we must teach that the State of Israel, the homeland of our ancestors and of generations of Jews still to be born, is a fundamental component of *K'lal Yisrael,* the Jewish people.

QUOTATIONS AND QUESTIONS FOR DISCUSSION

North American Jews and Israel

1. Once upon a time, Israel gave us our Jewish identity. Those who had lost their Judaic faith in the Holocaust created a new faith out of some politicized, socialized ideal, wrapped in the then unstained blue and white flag of Israel. Many found their Jewish *raison d'etre* in Israel.

-Balfour Brickner in "My Zionist Dilemmas,
Twenty Years Later," *Sh'ma,* 1990

Discussion Questions:

What is the "politicized, socialized ideal" of Israel?

Why would the establishment of a political entity give a Jewish person a reason to remain a Jew?

How soon after the Holocaust did the state of Israel become a recognized, political state?

How can a non-Jewish partner in an interfaith couple share in the Jewish partner's connection to Israel?

2. ... the demands which American Jews make upon the State are not the same as those of the people who live there. We need an Israel which in its existence, vitality and might validates our still fragile sense of Jewish life in the shadow of the death camps. We need a country which supports our claim to higher moral standards, illustrating for all to see Jewish teachings of social justice and compassion.... we need it, as well, to validate our own sense of what Jewish history has been and where it leads. In short, we need Israel to help us remain Jews....

- Balfour Brickner in "My Zionist Dilemmas,
Twenty Years Later," *Sh'ma,* 1990

Discussion Questions:

How does Rabbi Brickner describe the non-Israeli Jew's relationship to the country?

Why is the sense of Jewish life so fragile after the Holocaust?

Is it fair for non-Israeli Jews to demand ethical superiority from Israel in its political functioning?

Why would Israel be an anchor for a Jewish person's identity?

3. We are privileged to live in an extraordinary time, one in which a third Jewish commonwealth has been established in our people's ancient homeland. We are bound to that land and to the newly reborn State of Israel by innumerable religious and ethnic ties.... We have both a stake and a responsibility in building the State of Israel, assuring its security and defining its Jewish character.

- Centenial Perspective of the Central
Conference of American Rabbis, 1976

Discussion Questions:

What are Diaspora Jews' religious and ethnic ties to Israel?

Why do Diaspora Jews feel a responsibility to support Israel?

Do all Diaspora Jews feel this responsibility?

What is an American Jew's "stake" in the "security" and religious character of Israel?

How is an American Jew's sense of attachment and commitment to Israel different from or similar to an Italian or Irish American's attachment to his/her country of origin?

Is it possible to create "ethnic" ties to a country which one has adopted or embraced?

4. And turn in compassion to Jerusalem, Your city. Let there be peace in her gates, quietness in the hearts of her inhabitants. Let Your Torah go forth from Zion and Your Word from Jerusalem.

-prayer in the daily Jewish worship service

Next year in Jerusalem!

- final words of the Passover seder in the Passover Haggadah

Discussion Questions:

Why do Jews face the East when they worship?

What could be a psychological effect of including prayers for Israel in the daily ritual of worship?

Why do Jews in all parts of the world who have strong religious connections in their own communities still recite the words that the message of God will go forth from Jerusalem?

What is the metaphorical meaning of "next year in Jerusalem?"

5. After wandering in the desert for forty years, Moses and the Israelites finally reached the border of the land of Israel. At this point, two of the tribes (the Reubenites and the Gadites) decided not to enter the land of Israel, but to settle in the fertile lands of Jazer and Gilead. These tribes owned great numbers of cattle, and the land outside of Israel was more suitable for cattle raising. The tribes came to Moses, Eleazar the priest, and the chieftains of the community to ask permission to remain outside of Israel.

Moses reminded them of their communal responsibility saying: "Are your brothers to go to war while you stay here...?" Moses and the two tribes then worked out a compromise in which the tribes could fulfill their obligation to their fellow Israelites. If the men from the tribes promised to serve as shock-troops and go to battle in Israel, and help subdue the land, they could then return to their homes outside of Israel with clear consciences. Moses warned these "diaspora" Jews, "But if you do not do so [serve as shock-troops], you will have sinned against the Lord; and know that your sin will overtake you. Build towns for your children and sheep-folds for your flocks [here outside of Israel], but do what you have promised [go and make sure the rest of the tribes find a safe home in the land of Israel]."

-from the Bible, Numbers 32:1-24

Discussion Questions:

What message does this story have for Jews who live outside the geographical boundaries of Israel?

Do Jews who live in areas outside of Israel still have a responsibility to defend Israel?

According to this story, are Jews permitted to live outside of Israel for economic reasons?

How do Diaspora Jews still act as "shock-troops" for Israel?

Can non-Jews feel responsible for Israel's existence?

6.   For the Jew, Israel is a state of mind.

It is not only a piece of geography.

It is history.

It is theology.

It is memory.

It is Jewish tears and Jewish triumphs.

It is Jewish anguish and Jewish ecstasy.

It is childhood legends and Biblical verses.

It is the direction that we pray and the subject of our prayers.

It is exile and homecoming.

It is a burning Temple and a new flag at the United Nations.

It is Tisha B'Av and the 5th of Iyar.

It is a people restored and hope reborn.

-From "Israel and the Jew," author unknown

(Tisha B'Av is the ninth day of the Hebrew month of Av, and a fast day commemorating the destruction of the Temple in Jerusalem. The fifth day of Iyar is the Hebrew date for Israeli Independence Day).

Discussion Questions:

Many Diaspora Jews are buried with a bag of soil from Israel. Why does this connection to Israel even transcend life?

Does the author describe Israel in overly romantic terms?

Have you ever been to Israel? Describe your impressions, experiences.

How does Israel make Jewish identity more concrete for Diaspora Jews?

Do you feel a powerful connection to Israel? Do you want your children to feel this link with the country? Why?

ISRAEL SCENARIOS

Goals and Objectives

1. The scenarios are designed to help the participants understand the importance to Jews of Israel as a country, homeland, and link among Jews throughout the world.

a. *K'lal Yisrael*

It is always difficult to teach about "peoplehood," particularly when members of the group are likely to identify themselves primarily as Americans. The vignettes should be helpful in introducing the notion of being connected to a culture and civilization which has a 4000 year old history.

b. *Israel—the Homeland and the Political Entity*

Israel is also a refuge and homeland for the Jewish people—concepts difficult for the comfortable American (sometimes for the Jew just as much as the non-Jew) to comprehend. Why, for example, would anyone need a refuge or a homeland if one is an American citizen?

Israel is also a political body, very much the focus of current international politics. A participant (either Jewish or not) may ask, "Why should I care about a little country thousands of miles away?"

The scenarios are designed to facilitate participants' discussion regarding the realities of Israeli politics, the historical ties between Israel and the U.S. Government, and the bonds between the American Jewish community and our Israeli sisters and brothers.

2. The scenarios are also intended to help interfaith couples begin to see the world through a Jewish perspective. It is our hope, for example, that they begin to view what happens in Israel as relevant to their lives either as Jews or as the partner of a Jew.

a. *K'lal Yisrael*

Optimally, at the conclusion of an eight-week program, the participants will see themselves as part of a human continuum. In reality, we can hope that they begin to *feel* as well as intellectualize the role they play as part of a larger whole, as members of a group that somehow transcends their daily existence and environment. The scenarios are designed to help them understand their role as a link in the tradition and, perhaps, their responsibility for not breaking that link. It is also intended that they begin to formulate ways in which they can realistically form this link.

b. *Israel - the Homeland and the Political Entity*

The scenarios should provide an introduction to the historical role of Israel in the lives of the Jewish people. Participants should gain an understanding of the history of Israel, the process of the creation of the State of Israel, the major highlights of the life of the State of Israel, and current political issues facing Israel.

Scenarios

1. You are having a discussion over lunch with you coworkers during the Persian Gulf War. Your friend and colleague argues that the U.S. Government should not be spending money to send Patriot missiles and military personnel to Israel. Others agree that this is an unnecessary waste of the American taxpayer's money. How do you react?

2. The President of the United States has held a nationally televised news conference to announce that he will veto a congressionally approved bill to give the State of Israel a significant amount of money in loan guarantees. The government of the State of Israel has stated that resettlement of recent Soviet immigrants will be impossible without these loan guarantees. How do you react to this issue?

3. You are the Jewish spouse and work in a predominantly Jewish law firm. You have been approached by one of your colleagues to make a pledge to the UJA campaign. You want very much to make such a commitment, but your spouse demurs - not comprehending your need to support the UJA or local Jewish organizations in your community. How do you resolve the conflict? Do you ultimately make the pledge or not? What could be done to help your spouse understand the value of communal support and involvement?

4. You are the Jewish spouse in an interfaith couple that has raised your children as Jews. Your oldest has just been confirmed as a part of your congregation's educational program. She has been asked to participate in a confirmation class trip to Israel. The trip's expenses have been completely covered by the congregation, so money is not an issue. Your non-Jewish spouse, however, does not understand why your child - an American who happens to practice Judaism as a religion, should go to Israel, and argues angrily against her participation in the trip. You feel just as strongly that your child should have the Israel experience, especially under the auspices of the congregation. How do you resolve this conflict? Does your daughter go to Israel or not?

Discussion Questions

a. Do you feel a sense of connection toward Israel? How would you describe it?

b. Does your religious affiliation influence your political views? Why or why not?

c. Do American Jews have a responsibility to provide support to Jews in Israel? Why or why not?

d. Why or why not would you want your children to feel a bond with Jews in Israel?

e. How important is the existence of the land of Israel to you and your family?

f. Jewish identity for born Jews often focuses on ethnicity. For Jews-by-Choice, Jewish identity may revolve around religious thought. How can intermarried couples bridge this gap in Jewish experience when discussing Israel? How might this divergence in experience influence views toward Israel?

QUOTATIONS AND QUESTIONS FOR DISCUSSION

III. IN THE SHADOW OF THE HOLOCAUST

Partners in interfaith couples often express confusion over the mention of the Holocaust in the context of their relationship. Some couples view their love as a victory over the hatred and prejudice that the Holocaust exemplified. In addition to the terrible loss of over six million Jews, five million other souls also were victims of Hitler and those who helped him. Non-Jews may ask why Jews see the Holocaust as a particularly "Jewish" tragedy.

Ask participants to read "Intermarriage and the Holocaust" and discuss.

Intermarriage and the Holocaust
by Sharon Forman

The Holocaust weighs on the minds of modern Jews. The overwhelming hatred of Jews and the systematic destruction of a vast proportion of the world Jewish population has left an indelible mark in Jewish consciousness. The Nazis and those who assisted them murdered a third of the world's Jewish population. This "amputation" of such a significant part of the Jewish people is a loss whose pain is still sharply felt.

Parents and friends of the Jewish partner in an interfaith couple may view the marriage as the end of the Jewish tradition in a family. After so many Jews perished in the Holocaust, many Jews harbor a sense of responsibility to carry on a Jewish identity (even in families that do not observe any Jewish customs). Since 90% of children of mixed marriages do not marry Jews (statistics from the Council of Jewish Federations), the affiliation with Judaism often does end with a mixed marriage.

Emil Fackenheim admonished Jews living in the shadow of the Holocaust not to give Hitler a "posthumous victory." When Jews intermarry and cease to live as Jews or do not raise Jewish children, they may feel guilt or may be subject to other Jews' disapproval for their action.

In the mid 1800s, one of the early leaders of Reform Judaism wrote that intermarriage was "the nail in the coffin of the small Jewish race." After the Holocaust, this statement becomes even more emotionally charged.

Because the Holocaust is such a powerful part of the collective Jewish consciousness, it is often cited as a reason for being vigilant about preserving one's Jewish identity. Jews carry a sense of responsibility to those who lost their lives and feel compelled to remember the enormous tragedy so that it will never happen again.

Even if a Jewish individual does not participate in the "religious" ceremonies or worship of a synagogue, that person may still retain a strong sense of kinship with the Jewish people. A parent who seems to have no external commitment to Judaism or religious practice may protest a child's decision to intermarry. That parent may feel that he or she has failed in his or her responsibility to continue an age-old tradition and faith. The guilt is further compounded by the Holocaust, which shifted the "responsibility" of perpetuating Judaism onto those who escaped Hitler's deadly grasp.

Discussion Questions:

- How does Jewish identity differ from Christian identity?

- Can one be a Christian if one never attends church or never performs sacraments? Is a person still Jewish if he or she never attends synagogue?

- What are the dangers of focusing on the Holocaust as the central principle of one's Jewish identity?

- Do you feel connected to other Jews from different parts of the world?

- Do you think about the Holocaust frequently? How does the word, Holocaust, affect you?

- Do you remember learning about the Holocaust? How and when were you taught about this tragedy?

- Do you feel a connection to the Jews who perished in the Holocaust?

In the Shadow of the Holocaust

Primo Levi was an Italian, Jewish chemist who survived the Nazi death camps during the Holocaust. He has written a number of poems as well as novels touching on his experiences during and after the Holocaust.

This poem takes its title from the "Shema" prayer in Jewish liturgy. The "Shema" is found in the Bible and is often described as "the watchword" of the Jewish faith. The word shema means "hear!" The prayer proclaims the unity of the One God, and outlines how followers of the one God can best show their love for their Creator through teaching and remembering. The prayer's English translation can be found on the following page.

SHEMA

You who live secure
In your warm houses,
Who return at evening to find
Hot food and friendly faces:

    Consider whether this is a man,
    Who labors in the mud
    Who know no peace
    Who fights for a crust of bread
    Who dies at a yes or a no.
    Consider whether this is a woman,
    Without hair or name
    With no more strength to remember
    Eyes empty and womb cold
    As a frog in winter.

Consider that this has been:
I commend these words to you.
Engrave them on your hearts
When you are in your house, when you walk on your way,
When you go to bed, when you rise.
Repeat them to your children.
Or may your house crumble,
Disease render you powerless,
Your offspring avert their faces from you.

      10 January 1946
      Primo Levi
      Collected Poems
      Translated by Ruth Feldman and Brian Swann

Discussion Questions on "Shema":

What does the word "Shema" mean? Jews traditionally recite this central prayer of the Jewish faith daily and even as they prepare to die. How does this fact alter the way you read the poem?

How does the poet reinterpret the duties of a Jew from the original prayer?

How do Jews today follow Primo Levi's mandate to remember the Holocaust?

Do you feel a connection to the Jews who perished in the Holocaust?

Do you feel a connection to other Jews from different parts of the world?

How does the word "Holocaust" affect you?

Do you know any survivors of the Holocaust? What are their stories?

What are the dangers of focusing on the Holocaust as the central principle of one's Jewish identity?

שְׁמַע יִשְׂרָאֵל: יְיָ אֱלֹהֵינוּ, יְיָ אֶחָד!

Hear, O Israel: the Lord is our God, the Lord is One!

בָּרוּךְ שֵׁם כְּבוֹד מַלְכוּתוֹ לְעוֹלָם וָעֶד!

Blessed is His glorious kingdom for ever and ever!

All are seated

וְאָהַבְתָּ אֵת יְיָ אֱלֹהֶיךָ בְּכָל־לְבָבְךָ וּבְכָל־נַפְשְׁךָ וּבְכָל־מְאֹדֶךָ.
וְהָיוּ הַדְּבָרִים הָאֵלֶּה, אֲשֶׁר אָנֹכִי מְצַוְּךָ הַיּוֹם, עַל־לְבָבֶךָ.
וְשִׁנַּנְתָּם לְבָנֶיךָ, וְדִבַּרְתָּ בָּם בְּשִׁבְתְּךָ בְּבֵיתֶךָ, וּבְלֶכְתְּךָ
בַדֶּרֶךְ, וּבְשָׁכְבְּךָ וּבְקוּמֶךָ.

*You shall love the Lord your God with all your mind, with
all your strength, with all your being.*
*Set these words, which I command you this day, upon your
heart. Teach them faithfully to your children; speak of them
in your home and on your way, when you lie down and when
you rise up.*

וּקְשַׁרְתָּם לְאוֹת עַל־יָדֶךָ, וְהָיוּ לְטֹטָפֹת בֵּין עֵינֶיךָ, וּכְתַבְתָּם
עַל־מְזֻזוֹת בֵּיתֶךָ, וּבִשְׁעָרֶיךָ.

*Bind them as a sign upon your hand; let them be a symbol
before your eyes; inscribe them on the doorposts of your
house, and on your gates.*

לְמַעַן תִּזְכְּרוּ וַעֲשִׂיתֶם אֶת־כָּל־מִצְוֹתָי, וִהְיִיתֶם קְדֹשִׁים
לֵאלֹהֵיכֶם. אֲנִי יְיָ אֱלֹהֵיכֶם, אֲשֶׁר הוֹצֵאתִי אֶתְכֶם מֵאֶרֶץ
מִצְרַיִם לִהְיוֹת לָכֶם לֵאלֹהִים. אֲנִי יְיָ אֱלֹהֵיכֶם.

*Be mindful of all My mitzvot, and do them: so shall you
consecrate yourselves to your God. I, the Lord, am your God
who led you out of Egypt to be your God; I, the Lord, am
your God.*

XVI

The Jews I've felt rooted among
are those who were turned to smoke

Reading of the chimneys against the blear air
I think I have seen them myself

the fog of northern Europe licking its way
along the railroad tracks

to the place where all tracks end
You told me not to look

to become
a citizen of the world

bound by no tribe or clan
yet dying you followed the Six Day War

with desperate attention
and this summer I lie awake at dawn

sweating the Middle East through my brain
wearing the star of David

on a thin chain at my breastbone

Your Native Land, Your Life
by Adrienne Rich

Discussion Questions on Poem by Adrienne Rich:

Do you feel connected to those Jews who perished in the Holocaust?

Do you feel that all Jews who are alive today share a sense of "survivor's guilt" because they were not killed in the Holocaust?

Does this "guilt" manifest itself in Jewish life? If so, how?

How does the poet describe the tension between being a Jew and a citizen of the world?

What are the dangers of having one's identity defined by a catastrophe?

Describe some positive ways of identifying with the Jewish people.

Background to the Catastrophe

by Paula Hyman

PAULA HYMAN is Lucy Moses Professor of Modern Jewish History at Yale University. She is the author of *From Dreyfus to Vichy: The Remaking of French Jewry 1906–1939*.

The Jewish civilization of Europe, whose destruction *Shoah* carefully chronicles, had a history stretching back over 1,000 years. On the eve of the Holocaust more than half the Jews of the world lived in Europe. The nine million European Jews were a diverse group, living in a wide variety of political and cultural conditions.

Before the outbreak of World War II, fewer than 1.5 million Jews lived in Western and Central Europe, where they constituted a tiny proportion of the total population. West European Jews had contributed to the economic expansion of their countries and had often entered the urban middle class. Some had risen to prominence in the academic world, the arts, business and politics. Though as Jews, they retained their own religious, charitable and cultural institutions, they were virtually indistinguishable from their Gentile neighbors in dress, language and public behavior.

The approximately eight million Jews in Eastern Europe constituted a higher percentage of the general population and were more distinct and visible as a minority. More Jews lived in Poland than in any other European nation; in the 1930s they accounted for fully 10% of the Polish population and 30 to 40% of the populations of the large cities. The majority of East European Jews earned modest livelihoods as shopkeepers and artisans. Some had begun the process of cultural integration into the larger society, but most lived among their fellow Jews, spoke their own language (Yiddish) and maintained a traditional Jewish lifestyle.

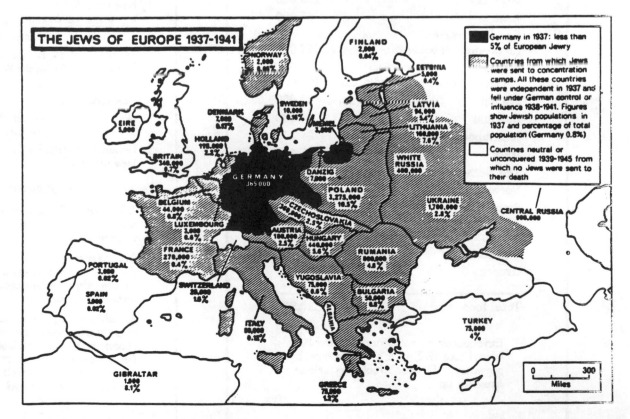

Despite mounting discrimination and anti-Semitism, the interwar era was a time of remarkable Jewish creativity in Eastern Europe. Many forms of Jewish culture, including journalism, poetry, theater, political movements, youth groups, Hebrew and Yiddish schools and rabbinic learning flourished up until the Nazi onslaught.

By 1933, Jews throughout Europe had achieved many goals for which they had been struggling for almost 150 years. In all the countries of Europe they enjoyed the rights of citizenship. Yet, despite their political and social advances, they found themselves particularly vulnerable. Economic depression and rising nationalism led many to blame the Jews for their misfortunes. Adolf Hitler took advantage of these trends and rose to power in Germany in 1933 partly on the basis of his anti-Semitic platform.

Between 1933 and 1939 Hitler—with little opposition—turned the Jews of Germany (and later Austria) into an impoverished and rightless minority by removing them from governmental positions, stripping them of citizenship and confiscating their property. On the night of November 9, 1938, known as the "Night of Broken Glass," a wave of anti-Jewish violence throughout Germany resulted in the destruction of Jewish stores and synagogues and the death of 92 Jews.

In most countries conquered by the Nazis, the Jews were forced to wear a yellow star, deprived of civil rights and property and concentrated together. The Jews of Poland were herded into crowded, walled ghettos in the major cities. Death rates in the ghettos were very high, owing to dreadful sanitary conditions and starvation-level rations.

When Hitler's Germany invaded the Soviet Union in June 1941, mobile killing units of the Nazi army began the first systematic extermination of the Jews. In January 1942, Hitler and his aides decided upon the "Final Solution to the Jewish Problem": the mass murder of all of European Jewry. From the summer of 1942 through the summer of 1944, as *Shoah* grimly records, the Nazis invested precious labor power and resources to deport Jews from all parts of Europe in sealed railroad cars to slave-labor and death camps. There the Nazis brutally worked and starved the able Jewish inmates to death and consigned women, children and the weak to immediate gassing and cremation.

When the camps were liberated by the Allies in early 1945, the entire Western world discovered how a civilized European nation had employed the most advanced technology to torture, dehumanize and murder a people in the name of ideology. After World War II, only 1.3 million Jews remained alive in Europe (outside the USSR). The European age of Jewish history had come to a tragic conclusion.

Estimates of Jewish Victims During the Holocaust

Polish-Soviet area	4,565,000
Germany	125,000
Austria	65,000
Czechoslovakia (in pre-Munich boundaries)	277,000
Hungary (including northern Transylvania)	402,000
France	83,000
Belgium	24,000
Luxembourg	700
Italy	7,500
The Netherlands	106,000
Norway	760
Rumania (Regat, southern Transylvania, southern Bukovina)	40,000
Yugoslavia	60,000
Greece	65,000
Total loss	**5,820,960**

Encyclopaedia Judaica, Jerusalem: Keter Publishing House, 1972, vol. 8, p. 889. Reprinted by permission of Keter Publishing House, Jerusalem, Ltd.

SUGGESTED READINGS

Lucy S. Dawidowicz, *The Golden Tradition: Jewish Life and Thought in Eastern Europe*, Boston, 1967.

Lucy S. Dawidowicz, *The War Against the Jews 1933–1945*, New York, 1986.

Paul R. Mendes-Flohr and Jehuda Reinharz, *The Jew in the Modern World: A Documentary History*, New York, 1980.

Martin Gilbert, *The Holocaust, A History of the Jews of Europe During the Second World War*, New York, 1986.

Raul Hilberg, *The Destruction of the European Jews*, 3 vols., New York, 1985.

Nora Levin, *The Holocaust: The Destruction of European Jewry, 1933–1945*, New York, 1973.

Howard M. Sachar, *The Course of Modern Jewish History*, New York, 1977.

DISCUSSION QUESTIONS

1. The Jews of Germany comprised a tiny percentage of its total population. What factors caused them to be singled out for persecution?

2. In the past, Jews could find refuge from discrimination by disassociating themselves from Judaism or changing their religion. Why were these options not open to Jews in Nazi dominated Europe?

3. Midway through *Shoah*, Lanzmann visits the Greek island of Corfu to interview Holocaust survivors. They describe their deportation to Auschwitz. Does it surprise you that Jews on a Greek island became part of the Nazi mechanism of death? How does *Shoah* chronicle the transport of Jews from many nations to the death camps?

QUOTATIONS AND QUESTIONS FOR DISCUSSION

IV. ADULT CHILDREN OF INTERMARRIAGE SPEAK

Questions for Discussion:

Adult Children of Intermarriage Speak

1. "Kids may feel alone in a certain social sense.... But I felt alone in a very basic family sense. I never felt I belonged anywhere. I didn't belong." (1, p. 261)

2. "I think my parents have one of the most beautiful relationships I've ever seen. I really admire them. What they have taught us children is to love and respect all people, and to think that they all have the right to believe as they wish." (woman raised as a Unitarian although her father was Jewish and her mother was Presbyterian, 1, p. 246)

3. "All my life I've been aware of being half and half. I feel like I'm on the fringes of things in a lot of ways. I'm half Jewish and half Christian.... I've wanted to know who I was ever since I was a teenager." (1, p.246)

4. "Yes, I was definitely confused by the whole thing, but the confusion wasn't exactly over who I was, it was more a result of the lack of knowing exactly what was expected of me as a child. That was the most difficult part, 'cause I never really knew what I was supposed to believe, think, and do." (the daughter of a Protestant mother and Catholic father, 2, p.190)

5. "Don't make your kid feel like she is nothing. Everybody wants to be something, to be called something, and it isn't good to be nothing." (sixteen year old, 2, p.210)

6. "I'm both. Lots of my friends are the same way, so it seems natural for me to be this way too. I think I have it good with both religions, and I feel more involved with both. I'm free to choose any religion, so I feel like I have a lot of freedom in my life. I see it as a positive thing for me growing up this way as a child." (teenage daughter of a Catholic father and Jewish mother, 2, p.201)

7. "You can't be both. You're neither and stuck and don't really know what you are. You are afraid if you say you are one or the other religion that you will offend someone, so you figure out ways to avoid the subject and not get into situations where you'll have to answer questions at all." (fifteen year old daughter of a mixed couple, 2, p.204)

8. "I see everything with two sets of eyes.... How I react to the newspaper - Israel, Washington, New York, AIWACS. I react from two different perspectives. It is confusing." (a Protestant minister who was raised in a Christian-Jewish family, 3, p.228)

9. "It's not like being a Democrat or a Republican. The feelings are there all the time. Every day something arises that reminds me of the fact that I'm two things, split." (3, p.227)

10. "I'm very lucky to be part of two worlds! I got twice as much heritage and more than twice as much life – and I love it." (4, p.72)

11. "I have felt like a schizophrenic (sic.) for most of my life! Or perhaps a giant piece of taffy, constantly being stretched and pulled to capacity in both directions.... For as long as I can remember, I have yearned to integrate, or magically fuse, my two halves, so I wouldn't have to choose one over the other." (an Episcopalian-educated woman, daughter of an Orthodox Jewish woman and a Christian man, 4, p.72)

Quotations are from the following sources:

1. Paul and Rachel Cowan, *Mixed Blessings,* Penguin Books, 1987.

2. Steven Carr Reuben, *A Guide to Interfaith Marriage: But How Will You Raise the Children?,* Pocket Books, New York, 1987.

3. Susan Weidman Schneider, *Intermarriage: The Challenge of Living with Differences Between Christians and Jews,* The Free Press, New York, 1989.

4. Leslie Goodman-Malamuth and Robin Margolis, *Between Two Worlds: Choices for Grown Children of Jewish-Christian Parents,* Pocket Books, New York, 1992.

Questions for Discussion:

Does having one religion in a family create closer bonds between the members of the family?

How can we enable a child of an intermarriage to feel connected to a certain religious group?

What are the advantages or disadvantages of having a sense of belonging to a religious group?

How can raising children according to one religion be an advantage for the child? a disadvantage?

What happens when both partners leave the religion with which they were raised? How are traditions transmitted? created?

What are possible results of children being asked to choose between parents' religions? Should this be avoided?

Do we give our children "choices" in other important areas of life? Identify some choices you feel can be made democratically and some you feel should be mandated by parents. Is it reasonable to give children a "choice" in their religious affiliation? Why or why not?

How can a parent reinforce a child's religious connection if s/he is not the same religion?

Can children being raised with two faiths feel "at home" in either a temple or church?

Would you or your partner be willing to be "half and half?"

If you are not prepared to be both religions, can you expect your children to integrate two very different religious responses?

Can a child believe in Jesus and still be a Jewish child?

Is it possible to integrate two religions successfully by emphasizing the universalistic characteristics of each?

What is the value of particularistic beliefs and practices?

Is it possible to maintain the integrity of a religion when symbols from various religions are blended?

THOUGHT STARTERS AND RESOURCE MATERIALS
ARTICLES FOR PARTICIPANTS

The following articles address topics of concern for interfaith couples. Culled from a variety of sources, these articles focus on issues which you will probably discuss in group sessions. On any given week you may wish to ask participants to read a specific article at home, record their reactions to the article (even if they only write names of emotions they experienced while reading), and then discuss the article in the group. In this way the articles may serve as excellent triggers for discussion. Alternatively, the articles may be given as hand-outs to extend the reach of a single session meeting.

Marriage of Christians and Jews

Ronald Osborne

Judaism and Christianity live and interact asymmetrically, and this is the cause of much of the difficulty Jews and Christians experience when they marry.

Osborne, Ronald. "Marriage of Christians and Jews." Plumbline. Volume 13, Issue 3. September 1985.

Reprinted with permission of author.

Jewish-Christian dialogue has yielded increased understanding and a greater sense of respect and mutuality between Christians and Jews, but it has not yet ameliorated the pain and conflict experienced by Jews and Christians when they marry each other, or try to stay married to each other, or indeed find that they cannot remain married.

I want to attempt to clarify some of these problems. My purpose is not to encourage or discourage Jews and Christians in marrying each other. It is to share some observations which may help name at least some of the problems so that, knowing their names, these problems might be managed.

My data come from several sources: from pastoral experience in guiding preparation for marriage by such persons, from marriage counseling, and from many conversations over the years with both Jewish and Christian colleagues and friends.

* * *

Judaism and Christianity live and interact asymmetrically. This fact is obscured by American religious pluralism which tends to regard all religions as variations on a common religious theme. I suggest this asymmetry is the cause of much of the difficulty Jews and Christians experience when they marry.

The theological dimensions of the asymmetry can be seen in the instance of worship. When Christians worship with Jews there is almost nothing they cannot affirm. They can participate fully without reservation in the liturgical life of the synagogue, Holy Day rituals, even family rituals. There is hardly anything which is religiously inaccessible to them, at least in theological terms. There may be cultural barriers. Some Jews may prefer not to have at least some Christians around in their synagogues or in their homes, and some Christians feel uncomfortable with some Jews. But the theological content of Judaism is not an offense or stumbling black (a *"scandelon"* as the New Testament calls it) to Christians. To be sure, Christians would want to say much more than what is said in Jewish affirmations, but they can *at least* say what Jews do.

The obverse is not the case. Christianity is not

The Rev. Ronald Osborne is chaplain at the University of Iowa, Iowa City, Iowa.

What does a couple do about on-going relationships to church and synagogue and family?

---

equally accessible to Jews. When Jews worship with Christians almost nothing is accessible, almost everything is problematic. "Old Testament" (even to call it that already denies Jewish understandings, since there is to the Jewish mind but one testament always old but ever made new) readings are selected in the Christian lectionaries to interpret New Testament experience. Even the Psalms gather Christian meanings. It is not enough to advise Jews to participate only in the Jewish parts of the Christian liturgy, because the "Jewish" content of Christian liturgy has a *publically* Christian meaning; thus, to participate at all might mean giving assent to these public meanings. Of course, the distinctively "Christian" content of Christian worship, "New Testament" readings, creeds, prayers, trinitarian invocations, acclamations and doxologies, are all utterly impossible to a Jewish participant, or at least to one with theological sensitivity and integrity.

This, of course, is not to say that Jews do not find ways to participate in Christian worship in ways they find comfortable. Sometimes just being present while not participating very directly in the worship service is a Jewish way of indicating support and affirmation of Christian colleagues and friends without claiming commonalities which do not exist.

One can state the asymmetry of worship abstractly, by simply noting that much Jewish theological content can be affirmed by Christians, very much less Christian theological content can be affirmed by a Jew. This can be put more strongly. Christians have persecuted Jews for not affirming more, and Jewish tradition has almost nothing positive to say about Christianity. It largely ignores it.

This asymmetry makes the planning of a marriage rite for Jews and Christians extremely problematic, and it complicates subsequent relationships enormously. What does a couple do about on-going relationships to church and synagogue and family? How are children reared religiously? How are important family events to be celebrated? What is the religious commonality in the marital relationship itself? What symbols interpret the relationship, give it meaning and depth, provide resources for hard times, celebrate the good? How is the relationship to be anchored in a ground of meaning which has tradition and community?

* * *

A second kind of asymmetry is cultural. While both Christianity and Judaism are lived through cultural forms, the relationship of faith to ethnicity is different for each. Each faith tends to misinterpret the other because of the difference.

Judaism is both an ethnic and religious phenomenon. In this century the ethnic and religious dimensions of Jewishness have been separated. Large numbers of Jews think of themselves as Jews and are thought of as Jews even though they have no palpable religious commitment. On the other hand, almost all persons who affirm Jewish religious beliefs and belong to Jewish religious communities of some kind are ethnically Jewish. Proselytes seem to adopt Jewish ethnicity quickly.

For Christians, at least in theological terms, there is no such thing as a Christian ethnicity. One is not a Christian because one's mother is, as is the case in Judaism. One is a Christian because one has been baptized and seeks to live out the meaning of the baptismal covenant.

Judaism survives and continues because of family relationships. The religion rides the back of ethnicity. Christianity survives and continues because each generation claims anew the Gospel.

Having said this it must be conceded that these theological distinctions may not seem very apparent in everyday life. A friend tells of attending a high school in an eastern city in which there were two ethnic groups, Italian Catholics and Jews. The two groups entered the building by separate entrances, took separate courses to the extent possible and maintained separate extracurricular programs. The Italians controlled sports, the Jews dominated debate and the chess and science clubs. To this person the relationship between religion and ethnicity seemed the same for each of these groups.

Another friend tells of living in a Jewish neighborhood in an eastern city adjacent to a Polish neighborhood. Both attended the same schools except that the Polish children who attended public schools were mostly children who had been expelled from the parochial schools. To this person the relationship of religion to ethnicity seemed the same except that Christians were perceived as persons with severe learning and behavior problems!

Because Jews come largely from urban areas where ethnic realities are important social facts, they probably have perceptions of the Christians which are colored strongly by the kinds of experiences noted above. They see the relationship of ethnicity to religion to be the same for others as for themselves.

Christians are less likely to have comparable perceptions, except, of course, for those groups in which ethnicity remains very strong. Christians are more inclined to see Judaism simply as another religious denomination, one of many voluntary religious communities.

The rub comes when Jewish and Christian teenagers leave home for college. Often enough, a Jewish youth who has only known Christians in ethnic terms meets a Christian youth who has only known of Jews second-hand through novels, and they fall in love. Each must struggle mightily to look beyond the culturally-given experiences they have had to understand the meaning of the other's identity.

I have had personal knowledge of relationships in which the Jewish partner is not religiously Jewish, but who nevertheless insists the children not be reared as Christians. One can understand the Jewish perspective. If Jewishness is largely cultural and there is a certain disenchantment with religion, or a secularization of religious belief, and if one cannot hope that much of the cultural Jewishness can be passed on in one's own family, one can at least keep a religiousness which one finds obnoxious from being propagated in one's own house. This reasoning, insofar as it is reasoning, seems perverse to the Christian partner. Considerable resentment accrues. There is something terribly unfair about not caring enough about one's own religion to embrace it and practice it, while denying to one's offspring the religious heritage of one's spouse, it seems to the Christian.

I know no one — no one who cares about religious meaning anyway — who has found a satisfactory strategy for resolving this conflict. My impression is that Jewish-Christian couples in which both partners have strong religious commitments find acceptable ways to rear their children. But when one partner is not religious and the other is, there are almost no good options. The strategy often pursued is that of raising children with exposure to both religious traditions but without commitments to either. While this is something which could be profitably studied empirically, my unsystematic observations suggest that parents seldom find this satisfactory. It appears that what happens is that the children are not exposed to either religious tradition sufficiently to feel religious meanings from the inside out. Since religion is caught, not taught, it is never caught. They, in fact, are raised as pagans.

* * *

There is also an asymmetrical way in which religious practice is institutionalized in Christianity and Judaism. For Jews the fundamental working entity for religious life is the family, which is where important religious celebrations happen. The synagogue, even though it has certain liturgical functions and has acquired meanings which once belonged only to the family, is fundamentally a school. The center of cultic life, the "priest figure" in Judaism, is in fact the Jewish Mother, although special roles are played by others, especially by elders. The Rabbi, an important person in the community, has very little cultic function. He is teacher and interpreter of the Torah, but less a priest than his own mother or wife.

For Christians the congregation in some form is the basic community entity. As important as family life is this larger family is the primary center for liturgical and cultic life. Even though this larger community may be organized in many different ways it remains a constant reality in Christian experience since the time the first believers "continued in the Apostles' teaching and fellowship and the prayers." The Rabbi, Priest, and Elder all become one person, the Bishop or the Priest who carries on all those functions. Other "ministers" have special representative roles, especially the Deacons, who extend the ministry of Christ's servanthood to the community and to the world. Family cultus, which is much less elaborate than in Jewish practice, is seen as supplemental to the liturgical life of the larger community, not the other way round. In fact, the Christian Eucharistic liturgy is the family Shabat meal of Jews with Christian meanings. Even the details of ceremonial are the same in some instances.

The equivalent institution to the Christian congregation or parish, therefore, is not the synagogue. It is the home.

A consequence of this institutional asymmetry is that when a Jew marries a Christian one of the basic constituative elements of Jewish identity, the Jewish home, is destroyed. There is a sense in which every Jewish-Christian marriage is to Jews a kind of genocide. It is like closing a church and more. One church more or less doesn't matter

Judaism survives and continues because of family relationships...Christianity survives and continues because each generation claims anew the Gospel.

much to Christians. Churches are not propagated by family relationships. They are gathered by the grace of the Spirit and perhaps some organizing efforts. But to Jews each opportunity to establish a new Jewish family makes Jewish identity and survival less fragile. Most Jewish families, however open-minded, thus find a marriage outside the Jewish community extremely troubling.

There are therefore very few Rabbis willing to cooperate in arranging Jewish-Christian marriages. And there will continue to be some families who will consider a child dead who marries outside the community. In theological terms there is a sense in which such persons are dead. For a Jew to remove himself by marriage from Jewish family life is almost like a Christian refusing to attend Mass, or more like self excommunication. It is to cut oneself off from the supportive context for Jewish identity. There is a sense in which there is no such thing as an individual Jew. A Jew by definition is part of a people and the constituative institutions of that peoplehood are Jewish families.

Christians find these attitudes simply unfathomable. They seem like religious and ethnic chauvinism to them and represent a rigidity and intransigence they find irritating and grating. A Christian family does not give up the Christian identity of one of its members even when that member marries outside the faith. Christian identity can only be surrendered by an intentional act of apostasy. Christians cannot understand why Jews do not see things the same way.

* * *

A final point of radical divergence between Jewish and Christian perspective which colors all relationships including marriage relationships is divergent perceptions of the meaning of the holocaust. For Jews that event has an importance like that of the Exodus or the Exile. It is nearly impossible to be Jewish and not struggle somehow with the meaning of that event.

Most Christians who think about the holocaust at all see it not as an issue about which enormous personal struggle is necessary. It is but one instance of evil among many. To be sure, it is an instance of enormous proportions, but evil often has enormous proportions.

Jews often perceive Christian treatment of the holocaust in this way as a kind of anti-semitism. It does nothing, they think, to own up to the complicity they see of Christians in the holocaust, or in the cultural propensities for it laid down by

centuries of church-inspired hostility and persecution.

Christians, when confronted by these perceptions, are perplexed. The holocaust violates Christian values as much as Jewish. Jewish preoccupations with the event seem to represent a kind of ethnocentrism in the extreme. Is not any act of brutality an evil to be renounced? Why renounce only those evils which affect Jews? The implicit blame of the current generation of Christians by Jews requires an ethnic understanding of Christianity Christian theology cannot countenance.

All of this spills over into marriage relationships, and all other areas of conflict are intensified. The holocaust turns the asymmetry into cacophanous dissonance. There is probably no way Jews and Christians can marry without hearing that dissonance.

* * *

Young adults have enormous difficulty handling all of these things. What we know of ego development and of cognitive, moral, and religious development suggests that most young adults simply do not have the emotional and intellectual maturity to deal with these matters very well. They are struggling with the discovery of their own identities and often have to do that over and against the claims of family, whose concerns are often perceived as efforts to reduce independence and autonomy.

For many young adults religion itself is problematic. Many keep their distance as they move from tacit acquiescence to the religiousness of childhood and youth toward owning an explicit faith of their own. Many move toward that position by a protracted period of religious disinvolvement. Occasionally young adults interpret religious matters in terms of a naive universalism. Differences between religions are simplistically blurred so that there is the absence of an ability to make judgments about many of the critical questions to be resolved.

Often the marital relationship proposed is not seen as part of a larger social and religious context. It is a very private affair between two people. Family and religion are all resented as intrusive. What the couple wishes to celebrate is not the covenantal love of their respective religious traditions, neither Jewish "Hesed" nor Christian "Agape," but the erotic and philial love of American Romanticism.

I have deliberately painted a rather bleak picture here, partly to balance what I think are the naive concepts which abound platitudinously in our culture. The fact is that when Jews and Christians marry, people experience pain. That pain is real...

The Hyphen Between the Cross and the Star

Reprinted by permission of Rabbi Harold Schulweis and KTAV Publishing House, Inc., from In God's Mirror, 1990.

THE HYPHEN BETWEEN THE CROSS AND THE STAR: MIXED MARRIAGE

Pope John Paul II's pastoral visit to America brought a revival of Christian-Jewish anecdotes in its wake. One such story tells of Cohen's conversion to Catholicism, for reasons unknown. The Knights of Columbus host a banquet in Cohen's honor. Called upon to speak, Cohen looks at his audience—devoted lay Catholics, priests, bishops, and monsignors—and begins his address, "Fellow goyim."

Jewish humor of this genre is meant to console. It implies that the conversion has not "taken". A Jew always remains a Jew.

The true challenge to Jewish identity comes less from outright conversion than from quiet "deconversion." It is not the cross but the hyphen that dissolves Jewish identity. The Judeo-Christian hyphen is turned into a sign of identity. Blue and white lights, green and red fixtures, hot-cross buns or latkes, all signal the same directions. The threat derives from the common notion that deep down, Judaism and Christianity are twin faiths without significant differences.

IN THE RABBI'S STUDY

The two of them—attractive, intelligent, young, and very much in love—enter my study. Sam, a Jew, and Peggy, a Christian. Their object is matrimony, and their goal is to find a rabbi liberal enough to officiate at the mixed union or alongside a liberal priest. Neither seeks conversion. They seek an "equal opportunity" cleric.

They each have a vague sentimental attachment to the faith in which they were raised and genuine filial fidelity to their parents. They have thought out the dilemma of raising children; they will offer the best of two religious civilizations. "If it's a boy, we'll have him both circumcized and baptized," they agree. They do not see conflict in this arrangement. Instead, they are convinced that the wisdom of both Old and New Testaments will enrich their lives and confirm the prophet Malachi: "Has not one Father created us? Has not one God made us?" (2:10). They take courage from how alike the sister traditions are. Towards their own and each other's beliefs and practices they offer benign neutrality.

The discussion wanders. At one point, perhaps out of frustration, I ask what they think of my officiating as both rabbi and priest. They are taken aback.

"You're not serious?" they ask.

"Well, let's play it out. I know the church sacrament, the nuptial blessings, and I certainly know the seven blessings of Jewish tradition," I reply.

Peggy finds such ecumenicism a bit much. She can't quite conjure up the union of surplice and tallit, swinging rosaries and knotted tassels. Still, if we have one Father, why not one rabbi-priest?

They are not slow to see how I have taken their approach to its logical, but absurd, conclusion. So Peggy goes on to explain that she is not a practicing Christian. Why then, I ask her, would she have her child baptized?

She answers with a personal anecdote about a cousin whose infant had died. "If that happened to me, I couldn't face the thought that my child was unbaptized." Unbaptized, her child would be suspended between heaven and hell. I ask about the status of her husband-to-be. Would an unbaptized Sam be subject to limbo or damnation, or would he be saved? A long and deep silence follows.

In that silence, I ponder the neglect of Jewish theology and philosophy in Sam's life. Sam's Jewishness amounts to casual observance of a pastiche of rituals, a vague sentimentality towards Jewishness, and an attachment to his Jewish parents. No Jewish map of the world, no distinctive view of human nature, God, or the quest for meaning.

The Hyphen Between the Cross and the Star

forty years before the destruction of the Second Temple, the veil of the Temple was torn from the top to the bottom. The Temple, the priests, the sacrificial system and the authority of the rabbis collapsed, while the instruments for communion with God fell exclusively into the hands of the true believers in Christ crucified and resurrected.

In Judaism, salvation is not for Jews alone. Those who do not believe our way or pray our way are not thrown out of the divine court. In rabbinic literature, heaven and earth are called to witness that "whether you be gentile or Jew, man or woman, slave or free man, the Divine Presence rests on you according to your deeds" (*Yalkut Shimoni, Tanna de-Vei Eliyahu*). In the Book of Jonah, the people of Nineveh are spared because of their deeds, not their conversion to Judaism; because of their turning from evil ways, not their acceptance of the Sabbath and festivals. Jews do not seek to convert the world to Judaism, but rather to convert the world to righteousness, justice, and peace.

THE EUCHARIST IS NOT MATZAH

"Whoever eats my flesh and drinks my blood has eternal life, and I will raise him in the last day" (John 6:53). This promise is ritualized in the eucharist, mass, or communion sacrament. The wine and wafer are transformed into the blood and flesh of Christ on the cross.[2]

By contrast, the wine of the Jewish *Kiddush* remains wine, and the challah of the *Motzi* remains bread. The Yiddish writer Y. L. Peretz told a story that reflects these radically different outlooks. On the day before Pesach, husband Hershl and wife Sarah find themselves without money to purchase matzah and wine for the Seder. Forlorn, Hershl goes to the market and stops to watch a traveling magician performing tricks in the square. The trickster produces matzot and a bottle of wine, and offers them to an amazed Hershl.

Hershl runs to the rabbi for counsel. Are the matzah and wine permitted for Pesach use, seeing that they were produced by magic?

The rabbi asks Hershl, "Does the matzah break? Does the wine pour?"

Hershl breaks a piece of matzah and pours a drink of wine. They perform naturally.

FAMILY AND SYNAGOGUE

For Sam, and for Peggy as well, all religions are the same. Preferences for a colored Easter egg or the roasted egg of a Seder, a swaying evergreen or a shaking lulav, are more matters of taste than of principle. It seems such a shame to dissolve a love because of a few residual ethnic memories.

In truth, however, the differences between Christianity and Judaism are profound. They entail basic world-views and values that affect them more than they think.

The world-view of most of the people with Christian backgrounds that I meet—like Peggy's—is woven out of the fabric of Christian doctrine and symbol. They understand the nature of original sin, damnation and salvation in the manner of traditional Christian theology. As we shall see, this is a far cry from Judaism—a gap too large for a hyphen to bridge.[1]

WHOSE PRAYERS ARE HEARD?

To begin with, Christianity is rooted in the dogma of original sin. "Original" does not refer to the invention of new sins, but inherited sin traced back to the Bible story of Adam and Eve. They rebelled against God, who forbade eating of the Tree of Knowledge. The "original sin" is transmitted to every living human action. It is no longer the result of an individual's choice; it is a congenital curse from which there is no human cure. Only by faith in the incarnation of the man-God and his unmerited kindness in dying for God's children is the stain wiped out. The crucified Christ alone can loosen Eve's children from the grip of Satan.

During the 1961 trial of Adolph Eichmann, when a Canadian Christian minister flew to Jerusalem to offer Eichmann the chance to confess his belief in Christ, reporters asked him whether Eichmann's confession would save his soul. The minister affirmed that it would. Asked whether the souls of Eichmann's victims would be saved without such confession, he answered, "No. No one comes to the Father but by me," says Jesus (John 14:6); as Reverend Bailey Smith restates it, "God does not hear the prayer of a Jew." Outside the church, no one is saved.

For many of the church fathers, Judaism was a vestigial anachronism, a "has-been" whose purpose was to prepare the path for the good news of the advent of Christ. In the gospels of Matthew, Mark and Luke, we read that on the day that Jesus died, some history of contempt for the "perfidious Jew" so virulent in the hands of the mobs as to defy even the restraints of higher church officials.

BAPTISM IS NOT CIRCUMCISION

Baptism and circumcision are rites with differing theological roots and psychological import. They are far from complementary dramas.

Baptism is based upon an anthropological pessimism. Human beings are born in the womb of sin. Since there is nothing a sinner can *do* to expiate that innate blemish, the sole recourse is to rely upon a supernatural Other, who has assumed the burden of suffering atonement for all others. As Luther expressed it, the believer becomes *velut paralyticum*, as one paralyzed, abandoning the conceit of his or her own deeds, utterly dependent on the self-sacrifice of the innocent lamb of God.

Baptism is crucial for Christian salvation. The Roman Catholic rite includes exorcism of the Prince of Darkness. The priest blows on the infant's face, ordering the spirit of Satan to depart. He moistens his thumb, touches the ears and nostrils of the infants, and asks the child's sponsors to renounce the power of Satan. Those who are baptized and who believe are saved; those who refuse are stigmatized by the inherited sin that remains indelibly inscribed in the unredeemed soul. We can understand Peggy's concern over her infant's baptism and her silence over its absence in Sam's life.

Circumcision is the initiation into the covenant of God and Abraham. The eight-day-old boy carries no baggage of sin into the world. Prior to baptism, the Christian infant is a pagan; by contrast, the Jewish boy is Jewish even before or without the rite of circumcision. The Jewish infant is born innocent, created and sustained in God's image. No eternal damnation hovers over him. As a Jew, he will be raised in a tradition that commands him to save lives rather than souls.

According to Christianity, humans sin because they are sinners. According to Judaism, a person sins when he or she sins. Of course, we do sin—not because we enter the world condemned as sinners, but because we are fallible human beings, and "there is no righteous human being who has done good and does not

"Then they may certainly be used for the Seder," the rabbi rules.

Matzah is matzah and wine is wine. No ritual item in Judaism is transformed into another substance. Nothing in the wine or matzah is intrinsically sacred. They are symbols to sanctify a festival and recall an event. The idea of the transformation of natural products into supernatural substances is alien to Judaism. After they have been used in the ritual, the remaining wine and matzah may be discarded. They possess no sacramental powers.

THE "OLD TESTAMENT" IS NOT THE JEWISH BIBLE

The Christian Bible includes the "Old Testament" with its "New Testament" but rearranges the order of the books. The Jewish Bible (Tanach) ends with the Book of Chronicles, a résumé of biblical history. The last verse in II Chronicles refers to King Cyrus of Persia, who is charged by God to rebuild God's Temple in Jerusalem. Cyrus, who in Isaiah 45:1 is referred to as a messiah—"the anointed one" (*mashiach*)—proclaims to the Jewish exiles: "Whoever is among you of God's people, may the Lord be with you. Go up!"

In the Christian reordering of the Hebrew Bible, the last books are those of the Prophets, which end with Malachi. Here the last verse reads, "Lest I come and smite the earth with a curse" (3:24). In this manner, the Christian order of the "Old Testament" has replaced the Jewish hope of return to Zion with the threat of Israel rejected. Thus Jesus is made to succeed and supplant the Hebrew prophets, and Israel's tragic destiny is foreshadowed. The old covenant is broken, and Israel depends for its redemption upon its acceptance of the new covenant and the resurrected Savior.

DEICIDE

Jews have a special taint in Christian thought. Guilt for the killing of Jesus is added to the contagion of original sin. The episode of the Roman procurator Pontius Pilate, who washes his hands of the bloodshed, and the stubborn mob of Jews who are crying, "Crucify him, crucify him," is dramatized in Easter Passion plays and in such commercial dramas as *Godspell* and *Jesus Christ Superstar*. The chilling words in Matthew 27:25, put into the mouths of the Jewish mob, "His blood be on us and on our children," augur the

Promised Land, without statue, icon, or shrine. David is found by the prophet Nathan to have sent an innocent man to war to be killed, so that the king might enjoy Bathsheba, the victim's wife.

The heroes of Israel are splendid, but not so special that they are to be obeyed without question. No sacrifice of intelligence is demanded. Consequently the people are all bidden to learn, know and ask questions. The rabbis declared that Ezra the scribe would have been worthy to be the bearer of the Torah if Moses had not preceded him (Tosefta *Sanhedrin* 4:7). Could that have been said if Moses were a man-God? The Israelite priest and high priest were to be honored, but not revered blindly. "The learned bastard takes precedence over the ignorant high priest" (B.T. *Horayot* 13a).

The Jewish Messiah is wholly human, mortal, and fallible. The Messiah's coming offers no excuse for being passive. As Rabbi Yochanan ben Zakkai taught, "If there be a sapling in your hand, when they say to you 'Behold the Messiah!' go and plant and afterwards meet him" (*Avot de-Rabbi Nathan* 31).

Jews live according to a different calendar. For them, this is not *anno domini*, the year of the Lord; the world is far from redeemed. The saplings in our hands are not to be put aside. We see poverty, bickering, jealousy, sickness and hunger. The Messiah has not yet come.

FAMILY

Peggy spoke warmly of the Jewish family. Family is one aspect of Jewish life that rabbis hear praised over and over by non-Jews. The primacy of family fits the horizontal world-view of Judaism. It is rooted in a tradition that makes no schism between love among humans and love between humans and God. In no Jewish religious text can one find the approach to the family that Jesus expresses in the Gospels of Luke and Matthew. "If any man come to me and hate not his father and mother and wife and children and brothers and sisters, yea and his own life also, he cannot be my disciple" (Luke 14:26).

In Judaism, Jews come to God through their families and friends, not at the expense of these relationships nor through the sacrifice of self. Divinity yields its nature through the love and care of human others and self.

By contrast, Jesus declared, "For I have not come to bring

FAMILY AND SYNAGOGUE

transgress" (Ecclesiastes 7:20). The sin is his or hers, the choice is his or hers, and the reparation to be done is his or hers.

No one can sin for another, cry or die for another, or absolve another. "Wash yourself clean," Isaiah addresses the penitent (1:16), "put away the evil doings from before My eyes; cease to do evil, learn to do well; seek judgment, relieve the oppressed, the fatherless, plead for the widow." The rabbis add, "Blessed are you, Israel. Before whom are you purified, and who purifies you? Your Father who is in heaven" (*Yoma* 8:9).

Whereas in Christianity, the relationship between self and God is vertical, the Jewish connection with God is horizontal. Horizontal human transactions call for reparation, forgiveness and apology for the injuries done to others. They cannot be skipped over by a vertical leap between the individual and God in heaven, ignoring the proper relationships with God's children on earth. The prophet Ezekiel makes it clear what the truly penitent is to do. "If you the wicked restore the pledge, give back what you have robbed, walk in the statutes of life . . . you shall surely live. . . . None of the sins you have committed shall be remembered against you" (33:15 ff.).

Baptism focuses on the paralysis of the human will, helpless without God combating Satan. The covenant of circumcision stresses that the human being can exercise control over his life. As God counseled the sulking Cain, "Sin crouches at the door, but you may rule over it" (Genesis 3:7).

Sam and Peggy must learn that circumcision and baptism are not a knife-or-water option, but ritualized dramas of values. They affect our relationships to God, world, neighbor and self. Baptism depends upon belief in a specific divine person who walked the face of the earth.

FLAWED FOUNDERS

Philosophers have noted a unique aspect of Judaism. The late Walter Kaufmann observed that Jinna and Buddha, founders of the sixth-century B.C.E. religions of Jainism and Buddhism, were worshipped in later years; Confucius and Lao-Tze came to be deified; the Greek heroes were worshiped as gods; Jesus was adored as God.

Only in Israel were the flaws of the religious founders openly revealed. Moses is buried in no-man's land, powerless to enter the

FAMILY AND SYNAGOGUE

peace on earth but a sword. For I have come to set a man against his father, a daughter against her mother, and a daughter-in-law against her mother-in-law." For Jesus, the believer is confronted with a hard, sharp break; either heaven or earth, either Christ or family, either Jesus or self. "He who loves father or mother more than me is not worthy of me" (Matthew 10:34 ff.).

In Christianity one cannot come to the Father except through the Son. In Judaism one cannot come to the Father except through the sons and daughters of the human family.

These are not easy teachings for Peggy and Sam to hear. But the differences in the birth traditions are not trivial. Theological differences are likely to cast large cultural and moral shadows.

Peggy and Sam may come to understand that true tolerance does not entail wholesale adoption of all traditions to sameness. They may come to see that conversion does not discredit a faith but flows from an awareness of the profound dissonance between religious cultures.

Their resolve to hold clashing traditions in one household not only distorts the uniqueness of each faith civilization, but compromises their own integrity. With the best of intentions, Peggy and Sam hope to offer their offspring the best of religion. But, to paraphrase Santayana, to attempt this would be trying to speak in general without using any language in particular. Judaism and Christianity are particular languages, with their own precious syntaxes, which when thrown together, produce a babble of tongues.

I am aware that there are Christian theologians who take a far more liberal view of original sin and damnation and salvation. I point this out to Peggy. But the more liberal views of modern Christian thinkers have not filtered down to Peggy. The interpretations of Paul Tillich or Reinhold Niebuhr or Hans Kung are as foreign to her understanding of Christianity as the Judaic interpretation I present to her. Peggy has not come to me for a course in Christian theology. I deal with Peggy as she presents herself, as she has been instructed by the church and religious school she attended.

Sam and Peggy have crucial decisions to make. If they build their lives on the narrow edge of the Judeo-Christian hyphen, they offer their children the fate of Disraeli. Converted to Christianity

The Hyphen Between the Cross and the Star

by his father, he became Britain's prime minister in the time of Queen Victoria, and yet he held pridefully the glory of his Jewish ancestry. Queen Victoria is reported to have asked him, "What are you, Disraeli? Which Testament is yours?" He replied with sadness, "I am, dear Queen, the blank page between the Old and the New Testament."

It is to be hoped that Sam and Peggy will learn to see and respect the difference between the Jewish and Christian outlooks and not lead their children to inherit the blank page. For all that Christianity and Judaism are alike, the hyphen between the Cross and the Star of David is no sign of identity.

NOTES

1. True, some modern and present-day Christian theologians interpret the doctrines of sin and salvation in a far more liberal manner. But their influence has not been wide, and so their views will not be included here.

2. How literally this transformation is understood remains a Christian debate that need not concern us here.

The Hyphen Between the Cross and the Star

Discussion Questions

How does Rabbi Schulweis describe his attitude toward officiation at a Jewish-Christian wedding? What are your reactions toward his statement about officiating as "both rabbi and priest?"

Contrast Judaism's and Christianity's traditional viewpoints toward the following ideas:

- original sin

- salvation

- transsubstantiation (the transformation of the wafer to the body of Jesus, and the wine to his blood)

- the "saving" nature of baptism

- the meaning of ritual circumcision

- attitude toward sages and Biblical figures

How do you interpret the author's statement: "Whereas in Christianity, the relationship between self and God is vertical, the Jewish connection with God is horizontal." (p. 174)

How do you respond to this statement: "Judaism and Christianity are particular languages, with their own precious syntaxes, which when thrown together, produce a babble of tongues?" (p. 176)

Why does Rabbi Schulweis say that "the hyphen between the Cross and the Star of David is no sign of identity?" (p. 177)

What are the author's reasons for not raising children with two faiths? Do you agree or disagree? Could you synthesize two distinct religious faiths and ideologies? Why or why not?

What emotions did you experience while reading this chapter? Is religion necessarily an emotional topic? Why or why not?

PARENTING

Crossover

Reprinted by permission of Judy Petsonk. Originally published in Hadassah Magazine, December 1991. Copyright c 1991 by Judy Petsonk. Judy Petsonk is the co-author, with Jim Remson of The Intermarriage Handbook: A Guide for Jews.

By Judy Petsonk

A little girl from an intermarried family told a friend, "I'm half Jewish and half cocker spaniel." A small boy said, "This week we visit my Jewish grandparents for Passover. Next week, we visit my Christian grandparents for Crossover."

Religion can be confusing for children. In an intermarried family confusion may persist. Children may reach adulthood with no clear religious beliefs or identity.

For *The Intermarriage Handbook* we interviewed 150 intermarried adults, and 43 offspring of intermarriage age 5 to 18. We concluded that if possible parents should choose a single religion for children (this should be a negotiated choice). Many people raised with no religion hunger for one. (One atheist home produced a Sufi, a Buddhist and two conversions to Judaism.) Many—certainly not all—offspring of two-religion homes spend much of their lives trying to figure out who they are.

For many intermarried couples, Judaism looks like the best choice—or compromise; as the foundation of Christianity, it has values both partners share. The 1970 National Jewish Population Survey by the Council of Jewish Federations found that 73 percent of intermarrieds start out intending to give children a Jewish education.

Yet statistics gathered in 1980 showed

Judy Petsonk is coauthor with Jim Remsen of The Intermarriage Handbook: A Guide for Jews and Christians *(Morrow Quill Paperbacks).*

that only 25 to 45 percent end up having a Jewish home (the larger number indicates conversionary homes). The August 1991 CJF survey shows that today when the rate of nonconversionary mixed marriages is 52 percent (compared to less than 10 percent in 1965) only 13 percent of intermarrieds affiliate with a synagogue.

How can an intermarried couple (or any couple) raise children to be active

For many intermarried couples, Judaism looks like the best choice— or compromise.

contributing members of the Jewish people?

• Have a consistent, happy Jewish homestyle in which both parents participate.

• Live in a neighborhood with a significant proportion of Jews. Participate in synagogue, religious school or other Jewish institutions.

• Choose neighborhoods and institutions where children will be fully accepted as Jews (Reform or Reconstructionist if the gentile mother has not converted to Judaism).

• Create wonderful memories. Celebrate the year-round holiday cycle with good traditional food, rituals, songs, stories, games, happy time with extended family. Talk about the ethical and spiritual meaning of each holiday. Young children are concrete; the symbols and activities in the home tell them who they are.

In many Jewish homes, identity cues are primarily cultural: chicken soup, jokes, books. But children of intermarriage are intrinsically bicultural. Two different cultures are part of the parents' personalities and will be passed on to children as naturally as hair or eye color. Thus symbols, stories and celebrations—especially Sabbath and the Seder—become more crucial in shaping Jewish identity.

There are at least three stumbling blocks to creating a Jewish homestyle: the Jewish parent, the gentile parent and the grandparents. To raise Jewish children, intermarried families must deal with their subconscious resistance.

The first obstacle is often the Jewish father. Many gentiles who marry Jews have rejected Christian doctrine and are attracted to Judaism: to the one God, the emphasis on ethics and family, the absence of dogma. On the other hand many Jews who intermarry are alienated and refuse to have anything to do with Jewish institutions. So they block the spouse's attempts to affiliate with a synagogue.

The second obstacle can be the gentile spouse. (I say "gentile" and "she" since the majority of intermarriages involve a Jewish man and a woman no longer actively Christian, but the issues also apply to gentile men and involved Christians.) At one of my workshops a woman voiced the key issues for the gentile: power balance, sense of adequacy and competence, and feeling the Jewish elements belong to you. "I have had to do 90 percent of the learning and 90 percent of the giving," she said. "I had to learn about all the Jewish holidays, the Yiddish words and inside jokes, how to cook the foods. But nobody in the Jewish family is interested in where I came from. It's as if I didn't have a past, as if I had no identity of my own."

The Jewish man often leaves child-rearing to his gentile wife. At first she assumes that raising children Jewish means teaching about one God and 10 commandments. But Jewish beliefs and ethical teachings are woven into a way of life. The gentile must acquire an entirely new culture. She feels unable to be a Jewish model since she didn't have a Jewish childhood. The Jewish spouse and community, reacting to the long history of Christian anti-Semitism, may feel threatened by her Christian past so they don't acknowledge it. She feels isolated and unappreciated.

She doesn't want to be a proxy, passing on someone else's heritage; she wants to give what's inside her, her own spiritual and moral insights, the traditions of her childhood. If she left religious teaching solely to the Jewish spouse, she would feel excluded from an important aspect of her children's life.

Grandparents are also an issue. "My parents believe faith in Jesus is necessary for salvation," the woman said. "How can I tell them my children won't be baptized and won't have Christmas? It seems like we're doing everything to please my husband's parents and nothing for mine." This woman's instincts are healthy because her background is not being honored. Children need to feel strongly connected to parents and grandparents on both sides, and vice versa. How can you meet these needs and still have a Jewish home?

The Jewish partner must take major responsibility for creating a Jewish homestyle. To make the transition from knowing what you don't want to figuring out what you do want, it is important to resolve ambivalent feelings about being Jewish.

Learn along with your children. Create your own Jewish "childhood"; store up new memories as you share stories and celebrations with children. Both Jew and gentile need to do this.

Learn and explore religion on an adult level with your spouse. Most adults need a philosophy to sustain them. Studying together, a couple develops the shared beliefs and values needed to be full partners in the moral upbringing of children. Children value traditions more when parents find meaning in them.

Join an intermarried couples group. Most Reform synagogues and Jewish family services have them. Talking with other couples brings out issues

CHOOSING JUDAISM

In addition to Judy Petsonk and Jim Remsen's *The Intermarriage Handbook*, you can refer to the following sources:

Mixed Blessings: Marriage Between Jews and Christians (Doubleday) by Paul Cowan and Rachel Cowan.

Intermarriage: The Challenge of Living With Differences Between Christians and Jews (Free Press) by Susan Weidman Schneider.

Your People, My People: Finding Acceptance and Fulfillment as a Jew by Choice (Jewish Publication Society) by Lena Romanoff with Lisa Hostein.

Between Two Worlds: Choices for Grown Children of Jewish-Christian Parents (Pocket Books, 1992) by Leslie Goodman-Malamuth and Robin Margolis.

Raising Jewish Children in a Contemporary World (Prima Publishing) by Rabbi Steven Corr Reuben.

more clearly, provides sympathetic support, helps you and your children meet other mixed-marriage families.

Take on one new holiday or home ritual at a time. Some resources: Stephen J. Einstein and Lydia Kukoff's

Stories, symbols and celebrations: Traditional Jewish foods and rituals tell young children who they are

Every Person's Guide to Judaism (UAHC); Anita Diamant and Howard Cooper's *Living a Jewish Life: Jewish Traditions Customs and Values for Today's Families* (Harper); Blu Greenberg's *How to Run a Traditional Jewish Household* (Jason Aronson); *Spice and Spirit: The Complete Kosher Jewish Cookbook* (Lubavitch Women's Organization); Irving Greenberg's *The Jewish Way* (Summit); Arthur Waskow's *Seasons of Our Joy* (Beacon); Behrman House's *Home Start* program; Jewish bookstores for stories, childrens' books, *Haggadot* and tapes.

Talk about your childhood experiences with religion. The gentile can begin to "own" Jewish ideas as she or he sees that most Jewish beliefs and values are the same ones she was taught as a child, such as the Golden Rule and the Ten Commandments.

Translate religious language from Christian to Jewish terms. By thinking about the essence of her or his beliefs, the gentile can generally share them in ways compatible with Judaism. Given the history of forced conversion of Jews to Christianity, most Jewish spouses would be uncomfortable with children being taught that Jesus loves them. Most would have no problem with children being taught that God loves them.

Give children a rich understanding of ethnic and family heritages on both sides. Use photo albums, stories, foods, music. Enlist grandparents as teachers of family history, values, culture. Show them you are passing along the most important things they taught.

Give grandparents clear ground rules. If you want your children to get gifts at Hanukka rather than Christmas, say so.

Develop a plan for the holidays. Think about meeting the emotional needs of each partner; develop traditions that bind the nuclear family; build bridges to both extended families.

At holidays these issues become pressing. Christmas is precious to most gentiles and they want to share it with their children. Yet because Christmas so dominates American culture, the Jew may fear—with some justification—that if children celebrate Christmas their Jewish identity will never take hold.

When children are being raised as Jews, it's better not to have a Christmas tree. As a widely recognized symbol of Christianity, it can undermine Jewish identity. One little boy told us he was "mostly Jewish and a little percent Christmas tree."

But gentiles who give up the tree often feel they have lost a precious piece of childhood. This loss must be dealt with. If possible, spend holidays with the Christian family or close Christian friends. Partake in the traditions there: cookies, presents, tree decorating. This does not undermine children's Jewish identity. On the contrary, it's important that they know their roots on this side. It also reassures gentile grandparents that they haven't "lost" their child or grandchildren.

Keep as many of the gentile family's traditions as possible, adapting them to be compatible with Judaism. Use sparkly lights and popcorn strings to decorate your *sukka*. Make Christmas cookies in Hanukka shapes. An Italian woman whose family made "stained-glass" greeting cards from colored tissue paper hangs beautiful tissue paper *menoras* all over the house at Hanukka.

Develop new family traditions to honor the gentile's holidays. At Christmas, decorate a neighborhood tree with food for the birds. Serve Easter dinner at a nursing home so staff can have the day off.

If the gentile parent would be miserable without the tree, have it—and enjoy it—rather than divide th[e] family. Consider a small but lovel[y] tabletop one. Make it a gift to the gen[-] tile parent. Exchange presents for th[e] whole family at Hanukka.

Give grandparents a role in you[r] holiday celebrations. For Hanukka one family asks the Italian grand[-] parents to prepare their traditiona[l] fried pastries.

Make your differences your strength[.] Teach children to understand view[-] points different from their own. Eac[h] of you should be able to give an in[-] formed, respectful explanation of th[e] other's traditions and beliefs. Answe[r] children's questions about religio[n] freely and fully. When explaining a[n] idea about which you and your spouse disagree, point out the areas where you agree, for instance: "We both believe God loves each person."

Many couples today plan to raise children in both religions. Unfortunately, dual-identity children often know little and believe less of either parent's religion. Fewer than 10 percent marry Jews; a Jew who raises his children in both religions is probably choosing not to have Jewish descendants.

It's possible to raise children as proud, committed Jews who also have a warm appreciation of Christianity. Children raised in this manner will not only be secure in their roots, they will have much to contribute to a Jewish people that is learning to survive in an open society. ■

WHY BE JEWISH?

Why make the effort to raise children Jewish? First, Jewish life is a wonderful way to transmit strong values. The bitterness of oppression becomes concrete during the Seder when you eat the bitter herbs and sweet *haroses* while telling the story of the liberation of the Hebrew slaves; and the brightness of freedom comes alive when lighting the Hanukka candles in the darkest time of the year. Second, Jewish life builds strong families. The Sabbath is a family day; the candle-lighting ritual tells your family your time together is sacred. Third, Judaism encourages education and intelligent debate and can help you to bring up thinking children. Fourth, Judaism gives children roots. Jews in touch with their heritage know who they are. Fifth, Judaism can give a wholeness and rhythm to your life. In Judaism there is an interweaving of spiritual life with the four seasons. Sixth, your help is needed. The Jews are a small people who have given much to the world. You and your partner can help ensure that this rich heritage survives.—J.F.

BO[RO]WITZ & MARGARE[T]

ⓤ

PAREVE[H]

MIXED MARRIAGE SOUP

WITH CHILDREN OF INTERMARRIAGE

NOT KOSHER FOR PASSOVER (MAYBE NOT KOSHER AT ALL)

hey are self-confident and tolerant, full of optimism. Their passion for Judaism is fueled more by faith than by nostalgia. They struggle for grudging acceptance by the religion they were born into and also have chosen. And in 2030, so they believe, they will constitute the majority of American Jews.

This is the self-described profile of the children of interfaith marriage who choose to be Jews, the parevehs,* as many call themselves, offspring neither milk nor meat, whose religious commitment must overcome the duality of their lives.

"Imagine a hundred of us in a room. One or two would have been born in the early years of the century; eight or nine would be baby boomers 30 to 50 years old; 40 would be teenagers and then you would see 50 babies crawling around on the floor," said Leslie Goodman-Malamuth, cofounder with Robin E. Margolis of Pareveh, an organization especially for the children of interfaith couples (see box, p. 37).

They see themselves as the coming wave of ethnic Jews, not unlike the earlier Eastern Europeans or Sephardim, internal mi-

* *Pareveh* is the category of kosher food that is neither milk nor meat.

We Are The Children You Warned Our Parents About

The children of interfaith marriage speak out

CHARLOTTE ANKER

grants revitalizing American Judaism by bringing new values, as waves of immigrants have always done. "If the Jewish community does sensible outreach to bring us in," Goodman-Malamuth continued, "instead of compelling us to struggle to get in, we will see the flowering of a new American Judaism that will grow and take in new people. We know how to be competitive in the marketplace of ideas. We bring a passionate belief in God and the Jewish people expressed in a tolerant manner. We see the universality of Judaism."

Pareveh recently conducted a survey of 185 adult children of interfaith marriage.* Nearly half the respondents identified with Judaism, while almost one-third called themselves Christians; the rest identified themselves as either secular or other. Virtually all have some sense of Jewish identity, the survey compilers report, describing themselves often in such hybrid ways as "semi-semitic, Jewish hillbilly" or "religiously Catholic, ethnically Zionist Jewish." The responses provide a window into the thinking of people drawn to Judaism but who often feel that Judaism doesn't want them.

"Rebuff" is a word that frequently appears in descriptions of interactions between Jewish organizations and parevehs.

"Our credentials are constantly checked," one Pareveh member said. "'Have you converted?' people ask us. 'Well, no, my mother, after all, is Jewish.' This is something Jews have a hard time accepting. We have to be especially committed and determined to remain Jews."

"When I hear a rabbi inveigh against intermarriage," another said, "I know that's my parents he's assailing."

Jewish legitimacy is a different issue for parevehs than for Jews-by-choice because parevehs come to Judaism in the belief that they already are Jewish. Requiring conversion often seems to them a denial of the Jewish parent whose religion they have already internalized and accepted.

Diane Traurig of Huntington Woods, Michigan, whose father was Jewish and mother Protestant, underwent a Reform conversion, the preparation for which

---

* The respondents were chosen from Pareveh's mailing list and from others located through ads in the *Los Angeles Times, Washington Post* and *New York Times* Book Review.

"moved me in a way that I embraced it as I never had anything before in my life." But she bristled when friends at the temple asked about her plans for her future as a *new* Jew. "I am a Jewish person, not a *new* Jewish person," she said. "I don't want to and I can't be called a Jew-by-choice."

Most parevehs are the children of Jewish fathers because, when their parents married the interfaith marriage rate for male Jews was much higher than for females. Today the difference in interfaith marriage rates for Jewish males and females is diminishing, although the figure is still higher for Jewish males. Because most parevehs have Jewish fathers, parevehs are, at least initially, drawn to Reform Judaism—and Reconstructionism, which was 15 years ahead of Reform—with its recent definition of a Jew based on patrilineal descent. Even so, acceptance is not easy. Reform Jews are far from unanimous on patrilineal descent and patrilineals are only considered Jewish by Reform Jews if they were raised Jewish. Many patrilineal parevehs were not raised Jewish, although as adults they consider themselves Jewish.

Even children born of Jewish mothers, if they were not raised Jewish, are often urged to convert, as was Robin Margolis, one of the founders of Pareveh. Parevehs—especially patrilineals—tend to say as little as possible about how they were raised, hoping the subject won't come up.

Parevehs, drawn to Judaism by its ritual and spiritual features, often choose Conservative or Orthodox Judaism. Here, patrilineals must convert; matrilineals are welcomed, if somewhat suspect. While having a Jewish mother may make someone a Jew in halachic (religious law) terms, this doesn't necessarily translate into people treating that person as Jewish, Pareveh respondents contend.

"Many more of us would happily convert if we didn't feel the Jewish community was making us do it in order to get rid of something illegitimate in their eyes," said Goodman-Malamuth, who converted in order to join a Conservative congregation. "And conversion does not eliminate our identity conflicts," she added.

Why do parevehs choose to be Jews?

Many say they feel a strong attraction to a religion that needs them: "The Jews need me most," is a frequent response.

The Shoah is clearly an impetus—one born of grief and a resolve akin to that which impels born Jews to return to tradition. But the Shoah has a special meaning for parevehs. They know, intensely, that being only half Jewish would not have allowed them to escape. "I knew I could be killed because I was Jewish," said Lydia Lewis, whose mother was Jewish and father Presbyterian, in explaining why she always felt more Jewish than Christian. "I knew there was no getting away from being Jewish; it's always with you."

Other parevehs are drawn by the spiritual element of Judaism, observing that born Jews often take for granted the spiritual pull of Judaic rituals.

Jewish intellectuality is another attraction. "Christian theology was the big stumbling block for me," said one pareveh. "There's an intellectual aliveness in Judaism that I never found in Catholicism," said Richard Conoboy, who has a Jewish mother but was raised as a Catholic because his Catholic father signed a promise to raise his son Catholic. "My mother went along with this, but later was sorry." Conoboy also likes the activist role that Reform Judaism takes in the community and the "questioning of all things, even religious doctrine."

Then there is the odd attraction of the Jewish sense of being a marginal people, part of society but not quite assimilated. This ambivalence strikes a responsive chord among parevehs, who often feel that they are not like everybody else. "The prospect of being different because one is a Jew is not a deterrent to us—we already are different," one pareveh said.

A recent trip to Israel at the age of 40 triggered in Lydia Lewis a desire to learn about her Jewish side and perhaps make a choice. For Lewis it was "a question of finding what heritage to identify with, not a religious decision....Israel just blew me away. From the minute the plane landed, it was an extremely emotional experience."

The parevehs interviewed were brought up at a time when there were no instructions for raising children in dual-religion households. Most of these parevehs are critical of the way in which they were brought up, as are most respondents in Pareveh's study.

They strongly oppose letting the children decide on a religion when they grow up. Letting the children choose puts them in the position of having to reject one parent or the other, parevehs say. "No matter how prepared they think they are, parents often freak out when this happens," says Margolis. "They become enraged to see their children become devout Jews or Catholics."

"My mother always said I could be what I want to be, but when I became Jewish she got terribly upset," is a typical statement. "Sometimes, under the pressure, the children go off and become Buddhists—then both parents feel rejected," said one pareveh.

A significant number of parevehs refuse to affiliate with any religion because they cannot bear to choose between parents. Some report that whenever they mention they are ready to make a decision, one or both parents react by "registering discomfort—the same discomfort that led to their being unable to make the decision when the children were young," says Goodman-Malamuth. "Strange as it may seem, we find middle-aged adults who say their parents won't let them choose."

Diane Traurig, raised in a family with no designated house religion, described how she would lie in bed at night and have terrible fantasies about having to choose between her mother and her father. Of her recent conversion to Judaism, she says, "If my mother were still living, I'm not sure I could have done it."

"I never wanted to be disloyal to either my mother or my father," said Lewis, adding that if her Presbyterian father were still alive, she, too, probably wouldn't feel so free to identify with her Jewish heritage.

Often, children raised with no religious or ethnic identity tend to go with the prevailing gentile culture, which they have experienced because it surrounds them.

But there are also dangers in the other direction. When an official house religion is chosen, the authorities of that religion often tell the parents they must have absolutely nothing to do with the other culture. "We know families who have been told by Jewish authority figures not only that the gentile spouse must convert but also, to avoid confusion, they must minimize exposure to the Christian family," Margolis reported. "Families have been advised that Christmas presents must be returned with a note saying that now that the parent is a Jew-by-choice and raising Jewish children, the gift is construed as an interference in the parent's attempt to raise the children. Can you imagine the heartbroken grandparents? The message is that half the family is contemptible or at least inferior to the half that adheres to the household religion."

"The child probably gets a subliminal message from the parent who feels that a part of his or her identity is wiped out," says Margolis. "I was totally cut off from my Jewish family. My mother was set on making me a total Episcopalian. When I found out I had a Jewish family, I defected. My two brothers are still devout Christians, but I feel strongly my mother should have had at least one kid for herself."

Whether parevehs are raised as Jews or Christians, they say they always have two halves. They assert that they are irrevocably tied to both their families and these ties cannot be undermined without endangering their psychological health.

But how can they be Jews and have a Christian half? "We have to learn to live with a duality inside ourselves," said Goodman-Malamuth. "It permeates every area of our lives, sometimes painfully."

"At times in my life, I've thought I was in limbo and fit in nowhere," said Diane Freedman of Saratoga Springs, New York. "At other times, I thought I had the best of both worlds."

"I've gone through a painful struggle being two people," Traurig said. "Now with my conversion I feel more whole, more complete. But I still can't disassociate from my Christian self; I am who I am. Last year I took a friend of mine along and we went to a reading of Charles Dickens' *A Christmas Carol.* It was very satisfying to me; I found I still needed something."

"When I am in a Jewish setting, I really experience that culture, but in a Christian setting, I see it through my father's eyes; it is not alien to me," said Margolis.

Most parevehs say parents should choose a house religion and commit themselves to it, but also provide ample exposure to the relatives of the religion not chosen. It is best if one partner converts, they concede.

"However, make it clear to the children being brought up Jewish that one part of the extended family has a Christian home," said Goodman-Malamuth. "'We may visit our Christian family and help them celebrate their holidays, but they're not our holidays.'"

If each parent feels strongly committed to his or her own religion, however, then the parents should raise the children with both religions—not with nothing—parevehs argue. Then the parents must steel themselves for possible rejection when the day comes that the child makes a choice. But at least the child will have a solid basis for the choice, they say.

Parevehs ask for outreach programs directed specifically at children of interfaith couples. Current outreach programs don't work for them, they say, because they are aimed at interfaith couples, Jews-by-choice or alienated Jews born of two Jewish parents. A program for parevehs would start with an assumption of their legitimacy as Jews, potential Jews or people with a valid interest in studying Judaism.

There are issues peculiar to parevehs that current outreach programs ignore, for example, how the adult child can help the parent, whose religion is not chosen, with his or her grief. "My father grieved deeply when I opted to go Jewish," said Margolis. "It took many talks over a long period of time before he could accept it and he had to do a lot of grieving first."

Set up programs for children, teenagers and college-age children of interfaith marriages and support groups for adult parevehs, respondents said. Find a way to say, "We know you're caught between two worlds; we understand that and want to help you." Introduce them to other children of interfaith marriages who have converted to Judaism. Make it clear that while they may need conversion at some stage of the process, conversion is only a way station along a continuum of Jewish life, not a ticket to legitimacy. Ⓜ

Intermarriage: A Sunday School Teacher's Perspective
by Susan Greenberg

It's Sunday morning. The sun filters through the windows, and my classroom is quiet as I prepare for today's lesson. I call it my "Being Jewish Is..." lesson. As I ready the room on this particular morning, I reflect on what a wonderful challenge it is to teach first grade at a Reform congregation. It truly is a challenge I look forward to each and every week. My lesson this morning is a solid one, based on a cumulative review of the curriculum covered thus far and strategically placed at the halfway mark of the school year.

The children begin to trickle in; bright eager faces, fresh from carpool. In my class it's double stickers for those who arrive early or on time. After all we have lots to do and limited time to do it. With morning formalities out of the way, tzedakah [charity] collected and our *shema* diligently recited, I announce today's lesson, "Being Jewish Is...," and I direct the class' attention to the giant Jewish star I have drawn on the board. Several hands immediately shoot up with ideas to fill it. Jonathan is raising both hands and obviously bursting with information to share. I, in my infinite, unsuspecting wisdom, call on him.

"I am Jewish and Christian," he announces to the class in a voice that is as unsure as it is challenging. Seventeen pairs of eyes turn to me to see what my response will be.... They know. Six year olds know this issue inside out–they live it. Every holiday season, every trip to Bubbe's or Grandma's, every birth of a sibling, even on their birthdays it comes up again and again. They may not know about the 52% intermarriage rate, but they know this issue quite well on their own level.

"I'm glad you mentioned you're Jewish because that is exactly what I want to talk about today," I say with a gentle smile, breezing right past the second part of Jonathan's statement.

I want to scream, not at this wonderful child, but at parents who choose to raise their children "both" ways. Do they understand that for this little boy there is never one answer? For all of his formative years there will never be one reassuring religious philosophy or system of values. There will always be two answers, two ways. This is great for problem solving in academia. But, when you are six and searching for where you belong, instead of ending up with the intended two ways to "choose," you end up with neither. You can't completely belong anywhere. I know. I've heard all the questions these children ask. Every Sunday school teacher has. Consider:

Did the Jewish God or the Christian God make me?

Is God angry if you have a Christmas tree?

Who's stronger, Jesus or God?

What prayers do I say today? (This is from a child who attends catechism on Saturday and Hebrew school on Sunday.)

My mommy says when I grow up I get to choose to be Jewish or Christian. Will she be mad if I choose Daddy's?

Which am I today?

Someday I have to choose Mommy's or Daddy's way....

If I'm Jewish and Christian now, when do I get to be just me?

These are questions, clearly, from children searching for a place to call home.

So why do I smile in response to Jonathan? I smile because, though his question inadvertently touched a nerve, I would die rather than make him feel cheated, slighted, or inadequate in any way.

My lesson goes well. We talk of things in our homes that make it a Jewish home – "We still have our etrog from Sukkot, but it's pretty moldy," says one honest child. We talk of God and Torah being the center of our existence as Jews – "Like a tree is to squirrels," observes a nature lover; of mitzvot – "613," a trivia expert quotes. We talk of Israel – "You know, our other half," adds another young voice. We talk of Abraham and his contemporaries- "Don't forget the women in the Torah!" says a favorite, free-spirited personality. And finally, as they start to squirm, I talk. I speak in my most sincere, teacher voice, the one I know they hear because it comes from my heart, and you can't fool kids.

I tell them: "Today, it is my job to teach you what it is to be Jewish, but someday I'll be gone, and you (I point to each one of them), you will be responsible for teaching your children what being Jewish means." (I note that they sit up a little straighter given this new information). "You will have to teach your children the wonderful, colorful things that go into being Jewish. This will be a most important job, because the most important thing we do is teach our children." It is amazing. Even at six, you can see in their earnest faces, the impression this makes.

We finish up the lesson with a craft — a Jewish star cut from tagboard and glued with brilliant, tissue-paper colored squares — a rainbow of colors that symbolize the kaleidoscope of things that make us Jewish. The children labor for thrity minutes, and as we pack up to leave, Jonathan approaches with his star. I see he has meticulously scrunched up the colored squares into balls and covered every square centimeter of the tagboard, with every imaginable color. I am about to heap a multitude of praise on him for a job so well done, when he looks up at me and says with confidence and trust, "You know, Mrs. Greenberg, I decided from now on I'm mostly Jewish!" He smiles broadly and turns to walk out. I think he is happy to have settled this in his own mind.

What a monumental decision to be asked to make constantly at six years old! How unfortunate that parents allow their own avoidance, indecision, or unwillingness to commit to impact their child's growing years. How do you explain to a parent that you are not giving your child the best of "both" worlds, but you are robbing him of the richness and fullness and sense of belonging fully to one?

Today I have been saddened and gladdened and saddened again, and as I pack up to leave, I wonder how many children have been too.

Questions for Discussion

1. How does the teacher feel about children who are raised "both" ways, as both Jews and Christians?

2. What are some of the difficulties the teacher claims these children will encounter if they are raised in two religious traditions?

3. Is it possible to be both Jewish and Christian?

4. Could you define yourself as both Jewish and Christian? Is it fair to ask your child to identify with more than one religious tradition?

5. Is it possible for a six year old to make the "monumental" decision of which religion to choose? Is it possible that a child may choose a religion based on whose religious school serves the best cookies for snack? What are your reactions to these questions?

6. How could a child's choice of religious affiliation affect his or her relationship with the parent whose religion is chosen, the parent whose religion is not chosen?

7. How does the writer suggest interfaith parents deal with this situation? Do you agree or disagree?

DECEMBER DILEMMA MATERIALS

The Christmas/Chanukah Conundrum: A Guide For Couples

"I get sweaty just thinking about it. We were climbing the stairs to our apartment, both thinking the same thing. The Christmas tree in our living room was a source of tension instead of joy, and we were both angry."

Nothing seems to stir up feelings quite like the holiday season which many of us associate with warmth and love. Celebrations that should be joyful may be the source of conflict, and it seems that there is no solution that will make everyone happy. Although there are no pat answers, the following suggestions may be helpful in beginning to communicate about "The December Dilemma:"

1. MAKE AN EFFORT TO DETOXIFY THE ISSUE. If at all possible, approach it with humor. This is a wonderful opportunity to poke fun at your own reactions, even if you're not feeling funny. Remember that laughing about something in no way diminishes the importance of the issue — it merely helps put it in perspective.

2. USE "I STATEMENTS" THAT DESCRIBE FEELINGS INSTEAD OF BLAMING. What your partner will be able to understand about your feelings may depend on how they're communicated. Try statements like, "I'm worried that my parents won't come to visit if they know there's a Christmas tree here," or "I feel like I can't be part of something that was very precious to me," rather than "You are so selfish in imposing your will."

3. REMEMBER THAT CHILDHOOD MEMORIES WILL REMAIN A PART OF WHO YOU ARE. Our past remains with us, no matter what religious choices we may make as adults. Encourage your partner to share memories of holidays and talk about their meaning. The holiday season is a time when we are often drawn back to our families, and it may be especially important to help one another find ways to share the current season with relatives and friends.

4. SHARE FEELINGS OF LOSS. If the issue of loss remains off limits, tension will mount and solutions will become even more remote. Anger, disappointment, jealousy, and sadness may all be reflections of loss. Even when we make conscious, rational choices about holiday celebrations, there may be powerful feelings related to compromise. Often the very acknowledgement of these feelings will shift the focus from looking back toward the past to looking forward with hope.

5. HAVE THE COURAGE TO MAKE ADULT DECISIONS IF THERE ARE (OR WILL BE) CHILDREN. Celebrating two sets of holidays may seem like the best of all possible worlds, but it may confuse children and complicate their sense of "Who am I?" It is easy for celebrations to become competitive, for unexpressed concerns to arise, and for families, seeking cohesiveness, to feel confused. Leaving the choice of religion up to children when they are "old enough" translates to "Choose Mom or choose Dad." No child is ever "old enough" for that choice.

6. CONSIDER THE POSSIBILITY OF AN `ANTHROPOLOGICAL' CHRISTMAS. Many families have successfully managed the December Dilemma by observing Jewish holidays in their own home, but sharing Christmas at the home of non-Jewish family. Children will not be confused if they understand that while theirs is a Jewish home, they may visit non-Jewish relatives on Christian holidays to help Grandpa George or Cousin Marcy celebrate their holidays.

The above tips are intended to be food for thought as the holidays approach. For further problem solving or discussion, your rabbi or your regional Outreach Coordinator can be important resources.

The Family

BY DR. RON WOLFSON

Reprinted by permission of the author. From his book, <u>The Art of Jewish Living</u>: Hannukah, Federation of Jewish Men's Clubs and University of Judaism, N.Y., 1990.

Confronting the December Dilemmas

My mother likes to tell a story about me, Hanukkah and Christmas.

December in Omaha, Nebraska was the height of the Christmas season. There was not a place you could go that didn't announce the fact that Christmas was coming. From the daily countdown in the newspaper of "shopping days 'til Christmas" to the incessant commercials on television, the holiday was everywhere. Our block became a virtual wonderland of sparkling lights outlining homes and trees. The stores and malls featured Christmas displays and merchandise. Even the front entrance of our public school was adorned with a huge Christmas tree. The strains of Christmas music filled the air. There was no escape.

To a little five-year-old Jewish boy, December was the first test of one's identity, the first realization that you were not like almost everyone else.

My mother had the answer! She would outdo Christmas. This explains the decorations, the presents each and

Dr. Ron Wolfson is Director of the Whizin Institute for Jewish Family Life at the University of Judaism, Los Angeles. He is the author of The Art of Jewish Living series of books published by the Federation of Jewish Men's Clubs and the University of Judaism. The Art of Jewish Living: Hanukkah is available from the FJMC, 475 Riverside Drive, NY, NY 10015.

every night, the piles of *latkes*, the Hanukkah *gelt*. It seemed to work, especially when our Christian next-door-neighbor, Mrs. Lamm, called to complain to my mother that I had been teasing her son Alan: "You only have Christmas for one day; we have Hanukkah for eight."

The plan worked marvelously until, one year, the fifth night of Hanukkah coincided with Christmas Eve, a fact of which I had been well aware. After the lights had been lit, the presents given, and the *latkes* consumed, my mother confidently tucked me into bed saying:

"Well, Ronnie, wasn't Hanukkah wonderful tonight?"

"Yes, Mommy," I dutifully replied. "Mommy?"

"Yes, honey."

"Mommy, can we take down the Hanukkah things - just for tonight - so Santa Claus won't know we're Jewish?"

A plea for more presents? A rejection of my nascent Jewish identity? I think not. Looking back, I believe it was a half-hearted wish not to be different, if just for one night.

How many of our children and grandchildren feel these same desires, these same pressures, these same dilemmas? Existing articles on "The December Dilemma" have considered the problem of Christmas in the public arena—at school, in the stores, in the neighborhood, thereby distancing the discussion.

This is no longer the case. When at least one-fourth of first marriages among born Jews are to non-Jews (and in some parts of the continent, the figure is *one-half*), the indisputable fact is that a large percentage of Jewish families have within their extended systems members who were not born Jewish and/or are not now Jewish.

All of a sudden, we are not just confronting Christmas in the shopping mall; we must respond to an invitation from a non-Jewish relative to celebrate Christmas with a part of our family. All of a sudden we are not just debating whether to sing Christmas songs in the school choir; we are asked to accompany a family member to Midnight Mass. It is one thing to say "no" to a child wanting to sit on Santa's knee, but quite another to refuse an invitation from in-laws to celebrate their holiday.

This new situation renders the term "December Dilemma" inadequate, for there is no single dilemma. Rather, there are a whole series of December Dilemmas - questions, situations, and alternatives that sensitive people must confront when struggling with the issues raised by the proximity of Christmas and Hanukkah. Fully one-third of the book *The Art of Jewish Living: Hanukkah* deals with these issues. Let us consider just a few.

JOY

THE CHRISTMAS DILEMMA

Unfortunately, the "Christ" has gone out of Christmas. "Good" Christians often do not know the deep religious significance of the Christmas tree, the Christmas wreath, Santa Claus, and the carols. The tree, an evergreen, represents the eternal life of Jesus the Christ, meaning "the Messiah." One of the fundamental differences between Judaism and Christianity is that Jews believe Jesus was a man, while Christians believe Jesus was the son of God, the Messiah. Its shape is ascending towards heaven, its star is the Star of Bethlehem, its sap is the blood of Christ. How about Santa Claus? He is not just some jolly old man with a stable of elves and reindeer somewhere north of Alaska. He is a fantasy figure derived from a Catholic bishop, Saint Nicholas, born in the third century, who was famous for giving unexpected gifts. The Christmas wreath symbolizes the crown of thorns Jesus wore to the cross, its green holly berries turning to red as he was crucified.

"But," your friends protest, "nobody believes that anymore." Ah, but that is not the point. The point is that by adopting Christmas and its customs, Jews are introducing symbols and traditions into their homes and into the lives of their children that are absolutely foreign to Judaism. There is no connection between Christmas and Hanukkah except that, because of the vagaries of the calendar, they come together at the same time of year. Christmas is the celebration of the birth of a Messiah whom Jews do not believe in and Hanukkah is the celebration of the right not to assimilate - the very thing that Jews who celebrate Christmas are doing!

So, why is it so difficult to say "no" to Santa?

THE PARENTING DILEMMA

It's December; the family takes its stroll through the mall and happens upon Santa's North Pole, and a wide-eyed three-year-old asks, "Can I sit on Santa's knee?" The Jewish parent's answer to the child will depend on several things: the intensity of the parent's Jewish commitments, the parent's assessment of how "influential" the visit to Santa might be on the child's Jewish identity, and, perhaps most importantly, the parent's ability to set limits.

No one wants his/her child to feel deprived of anything, especially if what the child wants, on the surface, seems so harmless. There is a deep-seated wish in many Jews to be accepted, to be part of the majority, to be equal in the eyes of society. If we deny our children Santa, will they feel left out, inferior, different, frustrated, envious? Moreover, many parents simply hate to say "no" to their children. We want them to have everything.

Yet, certainly our children ask us for many things which we refuse, not for some capricious use of parental authority, but because we value their health, safety and well-being. So, we occasionally say "no" to more candy, running across the street, or watching violent television shows. We say "no" when we believe we have the responsibility as parents to teach them, to guide them, to help mold their character and sense of identity.

Thus, many Jewish parents say "no" to Santa Claus and Christmas trees because they are not part of being Jewish as we are Jewish. You, my child, are Jewish. Christmas is not our holiday.

But, "just say no" doesn't seem to be enough of an answer. And this leads us to one powerful explanation of why Hanukkah has been elevated to the status of one of the most observed Jewish holidays.

Christmas is not our holiday. "Hanukkah is our holiday," the parent will rush to add. So, the first instinct is to offer an alternative to Christmas. Many parents are thankful that there is one. Yet, even more important may be the opportunity to seize this seemingly negative episode and turn it into a lesson in Jewish identity building and child development.

Early childhood educators tell us that one of the most crucial stages in socialization occurs when a child is between 18 and 30 months old and attends another child's birthday party. When the birthday cake is brought in, most of the little guests try to blow out the candles right along with the birthday child. As the child opens presents, little hands start to grab for the toys. Why do you think "party favors" were invented? To help children begin to distinguish what's mine and what's his/hers. Toddlers must learn the difference between celebrating one's own birthday and celebrating another's.

Thus, many Jewish educators will advise parents to give children who want to celebrate Christmas a very important message: Christmas is someone else's party, not ours. Just as we can appreciate someone else's birthday celebration and be happy for them, we can wonder at how beautiful Christmas is; but it is not our party.

And then, many parents make a perfectly understandable, but incomplete, leap. "Christmas is for Christians. They have Christmas. We are Jewish. We have Hanukkah." In an attempt to substitute something for Christmas, the parent offers Hanukkah. In fact, Hanukkah is even better than Christmas. "Christmas is only for one day. Hanukkah is for eight." So, now, as incredulous as it seems, the parental anxiety leads to the teaching that our party lasts longer, offers more presents, and is just as beautiful.

Of course, the problem is that it just isn't true. Hanukkah cannot hold a candle to Christmas. It is a minor event in the Jewish holiday cycle and has never, until recently, been viewed as a central celebration for the Jewish people. Therefore, the customs and ceremonies surrounding Hanukkah pale by comparison to those of Christmas - which is one of the two major holidays of Christianity.

The answer to the child is incomplete. "We're Jewish - we have Hanukkah" is only the beginning of the response. "We're Jewish and we have - Hanukkah, Sukkot, Pesah, Shavuot,

...urim, Simhat Torah, Rosh HaShanah, Yom Kippur, Lag BaOmer, Yom HaAtzma'ut, Tu BiShvat - and most importantly, Shabbat every week." The child who has experienced the building of a *sukkah* will not feel deprived of trimming a tree. The child who has participated in a meaningful Passover *Seder* will not feel deprived of Christmas dinner. The child who has paraded with the Torah on Simhat Torah, planted trees at Tu BiShvat, brought fresh fruits at Shavuot, given *mishloach manot* at Purim, and welcomed the Shabbat weekly with candles and wine and hallah by the time he/she is three years old will understand that to be Jewish is to be enriched by a calendar brimming with joyous celebration.

THE PUBLIC CELEBRATION DILEMMA

One of the terribly difficult problems for Jews during December is the celebration of Christmas as an official "legal" holiday. The problem has been greatly exacerbated by the recent United States Supreme Court decision that it is legally acceptable to put up Christmas trees and Hanukkah *m'norot* in public places. Incredibly, the decision rests on the view of the court that the Christmas tree and the Hanukkah *m'norah* are *not* religious symbols.

For Jewish children who attend public schools, the introduction of Christmas into the curriculum during the weeks preceding the holiday throws them and their parents into a yearly confrontation with their minority status. Numerous Jewish parents have marched into principals' offices when their children brought home Christmas art projects or tree ornaments; or, debated the singing of Christmas carols featured in annual winter concerts; or, agonized over taking roles in Christmas pageants.

More Jewish organizations with interests in this area have strongly pressed the case for separation of church and state as reason enough for the elimination of religious holiday celebrations in the public schools. They point out that Christmas is an important Christian holy day that not all students celebrate. They argue that Christmas plays which portray religious themes have no place in public schools. They maintain that neither Christmas nor Hanukkah should be celebrated in this setting.

Yet, most officials of the Jewish community realize that it is difficult, if not impossible, to police thousands of teachers throughout the land to prevent these celebrations. Much work is done to sensitize school personnel to the feelings of Jewish children at this time of year.

Alternative celebration suggestions are made: produce a "winter festival" that preserves the holiday atmosphere, but removes the religious connotations. Study about different religious celebrations around the world at this time of year. Use the holiday season as an opportunity to celebrate the brotherhood of humankind.

THE MARKETPLACE DILEMMA

One of the more interesting of the December Dilemmas is the confusion between Christmas and Hanukkah in the marketplace. In their rush to commercialize the winter holidays, entrepreneurs regularly confuse the meanings of Hanukkah and Christmas. We see evergreen trees sold to Jews as "Hanukkah bushes;" blue and white lights to decorate the home inside and out; "Hanukkah Harry", an ersatz Jewish Santa Claus who visits little Jewish boys and girls with Hanukkah presents; "Hannuklaus," a mixed image of Santa Claus, a *dreidel* and a Star of David; greeting cards with Santa lighting a *m'norah*; holiday displays of blue and white tinsel surrounding a *hanukkiah*; Hanukkah stockings in blue and white embroidered with *dreidels*, Star of David designs and the word *Shalom*. On the other hand, it has become increasingly clear, year after year, that the merchants and mass media mavens have finally discovered Hanukkah. Not long ago, it would have been unthinkable to see Hanukkah decorations in store windows, "Happy Hanukkah" greetings on television, or i n c l u s i v e "Season's Greetings" messages o n f a s t - f o o d packaging. Today, these things are a reality.

Should Jews be happy with the developing commercialization of Hanuk-

kah? There are those for whom the elevation of Hanukkah is repugnant. It forces comparisons that are difficult to make. It encourages the embellishment of a Jewish holiday for which there is little traditional ritual. Any such attempt to compete with Christmas is futile. Let's keep Hanukkah the minor holiday it is, de-emphasizing the decorations, the presents, and the public displays. Yet, there are others who have concluded, "If you can't beat 'em, join 'em." Fortunately, Hanukkah comes when it does. At least we have something to celebrate, too, at a time when it feels as if the whole world is geared to family gatherings, gift exchanges, and good cheer. And besides these Hanukkah-embellishers argue, have not Jewish holidays always held more or less importance and meaning for Jews depending on when and where they have lived? Purim, a celebration of the physical survival of the Jews, was a much more popular holiday in places and times where Jews lived under the threat of bodily harm. Hanukkah, a celebration of the spiritual survival of Judaism, is the ideal foil to a Christian holiday which, in its secular formulation, represents the threat of assimilation in our own day.

THE PSEUDO-CHRISTMAS DILEMMA

Adding to the confusion of the season is the fact that Christmas is the one day of the year when virtually every business and office is closed. For many Jewish families, it is an ideal opportunity for a family gathering. The temptation for these families to turn the day into a pseudo-Christmas is so convenient. What difference does it make that Hannukah was three weeks ago? The important thing is

that the whole family can be together and exchange gifts. Even a "pseudo-Christmas" celebration on December 25 is not consistent with Jewish law and custom. So, what are Jews to do on December 25? Many families do gather together for the day simply to enjoy each other's company. Some try to avoid Christmas altogether by leaving town on vacation or by pursuing favorite activities such as going to the movies.

THE FAMILY DILEMMA

One of the most profound changes in Jewish family life during the past 40 years has been the significant rate of intermarriage between Jew and Gentile. Intermarriage experts agree that the way in which a couple negotiates the Christmas-Hanukkah season often becomes the true test of the viability of such a marriage.

Even if the non-Jewish partner converts, and the couple celebrates only Hanukkah in the home, there is one complicating factor that cannot be dismissed: *The family of origin of a Jew-by-choice does not convert.* This is an extremely important point and raises one of the most challenging obstacles to resolving this particular December Dilemma: What do I do about celebrating Christmas and Hanukkah with my family when my family includes both Jews and Christians?

Before suggesting some options, it is important to understand how difficult, if not impossible, and perhaps undesirable it would be to ignore the fact that the non-Jewish grandparents cannot be expected to give up their religion. As grandparents, they will more than likely expect their now-Jewish child to respect their religion and their right to share their holidays with their grandchildren. To complicate matters, the parents of the born-Jew in the couple may be frantic about the possibility that their grandchildren might "celebrate" Christmas with their Christian counterparts. And, as in most family systems, they are likely to let their fears be known.

All this puts the Jew-by-choice and his/her spouse in a very difficult position. After talking to many intermarried couples and surveying the current (and growing) literature on the subject, here are some of the choices available, ranging from total avoidance to reasoned compromise:

1. Leave town for the holidays.
2. Do not recognize Christmas at all. Celebrate Thanksgiving, Fourth of July, Memorial Day - any non-religious holiday - with them.
3. Do not accept an invitation for Christmas. Send or bring gifts to the grandparents at another time.
4. Ask the non-Jewish grandparents to celebrate Hanukkah with you when Hanukkah occurs, not on December 25.
5. Visit the Christian grandparents for Christmas, but make it very clear that "this is grandpa and grandma's holiday, not ours. Nevertheless, we can enjoy sharing it with them." Just as Jewish parents or grandparents might invite Christian inlaws to a Passover *Seder*, "sharing" a religious holiday other than our own is quite different from "observing" it in our own homes.

SOLVING THE DECEMBER DILEMMAS

The Art of Jewish Living: Hanukkah features interviews with a number of Jewish families who discuss how they are resolving their December Dilemmas. Three important lessons emerge from their experiences:

1. The most important task in solving each dilemma is to set limits and determine borders. Where do you draw the line? Will you let your children watch Christmas television shows, but not sit on Santa's knee in the mall? Will you take the family to see the Christmas decorations in the neighborhood, but not participate in the public lighting of the *hanukkiah*? Will you go to Christmas dinner at a non-Jewish relative's home?

2. The most important strategy in reaching these decisions is to *communicate clearly*. Be consistent with your children. Be open with your spouse. Plan to have the discussion about Christmas or "pseudo-Christmas" in July, not on December 1.

3. The solutions to the December Dilemmas are likely to be worked out *over a period of years*, not all at once. It takes time for people to change their thinking about deeply held positions and desires. Above all, try to avoid confrontation. Muster all the patience, compassion, and understanding you can.

Coping with December Dilemmas can be an exasperating and difficult experience. Yet, it can also bring about a reaffirmation of one's Jewish identity in the face of pressures to assimilate into the cultural majority. And, is that not the very lesson of the holiday of Hanukkah? ☐

Being a Jew at Christmas

by Faye Moskowitz

"Jewish Christmas" – that's what my Gentile friends called Chanukah when I was growing up in Jackson, MI. in the 30's and 40's. Anachronistic, yes, but they had a point. Observing the dietary laws of separating milk and meat dishes was far easier for the handful of Jewish families in our little town than getting through December without mixing the two holidays.

Christmas was a miserable time for Jewish children in those days – a time of envy and cruel illumination of our difference from what seemed to us, everyone else. I secretly hung a stocking on a bureau knob in my bedroom one year and prayed that Santa wouldn't stumble when he came, and wake up my mother and father. Nothing short of quarantine could have kept us from catching Christmas fever. My parents were no help. Immigrants who fled pogroms in Russia and Poland, they were world-class outsiders. If T-shirts with mottoes had been in fashion then, our shirts would surely have read, "Keep a Low Profile." My mother would never have considered going to my school to complain about the Christmas tree in the lobby or the creche in our principal's office or the three life-size wise men, complete with camels, we cut out of construction paper in art and hung on our classroom walls.

If I still wasn't convinced that Christmas was coming after all those reminders, I had only to look at the Advent calendar hanging behind my teacher's desk, or to walk downtown where carols blared out over loudspeakers in front of the six-foot neon cross decorating our largest department store. And as for keeping a low profile, try it when yours is the only neighborhood house in work clothes while everyone else's is dressed for a party.

I was born in 1930 in Detroit, comfortable in the Jewish ghetto, knowing little about the outside world except for stories I'd heard. To me, being Jewish was as natural as the air I breathed or the water I drank. My parents and their parents and landsleit huddled together in an atmosphere that in many ways must have replicated the little town in Russia and Poland from which most of them came. Everything we needed to live a cloistered Jewish life was close at hand. So the first five years of my life were spent in a kind of Edenic innocence. And then, for whatever the sin, the Great Depression struck our family, we moved to Jackson, and for me knowledge began.

By the time we moved back to the Jewish section of Detroit in 1942, I was old enough to accept Christmas as a holiday other people celebrated. From Sunday school, from my parents, and from reading on my own, I had come to understand that Chanukah was our winter holiday, not a substitute at all but a festival that commemorates the miraculous tenacity with which light claims its primacy over darkness. In Jackson every element of my Jewishness had been thrown into sharp relief by the prevailing Christian customs and values. Back in the ghetto once more, I could stop measuring myself by the chalk marks of other people's standards. In a subtle way, I could relax again. With enormous relief I joined cousins who gathered at our grandparents' house, where we lined up to get Chanukah gelt from the uncles: quarters and half-dollars, and dollar bills perhaps for the older children. Mostly we ran around a lot, got very flushed, and ate latkes, plenty of them.

My own children were raised in a diverse neighborhood in Washington, D.C. The Ghost of Christmas Past clanked its chains for awhile, and sometimes I worried that our children might be seduced by Santa as I once was. So, being first-generation Americans and a little less rigid than our own folks, my husband and I made some concessions. While we never sank to the Chanukah bush (though we knew people who did), we lit the menorah, bought presents for each of the eight nights, and decorated our house with blue-and-white paper chains. In spite of all that, our kids were pretty disgruntled for most of December, but even their non-Jewish friends had to concede that we had something with those latkes.

For the past few years, with our children grown, my husband and I have been away from home during Chanukah. A December vacation suits my schedule, and we figure – rationalize – that Chanukah is a relatively minor holiday compared with Rosh Hashanah, Yom Kippur, or Passover. Last year we found ourselves in Venice during the holidays. Despite our excuses, we missed being home with our children. We asked ourselves if they would get together to light the menorah without us there to orchestrate the ceremony. We wondered if our celebrations in the past had come to mean anything more than the presents we gave one another. At that moment we would have traded any pasta dish, no matter how delectable, for potato latkes like the ones we ate at Chanukah as far back as we both could remember.

So perhaps that's why, with the help of guidebooks and faltering Italian, we threaded our way through the city's bewildering twists and turns until we suddenly emerged into a spacious square, which marks the old Jewish ghetto of Venice. The clip-clop of our heels on cobblestones and the flutter of pigeons punctuated a silence that might have existed for centuries or only on that particular day. "There's an old synagogue at the other end of the square," my husband said. "Let's go see if maybe it's open for visitors." We pulled at the heavy brass-studded wooden door, and far down a long corridor I heard the sound of many voices chattering in Italian. "I'm probably hallucinating," I whispered to my husband, "but I swear I smell latkes."

In that musty, crumbling building, the memories flooded back as clear as the icicles we licked in those nose-numbing December days of my Michigan childhood. Bundled against the cold, we walked hand in hand, my mother and father, my brothers and I, along the darkened streets of Detroit, where orange candles in brass menorahs bravely illuminated each front window we passed.

In my grandparents' vestibule, we shed our boots. The warmth of the coal furnace promised more coziness deep inside; there my aunts sucked in their bellies as they elbowed past one another in and out of Bubbe's tiny kitchen, from which they pulled a seemingly endless array of delicious dishes, as if from a magician's opera hat: platters of bagels slathered with cream cheese, smoked fish with skins of irridescent gold, pickled herring, thick slices of Bermuda onion strong enough to risk a double dare, boiled potatoes with their red jackets on, wallowing in butter. Best of all were the crisp potato latkes, hot from Bubbe's frying pan, to eat swaddled in cool sour cream, the contrasting textures and temperature indelibly printing themselves on our memory.

Though our mothers' cooking styles were virtually interchangeable, my husband and I used to quarrel every year about whose mother made the better latkes. My mother's potato pancakes were thin and lacy, delicate enough to float in their hot cooking oil. His mother's latkes, I pointed out at every opportunity, lacked refinement: colossal, digestion-defying pancakes the size of hockey pucks, each of them a meal itself. "Just the way I like them," my husband would tell me as he wolfed down yet another.

I never learned to make my mother's latkes. She died just before my husband and I were married, and when we came to Washington we took my mother-in-law with us, so her potato latkes won by default and became part of our children's Chanukah tradition (which is not to say I ever accepted them graciously).

Friends came each Chanukah and brought their children to celebrate with ours. We spun dreidels and exchanged small gifts, boxes of crayons, pretty bars of soap, cellophane bags of sour candies for grandma, who of course, provided the latkes. Early in the afternoon, she would begin grating potatoes on a vicious four-sided grater, the invention of some fiendish anti-Semite who must have seen the opportunity to maim half the Jewish population each December.

The trick was to finish grating just before the guests arrived, so the potatoes would not blacken, as they have a discouraging tendency to do. Meanwhile, as she mixed in eggs, matzah meal, salt, and baking powder, grandma heated the frying pan with enough oil to light the Chanukah lamps into the next century. The finished latkes were drained on supermarket paper bags that promptly turned translucent with fat. Still, we ate them - great, golden, greasy, dolloped with sour cream latkes - and our complaints became part of our Chanukah tradition, too.

The Venetian laktkes didn't taste very much like Grandma's, but there was enough resemblance to quell our homesickness. Walking back to our hotel, I thought of the fragile threads that stitch a people together. I thought of the Italian Jews whose hospitality we had just shared, this stubborn remnant of those lost in the Holocaust, mending itself with the continuity of old customs. I thought of Grandma tasting a bit of her childhood each Chanukah when she made the latkes, as her mother had made them before her. I prayed my grandchildren would remember who they were and where they came from. And then my mother, my aunts, my grandmother floated back to me, young and vibrant once more, making days holy in the sanctuaries of their kitchens, feeding me, cradling me, connecting me to the intricately plaited braid of their past, and even at this moment, looking down the corridor of what's to come, I see them opening their arms wide to enfold my children and grandchildren in their embrace.

The Jewish Journal, December 15-December 21, 1990

Chanukah Is The Time

Chanukah is the time to ask ourselves whether we have exhibited the vigor and the valor of the Maccabees.

Chanukah is the time to re-commit ourselves to the defense of our faith.

Chanukah is the time to intensify in our homes the warmth and the tingle which comes from religious observances.

Chanukah is the time to pledge new fealty to the temple which can never be destroyed by our enemies but which can be eliminated by our apathy.

Chanukah is the time to understand afresh the relationship between piety and sacrificial efforts on behalf of freedom.

Chanukah is the time to rejoice that human beings can launch satellites but must never become the satellites of other human beings.

December Dilemma: Jews and Christmas

by Rabbi Peter Weintraub

Q. *What does Christmas signify?*

A. It means literally a Mass for Christ, celebration of the birth of Jesus, the Christian Messiah. The Christmas story derived from the "New Testament." The Jews' non-acceptance of this testament has resulted in our persecution throughout the centuries.

Q. *Is Santa Claus a Christian symbol as well?*

A. The innocent-jolly-robust Santa Claus is a modern version of St. Nicholas, a third-century bishop who would go out at night and deliver gifts to the needy. He was canonized a saint by the Roman Catholic Church after his death, and his fame as the patron saint of schoolchildren rapidly spread throughout Europe and eventually to America.

Q. *Is it possible to take the Christ out of Christmas?*

A. When a Jew takes what has traditionally been a deeply religious experience for Christians and keeps the symbols but says that there is really nothing religious about them, that Jew is being both insensitive and disrespectful.

Q. *Do most Christians still consider these symbols to have religious content?*

A. Even if the majority of Christians do not take their religious symbols seriously, that does not give Jews license to adopt them and proclaim them secular or American symbols. How would we feel if Christians started wearing a talit or a yarmulka and "de-judaized" them for their own purposes?

Q. *How do devout Christians who have not lost the true meanings of Christmas react to seeing a "Chanukah Bush" in their Jewish neighbors' homes?*

A. The following letter illustrates how one devout Christian reacted to seeing a tree in her Jewish friend's home: "I ask myself what meaning the tree has for you? It cannot be a Christian religious symbol, since you have told me often that as a Jew you do not accept Christ. For you, it must then be no more than a pretty decoration. How can I help feeling resentful when you take my sacred religious symbol and make it a mere "decoration?" And when I hear you refer to it jokingly as a "Chanukah bush," I am ashamed. Ashamed for you. For your nervous laugh when you say it. For the look in your eyes that cannot quite hide your hope that I will "understand" - and your fear that I might not."

Q. *Won't Jewish kids feel deprived if they can't participate in Christmas celebrations?*

A. We have our own holiday which occurs approximately the same time of year as Christmas. Chanukah, once a "minor" festival, has evolved into a joyous holiday which allows us to give and receive gifts within a Jewish context. We have our own symbols like the Chanukiah and our own songs like "Rock of Ages." Children who feel the spirit of Chanukah do not miss Christmas.

CHAPTER 6

LOGISTICS

LOGISTICS

Much of the work of insuring that programs for interfaith couples are a success happens before the group actually meets. Interfaith couples are not always an easily accessible group, and careful preparation, publicity, and follow-up are crucial to the success of whichever program you choose.

SUPPORT FOR YOUR PROGRAM

You are most likely to be successful in attracting couples to your program if others share in the groundwork and implementation. Never plan a program in a vacuum: Who else should be included in your planning? Who might be a useful source of referrals? Are there potential co-sponsors in your area? Is anyone else doing similar programming? To whom should you turn for advice?

Your best resource before beginning to plan is your regional UAHC Outreach coordinator. She can help you with the answers to the questions listed above, and can offer expertise and advice on making your program a reality.

FEES

While the structure of fees and customs regarding charging for programs varies, the following guidelines may be useful:

1. There is usually no charge for synagogue-sponsored programs which serve members. Some congregations open programs to the community, and prefer to charge a nominal fee to non-members. Other congregations see this programming as a way to attract interfaith couples to the synagogue and, therefore, do not charge.

2. In general, there are no fees for most programs that are sponsored by Outreach, either on a community level or under the auspices of a particular congregation. The exception is the multi-session model, which often requires hiring an outside facilitator.

3. In most communities, facilitators for the multi-session model are paid $50 -$75 per session. To calculate the charge per couple, divide the per session fee by the number of couples you hope to attract and multiply by the number of sessions in your series. Be sure to include any additional expenses for refreshments, supplies, paid advertising, etc.

Asking couples to pay for the series beforehand will improve commitment and attendance, avoid unnecessary bookkeeping, and enable you to assess your program's needs realistically. Special arrangements should always be made for couples genuinely unable to pay.

RECRUITING

Consider using a variety of recruiting strategies, since each typically results in a few couples per group. Together, these approaches can result in sufficient numbers for your programs.

- *Referrals from Rabbis*

  The support of local rabbis can be of utmost importance to the success of your program. In addition to being effective facilitators or co-facilitators, rabbis are often the best sources of referrals. They are knowledgeable about the make-up of both specific congregations and the community, and often they are willing to write a cover letter for your flyer to be sent to a mailing list of couples with whom they've had contact.

It is important to remember that interfaith couples' groups can also be a valuable resource for rabbis, providing the opportunity for many more hours of discussion than any rabbi's schedule would allow for meeting with a couple privately. When a rabbi meets with a couple regarding a possible marriage, the rabbi has the opportunity to suggest these programs to the couple. In addition, participants in all groups are encouraged to avail themselves of opportunities to attend appropriate congregational Outreach programs.

- *Publicity*

1. Prospects Mailing With Follow-Up Calls
   Keep an ongoing list of prospective couples (from rabbi referrals, responses to previous publicity, past participants' referrals, etc.), with notes as to what future group they are interested in, feasible locations, etc. When it is time to begin recruitment for the next group, mail applications to the appropriate prospects and follow up with a personal phone call. These couples are your best source of participants, as they have already expressed an interest in the series.

2. Jewish Press
   Despite the fact that most prospective participants are not affiliated with congregations, many do read the Jewish paper or have parents or friends who pass on the information.

3. Mailing to Rabbis
   Before each new group, mail a letter to each local Reform rabbi to keep him/her aware of the next group and to ask for referrals.

4. Temple Bulletin Articles
   While this source may only provide you with a limited number of prospects, one couple each time would still be significant in recruiting. This source also serves to make congregants aware of Outreach programs.

5. Flyers at Temple Information Tables

6. Past Participants' Referrals
   At the end of each program series, ask couples to pass along the phone number of the facilitator to any couples they know who might be interested in future programs.

7. Miscellaneous
   - Community newspapers
   - Flyers at nursery schools
   - Current and past participants in "Introduction to Judaism" classes

- *Using Single-Session Programs as a Springboard*

The facilitator may want to consider serving as a speaker at a congregational Outreach program on a topic related to intermarriage. Be sure to have written information about multi-session groups available, including a form to turn in that evening with names, addresses, phone numbers, etc. to add to your prospect list. This approach can allow a couple to test the waters and see if the longer series would be appropriate for them.

The facilitator should look for any opportunity to speak in front of a group and describe the multi-session model. This can include being a speaker at a Friday night Shabbat service, or making a presentation before any organization or committee that is interested (e.g. a Reform Synagogue Council composed of local rabbis and lay leaders).

• Ongoing Recruitment

Recruitment is a perpetual process! Discuss the program at every opportunity. This will add to your list of prospect calls, even if no new group is scheduled for a while. Encourage couples to call to see what programming is right for them and to be put on the mailing list for the upcoming groups. Couples may remain on the prospects list for 6 months or more. They are often at a point in life where weddings, new jobs, or finishing college degrees necessitate a long waiting period before enrollment.

• "Specialized" Potential Participants

Are there some specific "target" groups you could recruit from your community? One example of such a population is a group comprised of young families, with babysitters provided for those with children. These groups may be held following Shabbat morning services - an easier time for parents with young children than an evening program where they are on their own to find sitters. Consider running a group for couples who already have children enrolled in Reform nursery schools or religious schools—many may have yet unresolved issues to discuss or concerns about implementing the plans they made earlier for the religious upbringing of their children. Work closely with your Temple educator for recruitment and referrals.

A NOTE ABOUT BEGINNING A PROGRAM IN YOUR COMMUNITY

It will take time for interfaith couples programs to become known. Building a solid reputation, and developing a network of referrals will not happen overnight. It will generally take longer to recruit enough couples to run the series in the beginning—allow for this. The first year, a given community may be able to hold one group, two the next, and three the third (e.g. Fall, Winter and Spring series). You may have some groups without sufficient enrollment. Keep in touch with these couples and contact them first regarding the next offering of the series. Over a period of time, you will be likely not only to have groups fill up, but also to have waiting lists for the next series.

EVALUATING SUCCESS

How do you measure success when "success" is intangible? While there is no quantitative measure for being certain that your program or group met all of its goals and was a meaningful experience for participants, using evaluation forms will provide you with useful feedback. The comments you receive can be invaluable tools for demonstrating the efficacy of such programs to boards or committees, and the feedback of participants is your greatest learning tool for future programs. A sample evaluation form is included in this chapter. It is most effective to allow time at the end of the program itself for the completion of evaluation forms. If participants leave your program with a form to be mailed back at a later date, the response rate is usually minimal.

SAMPLE "INFORMATION APPLICATION" FOR ONGOING RECRUITMENT

(Note to facilitator: To be completed by each participant. Information at the bottom of the form should be tailored to fit your needs.)

THE INTERFAITH COUPLES CONNECTION:
A JEWISH PERSPECTIVE ON INTERMARRIAGE

"The Interfaith Couples Connection" is an 8-week discussion group for intermarried couples and those contemplating intermarriage. This is an innovative program which will serve as a framework for open and frank discussions about concerns and issues related to intermarriage.

You will join other interfaith couples in a supportive, comfortable and non-judgmental setting to share your ideas and concerns about family holidays, raising children and other interfaith issues. During the course of the sessions, you will also have the opportunity to clarify questions which you might have about Jewish traditions, beliefs, and practices.

This program has been developed under the auspices of the Commission on Reform Jewish Outreach and is sponsored by the *(Region)* Council of the Union of American Hebrew Congregations.

For further information, contact: (name, address and phone number of Outreach Coordinator or appropriate contact.)

INFORMATION FORM

Name _____

Partner's name _____

Address/City/Zip _____

Phone: home _____ work _____

Occupation _____

Congregation (if applicable) _____

years married _____

Age & sex of children _____

Religion _____

Please briefly describe your religious training: _____

Please briefly describe the level of religious observance in your home as a child (holiday celebrations, attendance at religious _____

services, etc.) _____

_____

Have you taken an Introduction to Judaism class? _____

Other religious adult education courses? _____

If yes, what have you studied? _____

Have you been involved in other Outreach programming? _____

    If yes, describe: _____

Why have you decided to register for this program? _____

Date _____

••

New groups begin each fall, winter & spring. The cost of the seminar is $75.00 per couple and limited to eight couples.

    For more information, please contact the group leader:

please mail to: [insert address], & you will be contacted regarding upcoming groups.

Dear Nursery School Parents and
Parenting Center Participants,

Parents who do not share religious backgrounds confront difficult questions. Indeed every family with young children must make decisions about how to celebrate holidays, how to create their own traditions while respecting childhood and family traditions. For the intermarried couple, however, these questions may be particularly complex. Many parents ask questions such as:

How will we decide on a religious identity for our children?

How can we create love and respect for relatives who celebrate a different set of holidays?

How can I share my childhood memories if we choose to raise our children in a religion that is different than mine?

Is a religious identity necessary?

I don't believe in God. Aren't all people supposed to be good? Why create problems?

The_____Outreach Committee is offering an evening to allow Nursery School parents and Parenting Center participants to discuss issues like these with Rabbi_____ and _____ UAHC Outreach Coordinator. A discussion will take place on_____.

The Outreach Committee has been organized to help new Jews-by-Choice and intermarried couples explore the Jewish community, ask questions and deal with issues. We are sending this letter to all families involved in the Nursery School and Parenting Center. If this letter does not apply to you, please disregard it or pass it along to a friend. If you have any questions, please call _____.

Sincerely,

Rabbi _____

NEW YORK FEDERATION OF REFORM SYNAGOGUES

An Agency of

THE UNION OF AMERICAN HEBREW CONGREGATIONS

838 Fifth Avenue, New York, NY 10021-7064   Tel: (212) 249-0100

PRESENTS

TIMES AND SEASONS

A Jewish Perspective for Interfaith Couples

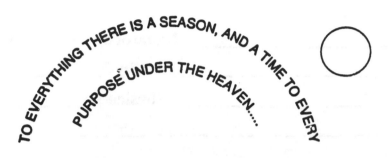

"This experience opened communications between us."
"Sharing our thoughts and feelings made us closer as a couple."

This seven-session workshop is designed for interfaith couples and will deal with the issues that occur as they build their life together.

* Discover ways of maintaining respect for your partner's religious background while deciding on new patterns for your life together.
* With support from the group, explore issues of personal concern.
* Learn how to make thoughtful and sensitive decisions in dealing with family members and holiday and life cycle celebrations.
* Discuss the options for raising children.

Beginning Wednesdays
Feb. 26
Mar. 4, 11, 18 and 25
April 1 and 8

Time: 6:30 p.m.–9:00 p.m.

Place: 838 Fifth Avenue
New York, NY 10021-7064

Cost: $125 per couple

Contact:
Ellyn Geller
212-249-0100

Make checks payable to:
N.Y.F.R.S. Times and Seasons

Send to:
Ellyn Geller
838 Fifth Avenue
New York, NY 10021-7064

TIMES AND SEASONS
A JEWISH PERSPECTIVE FOR INTERFAITH COUPLES

Registration Form

Name _____ Name of Spouse/Fiance _____

Address _____ City _____ Zip _____

Phone (Home) _____ (Business) _____

Occupations _____

_____

Birth Date _____ Birth Date _____

Years In Relationship _____ Children (If Any) _____ Ages _____

Description of Religious Upbringing _____

_____

What special needs do you have? _____

_____

_____

What are your expectations of this program? _____

_____

_____

Date of Registration _____

Please return to:

Ellyn Geller
Director
Outreach, Introduction to Judaism Classes

New York Federation of Reform Synagogues
Union of American Hebrew Congregations
838 Fifth Avenue, New York, NY 10021-7064
(212) 249-0100

Times & Seasons

A GROUP PROGRAM FOR INTERFAITH COUPLES

Times and Seasons was created in 1983 in response to the needs of intermarried couples. As part of the UAHC Outreach Program, Congregation Beth El is proud to be hosting this innovative program. Times and Seasons serves as a framework for open and frank discussions about the concerns and issues in interfaith marrigae. This group will explore religious and cultural issues partners confront in relationship, family life and religious invovlement while growing up, and concerns about the religious identity of children. It will provide an opportunity to clarify questions about Jewish traditions, beliefs and practices. Discussions will be within a supportive, non-judgmental environment.

WEDNESDAY, FEBRUARY 20 - MARCH 27, 1991 (SIX CONSECUTIVE WEDNESDAYS)

7:30 P.M. TO 9:30 P.M.

GROUP SIZE WILL BE LIMITED TO EIGHT COUPLES

CONGREGATION BETH EL
Arch & Vine Streets, Berkeley

Cost:
$60.00 per couple for all six sessions

For additional information and registration procedures, please contact Linda Walker, chairperson of the Outreach Committee, at 525-5074. Pre-registration is required.

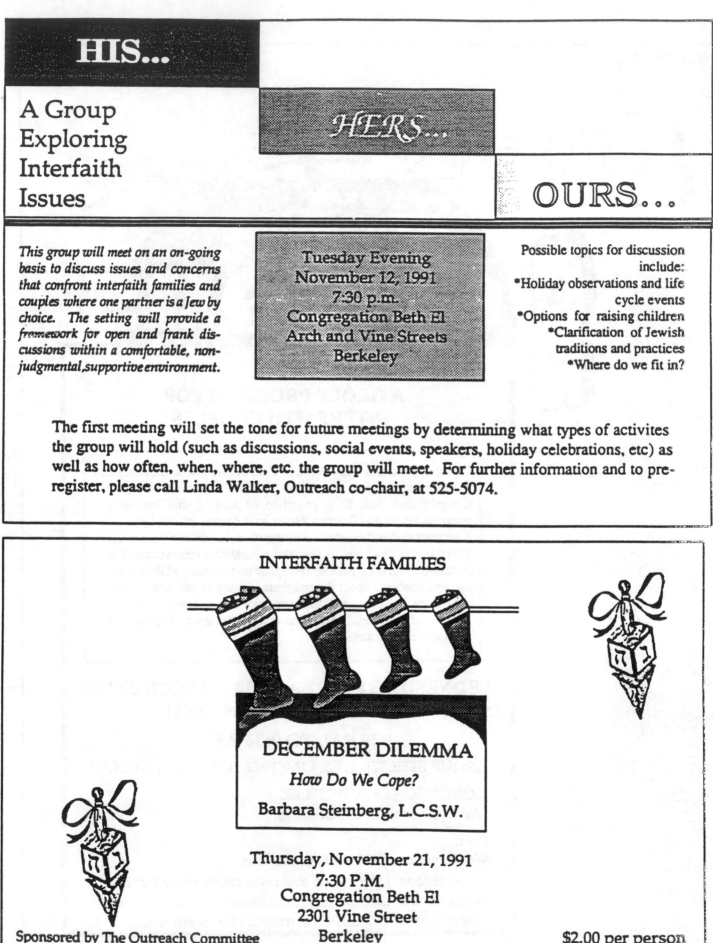

HIS...

A Group Exploring Interfaith Issues

HER S...

OURS...

This group will meet on an on-going basis to discuss issues and concerns that confront interfaith families and couples where one partner is a Jew by choice. The setting will provide a framework for open and frank discussions within a comfortable, non-judgmental, supportive environment.

Tuesday Evening
November 12, 1991
7:30 p.m.
Congregation Beth El
Arch and Vine Streets
Berkeley

Possible topics for discussion include:
*Holiday observations and life cycle events
*Options for raising children
*Clarification of Jewish traditions and practices
*Where do we fit in?

The first meeting will set the tone for future meetings by determining what types of activites the group will hold (such as discussions, social events, speakers, holiday celebrations, etc) as well as how often, when, where, etc. the group will meet. For further information and to pre-register, please call Linda Walker, Outreach co-chair, at 525-5074.

INTERFAITH FAMILIES

DECEMBER DILEMMA

How Do We Cope?

Barbara Steinberg, L.C.S.W.

Thursday, November 21, 1991
7:30 P.M.
Congregation Beth El
2301 Vine Street
Berkeley

Sponsored by The Outreach Committee

$2.00 per person

Temple Emeth Announces
DISCUSSION GROUP FOR
INTERFAITH COUPLES

The Outreach Committee at Temple Emeth invites all interested interfaith couples to join a new group where common concerns and interests will be discussed. Participants will have the opportunity to talk informally, make new friends, and set their own agenda.

The First Meeting is Scheduled for
SUNDAY OCTOBER 27, 12 noon to 2 pm
TEMPLE EMETH, TEANECK

Dru Greenwood, National Director of Outreach at the Union of America Hebrew Congregations, will facilitate the discussion. Rabbi Louis Sigel and Cantor Annie Borstein as well as members of the Outreach Committee will participate. Babysitting will be provided and refreshments will be served.

Reservations are Necessary for Baby Sitting Services
Call 833-1322 by Friday October 18th.

TEMPLE EMETH
1666 Windsor Road • Teaneck, NJ

Temple Emeth 57468 2x3 1/2 10/9
PYE

REFORM

CONGREGATION

KENESETH ISRAEL

OUTREACH

PROGRAM

Calendar of Events
1991-1992

*For any and all concerned with
the future of Judaism*

Reaching out to
Intermarried Couples and their
families, Jews-by-Choice, and all
who are interested in exploring
their Jewish identity

Programs
Activities
Workshops
Services...

HOW CAN I BECOME INVOLVED IN OUTREACH?

Please conctact Rabbi Deborah L. Pipe-Mazo, Keneseth Israel's Director of Outreach and Programming, at 887-8702

In each of the K.I. bulletins there is an OUT-REACH column which presents updates on the work of the OUTREACH committee and the K.I. OUTREACH program. Also, please take the time to browse through the new OUT-REACH shelf in the K.I. library.

If you would like to register for a program, or if you would like to be placed on the OUT-REACH mailing list, please fill out the form below.

Name _____

Address _____

Day Phone _____

Evening Phone _____

Programs of Interest _____

Please mail to:
Rabbi Deborah L. Pipe-Mazo
OUTREACH
Keneseth Israel
York Road & Township Line
Elkins Park, PA 19117

WHAT IS OUTREACH?

OUTREACH is a program which has the potential to impact the lives of all members of our congregation.

OUTREACH:

* welcomes those who seek to explore Judaism

* Invites born Jews to focus on issues relating to Jewish identity and attitudes toward the changing Jewish community

* welcomes Jews-by-Choice as full members of the Jewish community

* welcomes interfaith couples into the congregation and enables the non-Jewish partner to explore, study and understand Judaism

* educates and sensitizes the Jewish community concerning interfaith couples who have chosen Judaism

* enables children and young people to clarify issues, strengthen their Jewish identity and to examine the implications of interdating and interfaith marriage

* supports and sensitizes parents and grandparents whose children are involved in interfaith relationships

* encourages people to make Jewish choices through community support, adult education, the availability of OUTREACH resources in the K.I. library and informal programs focusing on the "how-to's" of Judaism

WHAT PROGRAMS DOES OUTREACH OFFER?
1991-1992

OUTREACH Brunch with Rabbi Maslin
Sunday, October 20th at 10:00 a.m.
"K.I., K.I. Rabbis, Interfaith Marriage and OUTREACH"

Introduction to Judaism
7:30 p.m. Mon., October 7th - February 10th
A course in basic Jewish concepts of theology, holidays, life-cycle events and history, serving as a pre-requisite for Reform conversion - but open to all who wish to learn. 18 weeks.

Parents of Interfaith Couples
7:30 p.m. Mon., October 7th - 28th
An issues-oriented group, led by Linda Steigman, M.S.S., for parents to explore and understand the dynamics of interfaith relationships in a supportive environment. 4 weeks.

Times and Seasons
7:30 p.m. Tues., Nov. 12th - Dec. 3rd
7:30 p.m. Tues., Feb. 4th - 25th
A forum for interfaith couples, facilitated by Sarah Barrett, M.S.W., and Rabbi Pipe-Mazo, to focus on issues which arise as a Jew and a non-Jew build a life together. 4 weeks.

Creating Jewish Memories
Sundays, 10:00 a.m.
Chanukkah - November 24th
Shabbat - February 2nd
Passover - April 5th
A series of workshops to learn about Jewish holidays in an enjoyable, hands-on environment.

OUTREACH Shabbat
Friday, May 1st

WHO CAN BENEFIT FROM OUTREACH?

* Jews-by-Choice and those interested in choosing Judaism

* Interfaith Couples and couples considering interfaith marriage

* Children of Interfaith Couples

* Parents of Interfaith Couples

* Born Jews exploring their heritage

* Any and all concerned about the future of Judaism

WHY SHOULD I GET INVOLVED?
Involvement in OUTREACH will help to strengthen the Jewish community

* Prior to 1965, Jews married other Jews 91% of the time. Since 1985, Jews have married within Judaism only 48% of the time.

* Over 600,000 children are the products of interfaith marriages.

* By the year 2000, over 50% of the children in Jewish religious schools will come from homes in which one of the parents was not born Jewish.

* Approximately 33% of all conversions take place after marriage.

For the Intermarried...

For Jews-by-Choice...

For someone you know...

OUTREACH

Stephen S. Wise Temple

WELCOME TO OUTREACH

The Stephen S. Wise Temple Outreach Program seeks to meet a wide variety of needs for those new to the Jewish Community. Our programs are open to Temple members and to the community at large. We invite you to join us in any of the programs described in this brochure, and to share the information contained in it with anyone you feel might benefit from Outreach.

THE PURPOSE OF OUTREACH

OUTREACH welcomes Jews-by-Choice as full members of the Jewish community.

OUTREACH welcomes intermarried couples into the Congregation. Outreach does not seek to convert non-Jewish partners. Rather, it enables them to explore, study and come to understand Judaism, thereby providing an atmosphere of support in which a comfortable relationship with Judaism can be fostered.

OUTREACH encourages people to make Jewish choices in their lives through community support and adult education, and by making the Jewish resources at the Temple readily available.

OUTREACH educates and sensitizes the Jewish community to be receptive to Jews-by-Choice and intermarried couples.

OUTREACH SHABBAT
DECEMBER 16, 1988, 8:30 PM

TIMES AND SEASONS

The Jewish perspective on intermarriage. This is a program which was created in response to the needs of the intermarried, to serve as the critical first step taken by unaffiliated intermarried couples, seeking to explore differences in their backgrounds. Times and Seasons groups meet for eight consecutive sessions and are limited to eight couples.

PARENTS OF THE INTERMARRIED

A support group which provides participants with a non-judgmental setting in which they can meet with others sharing similar concerns. Participants are given an opportunity to discuss the impact of their child's interfaith relationship on the family, and develop constructive responses to family dilemmas that may arise.

ONGOING EDUCATIONAL PROGRAMS AT STEPHEN S. WISE TEMPLE

The Holiday Workshop Series aims to make you feel competent and confident in observing the Sabbath and all the Jewish holidays in your home.

The Adult B'nai Mitzvah Class offers background in Jewish history, Bible, Hebrew reading, Jewish practice, and more, culminating in a group Bar/Bat Mitzvah service.

The Mountaintop Minyan is a Shabbat service and Torah discussion that provides a small, friendly, welcoming environment in which to learn and experience a sense of community. Meets the first and third Saturdays of the month, 10 AM in room in Hershenson Hall, followed by pot-luck lunch.

OUTREACH DISCUSSION GROUP

This group is designed to give Jews-by-Choice, intermarried couples, and those contemplating intermarriage, an opportunity to discuss with one of our rabbis, a variety of topics in a small, warm, supportive atmosphere. In the past, our conversations, topics of which are chosen by the group members, have included:

How shall we raise the children?
Relating to parents and in-laws, Jewish and non-Jewish.
Understanding how Jews relate to the State of Israel.
If I convert, what happens to the culture in which I grew up?
Holidays: Yours, Mine, Ours?

Join us in Taub Annex on any or all of the following Thursdays, 7:30 PM:

October 6, 1988
December 15, 1988
February 2, 1989
March 16, 1989
May 4, 1989
June 15, 1989

No sign-up needed. Come as often as you wish!

STEPHEN S. WISE TEMPLE

15500 Stephen S. Wise Drive
Los Angeles, California 90077
(213) 476-8561 (818) 788-4778

THE OUTREACH PUBLIC FORUM

The Outreach Public Forum is designed to help Jews-by-Choice, intermarried couples, and those contemplating intermarriage, as well as Jews by birth, explore the topics that cause the greatest number of questions and concerns for those entering the Jewish Community. All sessions are held in the Plotkin Chapel, Tuesdays at 7:30 PM. This year's topics:

WELCOME TO THE HIGH HOLY DAYS
September 6, 1988

An introduction to the High Holy Days intended to make participation at services more meaningful.

DECEMBER DILEMMA
November 15, 1988

How do we make sense of this often confusing season and maintain our religious integrity?

ASK THE RABBI
February 21, 1989

An opportunity to ask any and all questions about Judaism, the Jewish people, the Jewish community, intermarriage, conversion, and much more.

JEWS VIEW JESUS
April 4, 1989

Toward a deeper understanding of a Jewish view of Jesus: what is known about him, why his divinity was never accepted, Jewish Messiah concepts, interreligious respect and tolerance.

From time to time, interfaith couples have mentioned the need for
a place to which they could come and have an opportunity to discuss
issues facing them and share insights on such topics as family,
holiday conflicts, raising children, etc.

"LET'S TALK"

A DROP-IN CENTER FOR JEWISH INTERFAITH COUPLES

WILL DISCUSS

"CONVERSION: CAN WE EVEN TALK ABOUT IT ?"

Tuesday, December 17, 1991
North Shore Congregation Israel
1185 Sheridan Rd., Glencoe
7:30 - 9:00 P.M.

Co-Facilitators:
Rabbi Barry Block   Mimi Dunitz
N.S.C.I.   Assistant Direc

Please let us know if you will be dropping in (312) 782-1477

Sponsored by The Union of American Hebrew Congregations

"Let's Talk"

A Discussion Group for Jews-by-Choice and Interfaith Couples

From time to time, Jews-by-Choice and interfaith couples have mentioned the need for a place to which they could come and have an opportunity to discuss issues facing them and share insights on these issues.

Please join us this month to discuss:

Interfaith Relationships:
Are Our Differences Only Religious?
Do you ever feel your partner just doesn't understand you?
A discussion of attitudes, perceptions and expectations and their sources.

"Let's Talk"
Monday, January 27, 1992
7:30-9:00 P.M.
Adult Lounge
Temple Shalom
6030 Alpha Road
Dallas, TX 75240

Co-Facilitators:
Rabbi Nancy Kasten, Assistant Director, Union of American Hebrew Congregations
Debby Stein, Regional Outreach Coordinator, UAHC

Please let us know if you will join us in discussion: 214-960-6641.
Sponsored by the Union of American Hebrew Congregations

The Outreach Committee of Temple Beth-El presents...

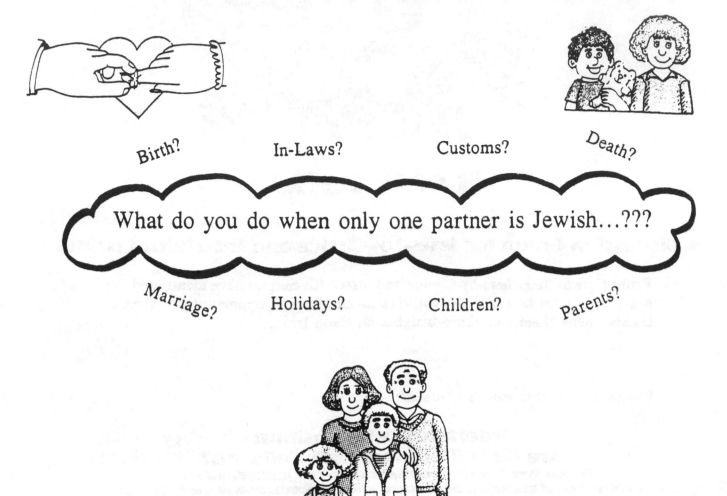

Birth?   In-Laws?   Customs?   Death?

What do you do when only one partner is Jewish...???

Marriage?   Holidays?   Children?   Parents?

A WORKSHOP ON LIFECYCLE EVENTS
(For people who have non-Jewish relatives)

You're invited to attend an informal get-together with some of us who are trying to sort out these issues. We might not solve all our problems, but maybe we can share some ideas on how we can cope with these situations, over coffee and cake.

Date:	Sunday, March 29, 1992
Time:	9:30 A.M. - 12:30 P.M.
Place:	Jerry and Roger Tilles 36 Fairway Drive Manhasset, NY 11030
RSVP:	Jerry - (516) 627-2487

PARTICIPANT EVALUATION

DATE: _____

	(1) Excellent	(2) Very Good	(3) Good	(4) Fair	(5) Poor
OVERALL, PLEASE RATE THIS WORKSHOP IN TERMS					
1. Relevance of Material Presented	___	___	___	___	___
2. Organization of Course	___	___	___	___	___
3. Maintenance of Interest and Involvement	___	___	___	___	___
4. Your Own Participation	___	___	___	___	___
5. Room Setting/Comfort	___	___	___	___	___
TO WHAT EXTENT WAS THE PRESENTER					
6. Knowledgeable about the subject matter presented	___	___	___	___	___
7. Able to hold your interest in the material being presented	___	___	___	___	___
8. Organized and effective in the delivery of the course	___	___	___	___	___
9. Able to incorporate handout material which enhance the course	___	___	___	___	___
10. Able to involve the participants in the course	___	___	___	___	___
11. HOW WOULD YOU RATE THIS PROGRAM OVERALL?	___	___	___	___	___

12. Would you recommend this program to a friend? (1) Yes _____ (2) No _____

Comments: _____

13. Will the information presented have an impact on your life? (1) Yes _____ (2) No _____

14. What did you think was the most helpful part of the program? _____

The least helpful? _____

15. How could the program's effectiveness be improved? _____

Page 2

16. Are there any courses/workshops you would like to see presented in the future? _____

17. Is there anything else you would like us to know? _____

Sex: Approximate Age:

(1) Female   (1) 16-20   (4) 36-45

(2) Male   (2) 21-25   (5) 46-55

                  (3) 26-35   (6) 56-65

Religious Background: _____

18. Would you like to be contacted by a synagogue near you?   (1) Yes _____   (2) No _____

19. Are there other couples you know who would appreciate receiving information on future groups? (Please provide names and complete addresses).

THANK YOU FOR YOUR COOPERATION

PARTICIPANTS EVALUATION FOR THE MULTI-SESSION MODEL

1. Wat was most helpful for you?

2. What was the least helpful to you?

3. What recommendations would you make for future groups?

4. Is there anything else you want us to know?

5. Would you like to be contacted by a synagogue near you?

6. Are there other couples you know who would appreciate receiving information on future groups? (Please provide names and complete address.)

Sample release for temple bulletins or newspapers

F O R   I M M E D I A T E   R E L E A S E

TIMES AND SEASONS: A JEWISH PERSPECTIVE FOR INTERMARRIED COUPLES

The Pacific Southwest Council of the UAHC is sponsoring a pilot
program for unaffiliated intermarried couples (and couples
contemplating intermarriage). The goal of the program is to
make the couples more comfortable with Judaism by focusing
on issues raised by Jewish holiday and life cycle obsevances
in a supportive environment. Theprogram, beginning in
October, will run for eight weeks. The cost is $50.00 per
couple.

If you would like more information about this innovative
program, or if you know anyone who might be interested in
participating, please call the UAHC office, (213)653-9962
and ask for Lydia Kukoff or Mickey Finn.

APPENDICES

Appendix A:

RESOURCES FOR FACILITATORS

The following articles provide background information and reference material for the facilitator on a variety of topics. While they are most likely not suitable for the entire group to read as a basis for discussion, they do offer the facilitator a broad perspective on relevant issues.

Contents:

All in the ˄Jewish Family   Egon Mayer

Outreach Statistics At-a-Glance

Judaism and Christianity: the Parting of the Ways.
The Start of the Rift

                                                    Michael Cook

What is patrilineal descent? The Reform movement's
policy on Jewish descent

Report of the Committee on Patrilineal Descent on
the Status of Children of Mixed Marriages

Some Thoughts on Officiation

Notes: Judaism as a Civilization

Questions Asked by Participants and Some Suggested
Responses

Additional Questions from Interfaith Discussion Groups

Ethnocultural Factors in Marital Communication
Among Intermarried Couples

                                                    Esther Perel

Intermarriage in Context

ALL IN THE ^JEWISH FAMILY

by Egon Mayer

Not so long ago the phrase "Jewish family" could easily conjure up a stereotypical image that would not be far from the reality of most American Jews. As recently as twenty-five or thirty years ago most American Jewish families consisted of two Jewish parents, themselves descendants of Jewish parents, probably just one or two generations away from immigrant ancestors from Europe, with their own two or three Jewish children. Stability and continuity were its hallmarks.

But the news about American families in general and Jewish families in particular has been news of rapid and radical change for the past twenty years. Changing life styles and family disruption have changed the complexion of the Jewish family. The rock-solid stereotype of yesteryear has given way to a much more kaleidoscopic image. The 1990 National Jewish Population Survey has provided rich statistical detail to what even casual observers have noted with increasing frequency over the past decade or two.

Divorce, intermarriage, childlessness, homosexuality, abortion, voluntary singlehood, and children out-of-wedlock have all added to the general fragmentation of the normative American family. Although Jews have always prided themselves on being "immune" to the social troubles of the wider society, in the past two decades these social forces have invaded Jewish family life as well.

jewish gays

Fact: A study of the "gay" community of San Francisco revealed that three per cent of that community is Jewish. That proportion equals the proportion of the Jewish population in the area in general. "Gay" synagogues have sprung up in the major centers of Jewish residence, such as New York, Los Angeles, and elsewhere. In the past year or two the Reform and Reconstructionist movements have taken decisive steps to "normalize" the role of gay men and women in all walks of Jewish life, including the rabbinate. The Conservative movement is at present struggling with how far to follow their lead.

divorce

Fact: Rabbinic associations of all three branches of American Judaism report a booming business in divorces. Correspondingly, Jewish centers throughout the United States have developed extensive programs for "singles" and "single parent families." According to the 1990 National Jewish Population Survey approximately 25% of all marriages of Jews have ended in divorce. Subsequently, about half of all who have gotten divorced have also remarried, fueling the growing presence of reconstituted families in the Jewish community.

small families

Fact: The average Jewish couple in their childbearing years is having less than two children (1.8 to be precise). Since slightly more than two are needed to keep the Jewish population at a constant level, concerned demographers fear that reproductive habits of the modern Jewish family will result in the erosion of the total Jewish population.

women pursuing careers

Fact: Young Jewish women are pursuing education beyond college in record numbers. They are almost as likely to pursue careers outside the home as their brothers and husbands – leaving the home as sort of an "empty castle." Since 1970 the percentage of Jewish married women with children under the age of 6 in the labor force has increased from about 15% to over 40%. "Who will raise the children?" is the question asked with increasing urgency by professionals and laypeople alike.

intermarriage

Fact: Since the mid-1970s the percentage of Jews marrying non-Jews has increased from about 30% to around 50%. This rate of intermarriage, argue many analysts, will have a devastating impact on both the quality and the quantity of Jewish life in the next few decades.

In short, the popular professional opinion is that the Jewish family is in trouble and the problems may be so serious that, unless drastic measures are taken, American Jewry might ultimately vanish. Consequently, the organized Jewish community has been on something of a "family kick" for the past couple of years: pushing young Jews to marry, to have more children, to stay married, and, above all, to marry Jews. Innumerable conferences and symposia have been organized by local and national Jewish organizations all bent on diagnosing and curing the troubles of the Jewish family. Perhaps because the obligations to marry and have children are firmly rooted in the mitzvah system of the Torah, the tone of these meetings is frequently conservative if not reactionary.

Thus, the troubles of the Jewish family are being "blamed" on individuals, men and women alike, for desiring personal advancement, pleasure in leisure time, and sexual fulfillment. The feminist movement has also received its share of the blame for changing women's minds about traditional roles and drawing them out of the home.

To remedy our ills, the critics tell us, we must do a kind of social *teshuvah*: to turn away from the general value system of American Jewry and return to the ways of our forefathers (and foremothers) where men remained in stable occupations in stable communities; where women remained at home, content to bear and raise large numbers of children; where the family was a large household of many members, often including several generations; where the well-being and integrity of the family superceded the wants of the individual.

Is American Jewry really bound to vanish because of the multiple tensions of career mobility, infertility, and intermarriage? And is return to an earlier form of family life the only solution to these problems? At the risk of offending the keepers of the conventional wisdom, I have reason to answer these questions in the negative. Here are the reasons for my optimism.

demise of family greatly exaggerated

Reports of the demise of the family in general and the Jewish family in particular have been greatly exaggerated. While it is true that the indicators of family disorders have been increasing in recent years for non-Jews and Jews alike, they have received far too much attention. The overfascination with signs of social ills has, on the other hand, tended to hide the pervasive normalcy of the family situation among the vast majority of American Jews.

According to a nationwide survey conducted in 1970, nearly ninety percent of American Jews between the ages of 30-60 were married. More recent polls of the American population at large reveal that: "After declining 10% between 1972 and 1976, the rate of marriages is now rising. Though the divorce rate is still climbing, so is the rate of remarriages. The number of people marrying for the second time has roughly tripled since 1960." (TIME, Nov. 21, 1977)

vast majority prefer married state

These facts suggest quite convincingly that for the vast majority of American adults, and especially for Jews, living in a married state is the preferred condition. Moreover, even those who remain technically single (and their numbers have, indeed, increased greatly since 1970) show a preference for "living with" a member of the opposite sex. In the same TIME magazine article we find: "And the people who have taken to living together (some 1.3 million, up 100% since 1970)...are inclined to talk about their loyalty to each other in much the same tones that newlyweds once used." The saying in the Torah (Genesis 2:18): *Lo tov heyot adam le-avado* – it is not good that man should live alone - seems to persist even in the modern consciousness.

the most private decision

Some of the other facts, such as the reluctance of young Jewish families to have numerous children or the increasing tendency of young Jews to marry non-Jews, which seem to cast such a gloomy shadow over the future of the American Jewish community must also be examined a bit more critically. The decision to have children is among the most private that a couple has to make. It is a decision that is hardly affected by the well-intentioned interference of parents, rabbis, community leaders, or even of government. Yet, it is a decision that is very sensitive to such social circumstances as job security, economic well-being, political stability, and a host of other influences. Demographers who study such matters have maintained that birth rates tend to have a cyclical pattern in the long run: peaks followed by valleys. The postwar "baby boom" was one of the peak periods. Many believe, on the strength of long scientific experience, that we are now witnessing the valley of that peak which, in turn, will be followed by yet another period of increase in the not-to-distant future. Thus, those who fear the erosion of the Jewish community because of "birth dearth" are likely to be mistaking a short-term pattern for a long-term one.

intermarriage does not always lead to assimilation

Perhaps the greatest fear for the future of the American Jewish community stems from the high and apparently rising rate of intermarriage among young Jews. It is feared that a high proportion of those young Jews who "marry out" and an even greater proportion of their children will eventually disappear as a result of assimilation. While no Jew who cares about his people can afford to minimize the potential negative consequences of intermarriage, the dire predictions based upon them should not be blindly accepted. The notion that assimilation follows on the heels of intermarriage is not an ironclad law of human nature. Certainly where intermarriage also involves the conversion of the non-Jewish mate to Judaism quite the opposite seems to occur. Both the convert and his or her spouse tend to become more committed to a Jewish way of life than is characteristic of American Jews in general.

Research which I have recently completed on the life styles of intermarried families reveals that even where no conversion has taken place on the part of the non-Jewish spouse, assimilation doesn't follow as an inevitable consequence. Jewish men and women cling far more tenaciously to their religious and ethnic heritage than do their non-Jewish spouses. Indeed, a great many of the non-Jewish spouses express an attraction for the Jewish way of life despite their reluctance to convert.

a self-fulfilling prophecy

To the extent that the organized Jewish community labors under the notion that assimilation follows "naturally" from intermarriage, nothing is done to help intermarried families retain their sense of Jewishness. As a result, the forecast of assimilation becomes a "self-fulfilling prophecy." Yet, this "prophecy" notwithstanding, many such families struggle mightily to retain a sense of Jewishness and to pass that sense on to their children. Thus, even the cloud of intermarriage which hangs so heavily over the future of the American Jewish community is not without its silver lining.

As we can see from the brief analysis of the facts, the American Jewish family is far healthier than its critics would have one believe. Indeed, I suspect that an exaggerated preoccupation with the ills of the modern Jewish family may actually discourage young people from forming families of their own. Truly, that would be the most cruel irony of all. Perhaps we might take the advice of Senator Daniel P. Moynihan who some years ago suggested, in another matter, that certain problems can be best solved with "benign neglect."

modern families more flexible

A nagging question remains: If the facts pertaining to the condition of the modern Jewish family are truly not so bleak, why do so many responsible analysts insist that it has a gloomy future? It cannot be denied that the Jewish family is changing rapidly, both in its structure and the functions it fulfills for its members or the community. It is smaller today than it has been for the past several hundred years. Parents and children, husbands and wives are far more flexible about the way in which they play their respective roles as well as the way in which they relate to one another. And all the members of the family are far more concerned with the welfare and happiness of their own little nuclear unit than they are with the community or the society around them.

sense of privatism

It is this sense of privatism, perhaps more than anything else, which has so profoundly altered the character of the family—especially the Jewish family.

Throughout history the family has been a virtual agent of the community in which it was embedded. The primary goal of mothers and fathers was to transmit the values and norms of the community to the next generation. The rules of family living, generally shared by the entire community, served to control the individual whims and desires of all its members. However, since the end of the Second World War, the family has undergone a metamorphosis. Once a primary agent of social control at the most intimate level, it has gradually become a haven from the controls of the larger social environment. It has become a private space in which men, women, and children feel freed (and seek to be freed) from the demands of job, school, club, and distant relatives.

change generates fear

To the extent that profound social change always engenders anxiety about the future, the mere fact that the family is changing has generated fear about its prospects. However, the proper understanding of the changing nature of the Jewish family is merely confused by the exaggeration of its troubles. It is also, and perhaps more so, confused by the mythicized images of Jewish family life in the past against which the modern Jewish family is inevitably compared either implicitly or explicitly.

distorted image of past Jewish families

In discussing the modern Jewish family, most writers and speakers portray it as a diminished form of the traditional Jewish family. The latter is seen as large while the former is small. The latter is seen as a harmonious little universe in which each member has clearly defined roles which they play happily, while the former is seen as a hotbed of psychological tensions (mainly stemming from each person's confusion about his or her proper role). The latter is seen as the warm locale in which several generations communicate their wisdom and curiosity to one another, while the former is seen as a sterile environment in which even two generations cannot communicate successfully. The latter is seen as a organic entity in which Judaism and the Jewish way of life is passed on from generation to generation, while the former is seen as a fractured vessel which can no longer contain, much less pass on, the heritage of our ancestors. If these contrasting images are taken seriously, and they are by many, one cannot help but be alarmed at the prospect of the modern Jewish family.

misleading comparison

However, the comparison is very misleading. It draws distinctions between the reality of the modern Jewish family with what is essentially a complex myth. Thus, a misrepresentation of the past results in a misunderstanding of the present and future.

The stereotyped image of the past is distorted by two myths. One of the myths is that the so-called traditional Jewish family was, at one time, a large multi-generational, pious, stable, and—at least by implication—a happy, culture-preserving entity. What makes this image a myth is not that there never were such Jewish families. Undoubtedly there were, and certainly there still are. What makes that glossy image a myth is the suggestion that, at least at one time, most or all Jewish families were of that kind.

knowledge of Jewish families in past generations sketchy

The preoccupation of social scientists with Jews is a relatively recent infatuation. Therefore, it is difficult to establish with any precision how the "average" Jewish family lived in previous centuries in Europe and other parts of the world. What little information we do have is mostly about the famous families of merchants, such as the Rothschilds, the Sassoons, or the Samuels. We also have some information about the families of famous rabbis, chasidic masters, and scholars. But these were all the tiny elite of a vastly larger downtrodden population. The records of these elite families in some cases come close to the idealized image of the traditional Jewish family. But the majority lived impoverished and fearful lives in rigidly controlled ghettos. Subject to sudden, disruptive changes in their economic circumstances as well as personal safety, life in these families was often a precarious balance between tension and control from which young people especially sought to escape as soon as possible.

Jewish family fragmented long ago

The colorful autobiography of the Bohemian philosopher, Solomon Maimon (1754-1800), provides a myth-shattering glimpse of the life and family circumstances of the so-called middle-class Jews of pre-Enlightenment Europe. It is clear from his account that the lure of the wider world, in such places as Paris, Berlin, London, and even Moscow or Warsaw, was a far more powerful magnet than the attractions of hearth and home.

We know that Maimon was not unique because soon after the French Revolution and the Emancipation the large masses of Jews left their ghettoized communities and the supposedly idyllic extended family systems of which they were part. They chose instead the metropolises of Europe and the budding cities of America. Rare is the European Jewish family of the nineteenth and early twentieth century whose members (brothers, sisters, cousins, etc.) were not spread out among the many cities of the continent and America. Thus, the supposedly closely knit, extended Jewish family was fragmented long ago into relatively isolated nuclear units. Moreover, this fragmentation was experienced as far less a tragedy than as a happy adaptation to circumstances of personal freedom and opportunity.

Jewish family—an evolving form

The second myth about the traditional Jewish family is that its form has been constant throughout history. Hence the modern Jewish family is seen as a break with an institutional form which has lasted unchanged for several thousands of years.

In a learned study which was excerpted in the JEWISH HERITAGE (Summer, 1972), Rabbi Herman Pollack has shown that, in fact, the Jewish family has undergone a steady evolution in both form and function from the biblical *mishpachah,* a semi-nomadic clan, to the modern nuclear family. Age at marriage, courtship patterns, family size, socialization practices, and other domestic arrangements varied greatly from one period of the Diaspora to another and from one society to another. For example, the family form of the Jews of Renaissance Italy was far more like our own families today (small, urban, rather liberal) than was the family form of the Jews of seventeenth-century Germany or Poland.

freedom and family size

In general, it seems that wherever and whenever Jews enjoyed relative political freedom and opportunity for economic advancement their families became small, mobile, nuclear units. What is remarkable is not that the Jewish family remained a fixed-frozen institution throughout the millennia. It didn't. Rather, it is remarkable that, in spite of its multiform adaptations to diverse cultural, political, and economic circumstances, it has continued to transmit, from generation to generation, a uniquely Jewish way of life.

shtetl family not synonymous with "traditional family"

It is one of the ironies of history that the vast majority of American Jews, about three-quarters of us, living in the most modern, technologically advanced and free society, happen to have our immediate ancestral roots in the repressed ghettos and backward shtetlach of Eastern Europe. In these mini-municipalities the harsh social restrictions imposed from without as well as from within tended to keep families close together. Mobility was virtually impossible, and the uncertainties of daily existence did make people highly dependent on their relatives.

Moreover, the hostility of the outside culture gave the family and the immediate Jewish community exclusive claim on the identity of the individual. Unfortunately, many who decry the fragmentary and culturally impoverished character of the modern Jewish family often compare it only with the family form which prevailed under the harshest conditions of Eastern Europe. They forget that the family form born of those conditions was not synonymous with "traditional Jewish family life" as such. Indeed, "traditional Jewish family life" is a record of successful adaptation to changing circumstances. Perhaps the only generalization one can make about "traditional Jewish families" is that they produced children who remained Jews and who, in turn produced Jewish children of their own.

It is the height of folly and historical distortion to suggest that those results can only be accomplished within a particular form of the family which happens to have emerged under the social conditions of Eastern European Jewry. Those who insist on this erroneous proposition can only increase the anxieties of modern American Jews.

self-realization not a threat to family

As we have seen earlier, despite the symptoms of increasing family disorders, the vast majority of America's Jews continue to opt for living in families with children who are raised as Jews. On the other hand, they also wish to partake of all the advantages that this great society has to offer. Young men and women enter adulthood with a rightful aspiration for professional and emotional self-realization. Their pursuit of comfort, security, and even pleasure is more to be celebrated than decried. The insistence that those pursuits are fundamentally antithetical to the perpetuation of Jewish life is false and dangerous. It is false because, in fact many American Jews—professionally successful men and women—have managed to remain committed Jews with "traditional" Jewish families.

What distinguishes the modern Jewish family from its precursors, perhaps more than anything else, is the ability of its members to consciously choose its form and cultural content. The inputs from the larger society compete heavily for the outcome of that choice. We can only hope that the inputs from the rich pool of the Judaic tradition, most liberally defined, will carry equal weight in the life choices of the modern Jewish families of the future.

Egon Mayer is Professor of Sociology at Brooklyn College, New York and Senior Research Fellow at CUNY Graduate School, New York.

OUTREACH STATISTICS AT-A-GLANCE

The following information may be useful in preparing introductory remarks for interfaith couples' groups. It is important to explain to couples why the Jewish community is so concerned about intermarriage and why couples may experience negative reactions to their marriage or childrearing plans. At the same time couples can be reassured that they are not alone in facing the issues that intermarriage raises. Reform synagogues welcome their participation and encourage their investigation of Jewish choices for themselves and their families.

1. Jews constitute only 2.5% of the population in the United States.

2. The intermarriage rate has increased dramatically over the past few decades. Prior to 1965, the rate at which Jews married someone who was not born Jewish and did not convert was approximately 9%. Since 1985, approximately 50% of Jews have married someone not born Jewish and not converted.

3. Reform congregations welcome interfaith couples. The vast majority provide in some way for the membership of non-Jewish spouses and encourage their participation in many facets of temple life. Eighty percent of Reform congregations provide Introduction to Judaism classes; 60% provide programming for interfaith couples; and two-thirds provide a variety of programs that address issues of intermarriage and conversion.

Sources:

Highlights of the CJF 1990 National Jewish Population Survey, Council of Jewish Federations, New York, NY, 1991.

American Jewish Yearbook 1989, AJC and Jewish Publication Society.

UAHC Outreach Census 1991, UAHC Commission on Reform Jewish Outreach, New York, 1991.

Wol. XIX, No. 3, December, 1973
"Judaism and Christianity: the
parting of the Ways"

During the reign of the Emperor Augustus (27 B.C.E.–14 C.E.), a certain Jesus grew up in Galilee, a northern region of the Holy Land. To the south lay Judea. Imperial Rome, which dominated the Mediterranean world at that time, had appointed Herod the Great as puppet king over the Holy Land, starting in 37 B.C.E. Upon Herod's death in 4 B.C.E., Palestine was divided among Herod's three sons. The son who received Judea failed so miserably that he had to be removed in 6 C.E. From then on, Rome sent over to Judea a series of governors called "Procurators." There were fourteen such governors in the next sixty tension-filled years, the best-known being the fifth, Pontius Pilate (26–36 C.E.).

Eventually, Jewish discontent with Rome's oppressive rule and heavy taxation was to explode in open and violent revolt. The Jewish rebellion against Rome (66–70 C.E.) was to bring terrible devastation to the land, enormous casualties, slavery for tens of thousands of Jews, and the destruction of the heart and center of the Jewish nation: Jerusalem and the Second Temple.

TWO MAJOR OUTLOOKS

But that is getting ahead of ourselves. Against this backdrop of history—of a once independent and sovereign Jewish nation chafing under foreign rule, a "different" nation clinging to its own religious laws and customs amid a pagan world, a nation forever recounting its past glories under Kings David and Solomon—the Jews of the land by no means appeared united in their religious and political views as to what should be done. Society was astir with many differing views, some people undoubtedly holding to various combinations of belief. But at least in the early decades of the first century, two outlooks predominated:

1. *A conservative view*—held by Jews who were generally satisfied with the *status quo* and hence discouraged

"Pontius Pilatus" (Pilate) name inscribed in a stone marker at Caesarea. He was the Roman governor over Judea from 26 to 36 C.E. during reign of "Tibereum" (Tiberius).

the start of the rift

BY MICHAEL COOK

about the author

Rabbi Michael J. Cook is assistant professor of Rabbinic and Intertestamental Literature at the Hebrew Union College-Jewish Institute of Religion (Cincinnati campus).

opposition to Rome. They belonged in the main to the wealthy aristocratic and priestly class. It was this class that formed the backbone of the sect or "party" called the Sadducees.

2. *A passivist view*—held by Jews who were unhappy about Roman rule but who nevertheless recognized the futility of rising against Rome. They thus advised the maintenance of law and order and the payment of Roman taxes. At the most, they suggested *passive* reliance on God himself to

overthrow Rome in His own good time. Many Pharisees—that is, the authoritative and apparently liberal interpreters of the Torah—probably held this view.

These were the two major outlooks of the day, but there were other views among the people, too:

3. *An activist view* called for *active* rebellion against Rome, insisting that no Jew could be loyal both to God and the emperor. This view found its greatest appeal at first in the Galilee region. And, as the decades rolled by, it was

P4 / **keeping posted** / DECEMBER, 1973

Destruction of Temple in Jerusalem by Roman forces under Titus in the year 70, as imagined by a 17-th century artist. Jews held out at Masada for 3 more years.

the mushrooming of this viewpoint which culminated in the great Jewish rebellion against Rome in the years 66–70 C.E.

4. *A messianist view.* Some Jews, while fervently sharing the activist wish that Roman shackles be broken in the *very near* future, nevertheless felt plans for rebellion were doomed to failure. Only with God's dynamic intervention could Roman might be smashed. These Jews expressed their longing for freedom by yearning for a "Messiah," an "anointed one," an agent of God on earth through whom Rome soon would be overthrown.

MYSTICAL IDEAS

There were various strains of "messianists." Some were "political messianists" who expected as Messiah a human king or military figure descended from King David. He would expel Rome and then usher in a new era of Israel's independence. Other messianists were of a more mystical bent. We can call them "apocalyptic messianists" because their prophet-like leaders claimed God had "revealed" to them from the heavens the secret wisdom that the world would soon come to an end in a vast fiery cataclysm. To them, the ultimate enemies were Satan and cosmic forces of evil; Rome was Satan's agent here on earth. A cosmic war was coming—a war between Good and Evil, Light and Darkness, God and Satan. The Messiah would assist in the struggle, leading to the final victory of God, and the arrival of a new age into which all deserving mankind would march following their resurrection. Since the sights of these visionaries focussed not only on this world but on the universe at large, the Messiah they conceived of was in some ways a supernatural figure, a more-than-human Messiah.

Starting around the year 30 C.E., there appeared on the scene yet another strain among the Jewish messianists — we do not know their number, but it cannot have been very large—who went beyond the usual expectations and claimed that *a Messiah had already come, had recently died, and had risen from the dead. His name was Jesus.*

STERN ROMAN VIEW

A critically important point arises: How did Rome view the messianists? How would an occupying power, in this case the "Kingdom of Rome," look upon those who preached the coming of a "Kingdom of God"? The answer is that Rome did not distinguish between the messianists and the activists. No matter to what extent *we* might regard the "Kingdom of God," the Messiah, and resurrection as *religious* beliefs or concepts, to Rome all of these were ingredients of *political* subversion and had to be dealt with swiftly and, if necessary, brutally.

Jesus was neither the first nor the last person to be hailed as the Messiah, but historically he has been the most important. The relatively small size of his initially Jewish following probably diminished when he—as perhaps other messianic figures, too—was crucified by Rome. For, among many Jews, his death would have been seen as implying the failure of his mission and the falsity of his credentials as Messiah. Nevertheless, a small group of Jews remained convinced that his mission had not failed, that he had been resurrected (raised from the dead), and that he would soon return to complete his task. Implicit in their belief was the idea that Jesus in some sense had to be divine. Eventually, the title "Christ" (the Greek form of the Hebrew word for "messiah") was applied to him; and later believers in Jesus as the Christ came to call themselves "Christians,"

GENTILES OF ASIA MINOR

The Jews who comprised this new movement in Palestine soon faded from history—both they and their "church." How then has Christianity survived? The answer is that very rapidly—perhaps within a single decade—the early Christian belief spread into areas *outside* Palestine, becoming very popular among the gentiles of Asia Minor and beyond. There it flourished by developing into a new form which was to become the basis of *modern* Christianity. We see it as a *new* form because Christianity among the gentiles of Asia Minor was quite different from the movement founded by Jesus' disciples and earliest followers. For the original Christian believers in Palestine had all been Jews who abided by the Jewish way of life. The gentile Christians in Asia Minor, however, were influenced not by the Jewish way of life but by the religious and philosophical beliefs of the Greek-Roman world. So different was the Christianity of these gentile believers in Asia Minor from that of the original Jewish believers in Palestine that it is almost as if Christianity had experienced a second beginning.

So what exactly was so different about gentile Christianity in Asia Minor? We can trace the answer to certain religious and philosophical beliefs prevalent in the Greek-Roman world of the first century, beliefs about man and his nature. Man was here seen as made up of two parts, body and soul. The material body was impure and evil; the spiritual soul was pure and good. The soul, it was believed, had somehow migrated down to earth from its true home in the celestial world and then on this ugly and unhappy earth had become imprisoned in wicked flesh. The "pure" soul was now helplessly subject to the body's lusts, passions, and death. Consequently, man found himself entrapped in a state of continuous sinfulness and consumed by a fear of death.

QUEST FOR "SALVATION"

In response to these prevailing Greek notions, many of the "mystery religions" in Asia Minor and beyond claimed to

Gates of Nicanor and the Court of Women in the Temple. Model by Dr. Avi-Yonah.

offer man's "pure" soul precisely the kind of rescue and reconciliation with the celestial world for which it yearned —in other words, "salvation." It was these religious and philosophical notions which so greatly influenced the newly developing gentile Christian communities of Asia Minor and which shaped the course of later Christianity. For, because of these ideas, the original *Jewish* messianic expectations of the early Jewish Christians in Palestine were now "translated" by the gentile Christians of Asia Minor into a new set of religious beliefs grafted onto the Greek search for "salvation." In other words, Christ Jesus now came to be worshipped as an essentially different kind of figure, not as the *Jewish* Messiah but as the gentile Christian "Savior" of all who would accept him and receive "salvation" before the inevitable and imminent end of the world.

Just as the original notion of "Messiah" had been transformed by gentile Christianity, so now the original notion of Jesus' resurrection took on more complex significance. In this, the first of all resurrections, gentile Christian missionaries now claimed, lay the means by which every soul could escape bodily enslavement. By having faith in the resurrected Jesus as the Savior, anyone —Jews and non-Jews—could be swept along in Jesus' victory over evil, death, and Satan and thus find individual salvation.

JEWISH REACTIONS

Christianity's adjustment to the Greek-Roman world naturally made it all the more appealing to pagan peoples. But gentile Christianity failed to make any serious inroads among the Jews of Palestine or Asia Minor. Why? There are many reasons, among them:

1. Until the beginning of the second century, there were very many Jews in Palestine, especially leadership elements, who did not believe in the *imminent* (that is, "in the very near future") coming of a Messiah. Moreover, when the Jewish rebellion against Rome collapsed in the year 70, the people reeled under the terrible consequences —and messianic fervor for a time subsided. Only in the early second century did messianic momentum again begin

to be generated, penetrating all levels of Jewish society. This resulted in a second and final major revolt against Rome—the ill-fated Bar Kochba uprising in 132–135 C.E. Many Jews, including the great Rabbi Akiba himself, now expected the imminent coming of the Messiah—but they perceived that Messiah to be Bar Kochba, not Jesus.

2. Even among those Jews who had all along held a Messiah concept, many in Palestine expected as Messiah a powerful military and political king descended from David. But, in the early days of Christianity, no extraordinary claims were made about the birth or ancestry of Jesus—and he did not resemble a king or military figure.

3. The Messiah of Christianity had been crucified. In Jewish eyes, this was a humiliation unbecoming to the genuine Messiah who, as God's anointed, was to enjoy victory and not suffer defeat.

4. Christian believers soon appropriated Jewish Scriptures (often in the Greek translation) as their own. By studying the sacred text in the light of their beliefs, Christians claimed to find many passages which "predicted" the coming of Christ Jesus and also the making of a "new covenant" by God with all who accepted Jesus as Savior. Jews have never taken kindly to such Christian re-interpretations.

Foundations of a tower of Herod's Antonia fortress where Jesus may have been held.

Latin marker found in Israel, identifying Roman Tenth Legion ("Leg. X Fretensis"), which was sent to quell revolt and occupy Jerusalem from the 1st to 3rd centuries.

5. At the same time, largely through the influence of a Jew and former Pharisee, Paul of Tarsus (a city near the southeast coast of what is now Turkey), most gentile Christians in Asia Minor had come to regard as valueless especially the *legal* prescriptions of the Law of Moses (the Torah). Paul claimed that obedience to the Torah could not guarantee salvation; rather, salvation was attainable only through acceptance of and faith in Christ Jesus.

SIN AND ATONEMENT

What led Paul to this attitude? It will be recalled that, to the minds of many reared in the Greek-Roman environment, man would seem to be, by his very nature, a sinful creature. For "sin" was not so much a man's evil *deed* as it was man's natural condition. After all, his "pure" soul was imprisoned in a sinful body. Paul held that man thus could never hope to atone for his own sinfulness—for how could he conquer his own nature? To believe that a person could atone for his own sinful condition *through any efforts of his own*—as, for example, by obeying the laws of the Torah—was, accordingly, a delusion. But Paul eagerly announced that what

man could not *himself* accomplish—namely, salvation—could still be accomplished *for* him! Only *God*, however, was powerful enough to atone for mankind's sinfulness, and Paul held that the death of Christ Jesus was that act of Divine atonement.

We Jews have rejected this gentile Christian view. For Judaism, as shaped by our Rabbis in Palestine, conceived of the body as a gift of God; to this day we regard the body as holy—and wholesome—not as a prison from which to escape. Any inclination by man to commit a wrongdoing, we hold, resides not in his body but in his heart or mind; and this inclination can be overcome by a change of heart or mind. Thus, man *by himself* does indeed possess the power to atone for his own misdeeds, and we Jews have *in our Torah* the guidance directing our hearts and minds to righteous living.

6. To many Jews in the first century, the emphasis in Judaism would have rested on what a Jew must *do*—that is, walk uprightly by fulfilling the *mitzvot*, the commandments. Christianity introduced a seemingly alternative emphasis on *believing*; and as we have said, Jews

simply could not accept certain Christian beliefs—especially that a divine being had taken for a time the form of a man (incarnation), had died, and was then resurrected. Equally foreign to Jewish monotheism was the growing tendency in Christianity to place Jesus in what appeared in Jewish eyes to be a role of divine intermediary between God and man.

THE PARTING OF THE WAYS

The earliest segment of Christianity, the Jewish Christians, were a relatively small Jewish sect in Palestine whose distinction from other Jews was their belief not that the Messiah would one day come but rather that he had already come, had died, and would soon return. Otherwise, for a number of decades, these Christians probably continued to worship with their fellow Jews in the same synagogues, generally using similar liturgy and abiding by the Torah. What became of them we do not know—they vanished from history.

But, whether or not we ever discover what became of them, it is not to these earliest Jewish Christians in Palestine that we trace the fundamental parting of the ways between Christianity and Judaism. That separation came about because Christianity took root in the Greco-Roman world of Asia Minor and flourished there in a *new form*—a form which had little in common with Judaism. The influence of Greek environment and thought, especially as regards the nature of man and the need for salvation, directed the course of

Rome issued victory coin, "Judea Capta," after Jerusalem fell in 70 C.E.

developing Christianity further and further away from Judaism, its mother religion. Moreover, the successful missionizing of gentiles in Asia Minor, especially by Paul of Tarsus (died about 64 C.E.), coupled with the Jewish rejection of Christian preachings, resulted in Christianity's gaining most of its new adherents from gentile ranks, from pagans who became Christians without first being or becoming Jews.

The four Gospels and Acts, opening the New Testament, all seem to have been written by gentile Christians in Asia Minor over a period of about forty to perhaps one hundred or more years after the death of Jesus. Given the gentile makeup of Christianity in *their* day and *their* environment, it seemed evident in *their* eyes that Jesus of Nazareth *must* have turned from the Jews, whom they saw rejecting him, to the gentiles whom they saw eagerly welcoming him. By contrast, from our perspective today, it would seem that Paul, not Jesus, had done the turning to the gentiles.

PERSISTENT QUESTIONS

The authors of the Gospels and Acts were separated from Jesus by time, geography, culture, and religious background. Accordingly, while their works certainly must be considered historical sources, the history they reflect is a mixture of the later times and religious climate in which they were written as well as of the earlier times they seem to describe. Because it is all too often difficult, if not impossible, to separate the two, we are left with many uncertainties about Jesus himself. Especially fascinating are these questions in particular: Who precisely did Jesus *himself* think he was? And what, exactly, did he *himself* believe or intend? §§

REPORT OF THE COMMITTEE ON PATRILINEAL DESCENT
ON THE STATUS OF CHILDREN OF MIXED MARRIAGES

The purpose of this document is to establish the Jewish status of the children of mixed marriages in the Reform Jewish community of North America.

One of the most pressing human issues for the North American Jewish community is mixed marriage, with all its attendant implications. For our purpose, mixed marriage is defined as a union between a Jew and a non-Jew. A non-Jew who joins the Jewish people through conversion is recognized as a Jew in every respect. We deal here only with the Jewish identity of children born of a union in which one parent is Jewish and the other parent is non-Jewish.

According to the Halacha as interpreted by traditional Jews over many centuries, the offspring of a Jewish mother and a non-Jewish father is considered a non-Jew. To become a Jew the child of a non-Jewish mother and a Jewish father must undergo conversion.

As a Reform community, the process of determining an appropriate response has taken us to an examination of the tradition, our own earlier responses and the most current considerations. In doing so, we seek to be sensitive to the human dimension of this issue.

Both the Biblical and the rabbinical traditions take for granted that ordinarily the paternal line is decisive in the tracing of descent within the Jewish people. The Biblical genealogies in Genesis and elsewhere in the Bible attest to this point. In intertribal marriage in ancient Israel, paternal descent was decisive. Numbers 1:2, etc., says: "By their families, by their fathers' houses" (*le-mishpehotam le-veit avotam*), which for the rabbis means "The line (literally: `family') of the father is recognized; the line of the mother is not" (*mishpahat av keryuyah mishpahan: mishpahat eim einah keruvah mishpahah: Baba Batra 109b, Yebamot* 54b; cf. *Yad, Nahalot* 1:6).

In the rabbinic tradition, this tradition remains in force. The offspring of a male *kohen* who marries a Levite or Israelite is considered a *kohen* and the child of an Israelite who marries a *kohenet* is an Israelite. Thus *yihus*, lineage, regards the male line as absolutely dominant. This ruling is stated succinctly in *Mishnah Kiddushin* 3:12 that when *Kiddushin* (marriage) is licit and no transgression (*ein avera*) is involved the line follows the father. Furthermore, the most important parental responsibility, to teach Torah, rested with the father (*Kiddushin* 29a; cf. *Shulchan Aruch Yore De-ah* 245:1).

When, in the tradition, the marriage was considered not to be licit, the child of that marriage followed the status of the mother (*Mishnah Kiddushin* 3:12, *ha-velad Kemotah*). The decisions of our ancestors thus to link the child inseparably to the mother, which makes the child of a Jewish mother Jewish and the child of a non-Jewish mother non-Jewish, regardless of the father, was based upon the fact that the woman with her child had no recourse but to return to her own people. A Jewish woman could not marry a non-Jewish man (cf. *Shulchan Aruch, Even Ha-ezer* 4:19, *la tafsei kiddushin*). A Jewish man could not marry a non-Jewish woman. The only recourse in rabbinic law for the woman in either case was to return to her own community and people.

Since Emancipation, Jews have faced the problem of mixed marriage and the status of the offspring of mixed marriage. The Reform Movement responded to the issue. In 1947 the CCAR adopted a proposal made by the Committee on Mixed Marriage and Intermarriage:

> With regard to infants, the declaration of the parents to raise them as Jews shall be deemed sufficient for conversion. This could apply, for example to adopted children. This decision is in line with the traditional procedure in which, according to the Talmud, the parents bring young children (the Talmud speaks of children earlier than the age of three) to be converted, and the Talmud comments that although an infant cannot give its consent, it is permissible to *benefit* somebody without his consent (or presence). On the same page the Talmud also speaks of a father bringing his children for conversion and says that the children will be satisfied with the action of their father. If the parents therefore will make a declaration to the rabbi that it is their intention to raise the child as a Jew, the child may, for the sake of impressive formality, be recorded in the Cradle-Roll of the religious school and thus be considered converted.

Children of religious school age should likewise not be required to undergo a special ceremony of conversion but should receive instruction as regular students in the school. The ceremony of Confirmation at the end of the school course shall be considered in lieu of a conversion ceremony.

Children older than confirmation age should not be converted without their own consent. The Talmudic law likewise gives the child who is converted in infancy by the court the right to reject the conversion when it becomes of religious age. Therefore the child above religious school age, if he or she consents sincerely to conversion, should receive regular instruction for that purpose and be converted in the regular conversion ceremony. (Vol.57, *CCAR Annual*)

This issue was again addressed in the 1961 edition of the *Rabbi's Manual:*

Jewish law recognizes a person as Jewish if his mother was Jewish, even though the father was not a Jew. One born of such mixed parentage may be admitted to membership in the synagogue and enter into a marital relationship with a Jew, provided he has not been reared in or formally admitted into some other faith. The child of a Jewish father and a non-Jewish mother, according to traditional law, is a Gentile; such a person would have to be formally converted in order to marry a Jew or become a synagogue member.

Reform Judaism, however accepts such a child as Jewish without a formal conversion, if he attends a Jewish school and follows a course of studies leading to Confirmation. Such procedure is regarded as sufficient evidence that the parents and the child himself intend that he shall live as a Jew. (p. 112, *Rabbi's Manual.*)

We face today an unprecedented situation due to the changed conditions in which decisions concerning the status of the child of a mixed marriage are to be made. There are tens of thousands of mixed marriages. In a vast majority of these cases the non-Jewish extended family is a functioning part of the child's world, and may be decisive in shaping the life of the child. It can no longer be assumed *a priori,* therefore, that the child of a Jewish mother will be Jewish any more than that the child of a non-Jewish mother will not be.

This leads us to the conclusion that the same requirements must be applied to establish the status of a child of a mixed marriage, regardless of whether the mother or the father is Jewish.

Therefore:

The Jewish status of the offspring of any mixed marriage is established through appropriate and timely public and formal acts of identification with the Jewish faith and people. The performance of these mitzvot serves to commit those who participate in them, both parent and child, to Jewish life.

Depending on circumstances,[1] mitzvot leading toward a positive and exclusive Jewish identity will include entry into the covenant, acquisition of a Hebrew name, Torah study, bar/bat mitzvah and Kabbalat Torah (Confirmation).[2] For those beyond childhood claiming Jewish identity, other public acts or declarations may be added or substituted after consultation with their rabbi.

---

1. According to the age or setting, parents should consult a rabbi to determine the specific mitzvot which are necessary.

2. A full description of these and other mitzvot can be found in *Shaarei Mitzvah.*

OFFICIATION

Some Questions and Answers

Any discussion on the issue of the rabbinic officiation of intermarriage must be preceded by a reminder that the ultimate policy guidelines are generated by the Central Conference of American Rabbis, and individual rabbis then decide what their particular policy will be. The following is an attempt to respond to some questions which are frequently raised concerning this complex issue. The issue of rabbinic officiation is outside the purview of the Commission on Reform Jewish Outreach. Outreach — providing a welcome to the Jewish community and to Jewish life for non-Jewish partners — is a mandate of Reform Judaism that is independent of a rabbi's decision about officiation.

1. What was the Central Conference of American Rabbis' 1973 resolution of the Committee on Mixed Marriage?

The CCAR, recalling its stand adopted in 1909 "that mixed marriage is contrary to the Jewish tradition and should be discouraged," now declares its opposition to participation by its members in any ceremony which solemnizes a mixed marriage.

The CCAR recognizes that historically its members have held and continue to hold divergent interpretations of Jewish tradition.

In order to keep open every channel to Judaism and K'lal Yisrael for those who have already entered into mixed marriage, the CCAR calls upon its members:

– to assist fully in educating children of such mixed marriages as Jews;

– to provide the opportunity for conversion of the non-Jewish spouse; and

– to encourage a creative and consistent cultivation of involvement in the Jewish community and the synagogue.

2. What are some of the arguments advanced by the Subcommittee on Mixed Marriage to the Task Force on Reform Jewish Outreach in favor of Rabbinic Officiation?

a) Rabbinic officiation at intermarriages enhances the possibility that children will be raised as Jews and the non-Jewish spouse will be more likely to consider the possibility of conversion at some later date.

b) When a rabbi refuses to officiate at an intermarriage, the couple may be alienated from the synagogue. The person of another faith, or of no professed faith, who requests that a rabbi officiate at his/her marriage has already made a first positive decision toward Judaism.

c) A refusal to officiate cannot be reconciled with Reform Judaism's emphasis upon interfaith dialogue and the prophetic message of universal brotherhood.

d) Rabbis can create wedding ceremonies appropriate to the occasion rather than utilizing the traditional Jewish ritual.

e) It is time to stop being concerned over the reactions of Orthodox and Conservative Judaism to the practices of Reform. Over the years, Reform Judaism has made numerous decisions which contravene Jewish law. In our pluralistic society, a significant percentage of Jews now marry persons born outside our faith. These marriages are increasing regardless of the rabbinic stance. We cannot afford to reject such a large proportion of our young people and their parents.

f) Both the 1973 CCAR resolution and the statements found in the Rabbis Manual have exerted powerful pressures upon rabbis to refrain from officiation at intermarriages lest in doing so they jeopardize their futures as members of that body.

g) Outreach begins before a marriage takes place. An outreach program which is intent upon reaching out to couples in an intermarriage but which disapproves of rabbinic officiation at intermarriages is a contradiction in terms.

h) Rabbis should be permitted to officiate at intermarriages in the sanctuary of the congregation. Such an act would increase the chances of the non-Jewish partner's conversion to Judaism.

3. What are some of the arguments advanced by the Subcommittee on Mixed Marriage to the Task Force on Reform Jewish Outreach in opposition to Rabbinic Officiation?

a) Premarital promises regarding the religious upbringing of children are prone to change subsequent to the birth of a child. Often commitments to educate children as Jews or to convert oneself are not voluntary but concessions to pressure brought to bear by the Jewish partner and the Jewish partner's family.

b) A growing number of intermarried couples have affiliated with synagogues and are raising their children as Jews despite the fact that they were not married by a rabbi.

c) The preservation of one's particular Jewish identity is both consistent and necessary if the integrity of other cultures, ethnic groups and faith communities is to be defended.

d) The rabbi is the symbolic representative of Judaism and of the continuity of the Jewish tradition. To tailor ritual to fit the religious needs of the couple is to subvert the basic assumptions under which both Judaism and the State have granted the rabbi the prerogative to serve as an officiant in the first place. The rabbi's participation in the ceremony is construed by the Jewish partner and the Jewish family as a sign that the wedding is a Jewish wedding thereby assuaging the family's discomfiture at the reality of an intermarriage.

e) It is not a question of Reform versus Orthodox interpretations of Judaism. It is a question of Jewish survival and the sanction of behavior which violates the purpose and meaning of Jewish marriage and rabbinic responsibility.

f) The CCAR has always permitted the free exchange of positions and points of view. The 1973 resolution clearly recognizes that members may hold divergent views regarding officiating at intermarriages.

g) The Outreach program stands on its own merits. There is no inconsistency whatsoever in a program designed to deal with the religious needs of couples after their marriage and the affirmation that a Jewish marriage is involving men and women who are committed to Judaism as a personal way of life.

h) To solemnize a wedding between a Jew and a non-Jew in a synagogue sanctuary is to transform a sacred moment in the life cycle of the Jewish people into an act of hypocrisy.

4. Where can further information be obtained regarding the ongoing rabbinic debate on officiation?

a) The "Committee of 100" published a booklet entitled "Reform Rabbis and Mixed Marriage," on why rabbis should not officiate at intermarriages. A copy of this booklet can be obtained by writing to: "Committee of 100," Congregation Keneseth Israel, Old York Road at Township Line, Elkins Park, PA 19117.

b) Rabbi Eugene Mihaly's *Teshuvot (Responsa) on Jewish Marriage* (Cincinnati, Ohio 1985), which suggest that support for rabbinic officiation can be found within the rabbinic tradition, is a response to the statement of the "Committee of 100."

5. What about synagogue policies regarding the participation of non-Jewish members in various rituals, on committees, the Board of Trustees, etc.?

A suggested constitution and by-laws for congregations affiliated with the Union of American Hebrew Congregations was adopted by the Joint Commission on Synagogue Administration of the UAHC and the CCAR in 1968, and amended in 1970 and 1984. A copy of these guidelines can be obtained through the UAHC Department of Synagogue Management.

In addition, while each congregation determines its own specific policy on the role non-Jews may play in the areas of membership, governance and ritual participation, the vast majority (88%) of Reform congregations do provide in some way for the affiliation of non-Jewish spouses. Most encourage participation on temple committees and find a way to honor a non-Jewish parent on the bimah at life-cycle occasions, but most reserve particularistic blessings for Jews. *The Role of the Non-Jew in the Synagogue: A Resource for Congregations* (available from the UAHC Press) gives further information in this complex area.

SOME THOUGHTS ON RABBINIC OFFICIATION AT INTERFAITH MARRIAGES

1. "We believe that intermarriage is neither good nor bad, just as we believe that the marriage between two Jews, in itself, is neither good nor bad. The moral worth of a marriage always depends on the quality of the human relationship.... We believe that rabbis who officiate at intermarriage ceremonies demonstrate their commitment to human freedom, dignity and love. We hope that more rabbis will choose to affirm these values." (Society for Humanistic Judaism)

2. "The CCAR, recalling its stand adopted in 1909 "that mixed marriage is contrary to the Jewish tradition and should be discouraged," now declares its opposition to participation by its members in any ceremony which solemnized a mixed marriage.... The CCAR recognized that historically its members have held and continue to hold divergent interpretations of Jewish history." (CCAR 1973)

3. "(Intermarriage) represents a potential drain on the numeric strength of the Jewish people and on its inner commitment. Whether I like it or not, my officiation would be seen as a seal of approval and would, therefore, become encouraging of intermarriage." (R. Alexander Schindler)

4. "Obviously there is a great satisfaction in meeting the needs of the couples, but when at least two-thirds of my marriages are mixed marriages, I've got to wonder what it says to the Confirmation child or Bar Mitzvah about carrying on Judaism? I can't forget David Einhorn's classic line that mixed marriage is the nail in the coffin of Judaism. It haunts me." (R. Ken Segal)

5. "It finally dawned on me that sometimes a given mixed marriage may actually serve the interests of the Jewish community... There are clearly situations in which mixed marriages *will* result in Jewish continuity and *will* strengthen the fabric of Jewish life. In such situations, I would argue that rabbis should be present for these couples, playing the role of *mekarev*, drawing them near to Judaism and the Jewish people, not estranging or rejecting them. The unfortunate aspect of this posture is it means that we need to assess each relationship on its Jewish merits. The role of assessor is downright uncomfortable. For the sake of Judaism and the Jewish people, however, it surpasses the more categorical position." (*Meditations of a Maverick Rabbi*, by R. Al Axelrad)

6. "... as long as the Jewish partner had a firm commitment to Judaism, the couple intended to have a Jewish home and the non-Jewish partner has no conflicting faith commitment." (R. Edgar Magnin)

7. "When officiating at a marriage ceremony, the rabbi acts as representative of the Jewish people and the Jewish heritage. What the rabbi does or does not do has an effect on the totality of Jewry and on our people's potential for survival in the midst of an over-whelmingly non-Jewish society." (Committee of 100)

8. "Certainly we as Reform Jews must state boldly and clearly, as we have numerous times declared, that in all cases involving the relationship of Jew and non-Jew, interfaith marriage, or the status of the children of such unions, the talmudic halakha is not operative. It is null and void. It is not *dat Moshe we Ysrael*. Its principles cannot, must not, be used. It is contrary to the higher impulses of traditional Judaism itself, contrary to the demands of God as Judaism perceives them. The literal halakha in this total area must be categorically rejected." (*Responsa on Jewish Marriage*, by R. Eugene Mihaly)

NOTES: JUDAISM AS A CIVILIZATION

Explain that this topic is intended to clarify the meaning of Judaism. The following presentation represents the facilitator's understanding of Judaism and will not necessarily be shared by all Jews. However, by learning what Judaism means to most Jews, the non-Jewish partner will better understand his/her loved one.

1. The Western world has incorrectly defined Judaism as a religion in the same way as Christianity, Islam, and Buddhism are defined; Judaism is both a religion and a culture/civilization.

2. A civilization is comprised of many components, most importantly: people, land, language, culture, history, theology, ritual, literature, cuisine. Viewed this way, religion is only one part the larger Jewish civilization—and not always the most significant part for every Jew. (For more information, see Mordecai Kaplan's *Judaism as a Civilization.)*

3. Seeing Judaism as a civilization helps us to understand the inconsistencies we observe in individual Jews who possess a strong Jewish identity, feel connected to Judaism and the Jewish people, but are not religiously observant. Some Jews express their Judaism through cultural, social, even culinary means and not through worship and ritual.

4. Being aware of Judaism as a civilization enables us to understand the meaning of Peoplehood in Jewish life. Peoplehood, comprised of both religion and ethnicity, has played an important part in the Jewish historical experience.

For most of their history (except the last century or two), Jews were separated from the larger non-Jewish world, living in a closed, autonomous society governed by Jewish law and self-regulated by Jewish communal institutions. Certain primary Jewish laws and customs, such as *kashrut* (dietary regulations), ritual dress, and observances, helped to support the cohesiveness and distinctiveness of the Jewish community: anti-Semitism served to maintain the separateness of Jew and Gentile.

Today, most of these internal and external barriers have disappeared. Jews dress, eat, speak, and grow up in the same environment as non-Jews: Jews and non-Jews work together, date one another, fall in love, and marry. In fact, Jews and non-Jews from similar socio-economic backgrounds may have more in common than liberal Jews have in common with Orthodox Jews.

5. Viewing Judaism as a civilization allows Jewish participants to evaluate their identity in a new context and helps non-Jews understand the feelings of their loved ones and those Jews who may make them feel unwelcome. This does not justify antagonistic behavior; but it may help explain the sense of being an "outsider" experienced by many non-Jews around Jewish family members.

6. Ask for questions and/or reactions during key points in the presentations.

Note: Be sure to refer back to this discussion of Judaism as a civilization whenever group discussion focuses on childrearing and taking the "best of both religions." Participants may find it difficult to accept that Judaism cannot be viewed solely as a belief system, like Christianity: it will be necessary to remind the group that Judaism encompasses much more than a system of belief.

QUESTIONS ASKED BY PARTICIPANTS AND SOME SUGGESTED RESPONSES

I. INTRODUCTION

• *Note to Facilitator:* During the course of the group you will probably be asked many questions directly by group members, since an important aspect of this group is informational and you are perceived to be the resident "expert." In order not to be trapped into feeling put on the spot and offering apparently instant solutions, we suggest that you consider the following when a direct question is asked of you:

1) Before answering, open the question up to the group. Asking "What do you think about Susan's question?" "Does anyone have any ideas about this?" "John and Ellen, you talked about similar concerns last week. Have you had any further thoughts that might be useful to Susan?" will promote group process and facilitate a full discussion of the issue raised.

2) Be sensitive to *how* the question is asked. If the person seems distressed, don't be afraid to acknowledge it. Examples: "Mary, you seem to have some pretty strong feelings about these issues..." or "This seems to be a painful topic for everyone." Commenting on feelings will provide participants with the opportunity to talk about Judaism and their relationship with an awareness of their own emotional process.

3) Don't be afraid to acknowledge that you don't have all the answers, and that there are many aspects of relationships that aren't always predictable.

4) You may notice that your answers to some of these questions will change from group to group, or even according to the particular individual within the group who has asked the questions. Many of these responses are highly subjective, and your own thinking will probably change somewhat over time.

II. MY PARTNER AND I

WILL LOVE ENDURE WITH THE DIFFERENCE IN OUR BACKGROUND?

"Part of the difficulty of making any long-term commitment to another person is that relationships come with no guarantees! Differences in background often mean that couples have to develop special sensitivities and deal with complex issues. I think it's important to acknowledge that all of you in this group, just by deciding to participate, have taken the first step toward a deeper understanding of one another and are starting on the right foot."

WHAT COMPROMISES SHOULD WE MAKE? SHOULD WE AGREE TO GIVE "EQUAL TIME" TO EACH OTHER'S RELIGIOUS BELIEFS?

"Through our Outreach efforts over the past few years (which we have discussed in other sessions), we have learned to help couples look at those very issues. Since every couple is different there just aren't any magic solutions. You probably noted that even within this group there are some striking differences in the ways that you approach issues we have discussed." OR: "You have probably noticed that I've said very little about working out the logistics of his and her religions in the home. That's because, in my experience, that plan doesn't seem to work very well. It is difficult when dealing with issues such as these to define parameters which guarantee "equal time" and pat solutions. In addition, what may seem to be an acceptable arrangement for both partners now becomes unmanageable when there are children. Can you imagine a child going to Shabbat services on Friday night, Jewish religious school some Sundays and Christian Sunday school on alternate weeks, and Hebrew School on Tuesday afternoon? The poor kid will be confused and exhausted!"

HOW CAN I EDUCATE MY SPOUSE ABOUT TRADITIONS AND HOLIDAYS IN A NON-THREATENING WAY?

"Let's start by asking the group. You're all spouses (or spouses to be) and you all probably have the same question. What do you think? Let's talk about the word 'threatening' for a minute. What does that mean? What would be threatening to you personally? I think the formula is really simple: From my perspective you might begin by discussing any religious activity beforehand with your partner. Would he or she like to participate? In what way? What could you do to make that experience as comfortable as possible? It may be a matter of sharing some information before the event. Or, just as important, it may mean simply that you let him or her know that you understand that there will be some discomfort and awkwardness. This doesn't always need to be articulated verbally — sometimes a hand squeeze will do."

III. RELIGIOUS IDENTITY AND MARRIAGE

HOW CAN I HAVE MY RELIGION WITHOUT STIFLING HIS OR HERS?

"I have to say honestly that I don't know the answer. I'm not sure this is possible. What do you think?" OR "We seem to be back on this theme of his and hers religions again. Suppose my answer to your question was a simple No! Where would we go in our discussion from here?"

HOW CAN WE PRACTICE OUR SEPARATE FAITHS AND STILL HAVE A UNIFIED HOME?

"Mary, I'm touched by your determination to solve potential problems early so that they don't become stumbling blocks in your relationship later on. We have been talking about this for two weeks now, and so far no one has been able to come up with an answer. To talk about 'separate faiths' and 'unity' seems like a contradiction in terms. Perhaps the answer lies in the word 'home.' Do you think that there is a way that you could agree to have one religion in the home, thereby making it unified? Let's talk about that idea to see if it helps us begin to get a handle on this...."

HOW DO I DEAL WITH MY FEELINGS ABOUT GIVING UP PART OF MY IDENTITY AND HERITAGE?

(*Note to facilitator:* Clarify what "giving up" means. Has this issue been discussed in the group? What is to be given up, etc.).

"What are your feelings right now as you're asking this question?" Then: "How do you imagine you'll feel in the future?" "I was pleased to see last week how critically the group was examining religious commitment on both sides. I wonder if that discussion put you in touch with aspects of your religious identity which you hadn't thought about for awhile..." "Are you going to have to deal with those painful feelings all by yourself? Who could help you?"

CAN MY NON-JEWISH SPOUSE EVER APPRECIATE MY JEWISH IDENTITY?

"Absolutely! Your Jewish identity is a part of what he or she fell in love with, even though neither of you realizes it. Fuller understanding is something that will happen over time, with exposure to some of the kinds of experiences that shaped your Jewish identity: holidays, life cycle events, and involvement with a Jewish family. It's a wonderful opportunity for you to be his or her teacher." OR: "I'm not sure what you're asking, Mark. Are there parts of your Jewish identity that Helen doesn't understand?" (What are they? Refocus the group discussion). "It's often hard for non-Jews to understand why Judaism is so important to us when we may go to synagogue only rarely. We seem to have automatic antennae for anti-semitism, and we seem to be concerned about intermarriage. It doesn't make a lot of sense on the surface. But usually such issues can be explained very simply through a combination of frank discussion, education, and encounters with Jews and Judaism. All of which we're doing here! Aren't you glad you came?!"

HOW MAY WE, AS A COUPLE (CHRISTIAN AND JEWISH), PRESERVE THE BEST OF OUR INDIVIDUAL RELIGIONS AND STILL RAISE A JEWISH CHILD IN A HARMONIOUS WAY?

"When a choice is made for the religious identity of a child in an intermarriage, there is always fear of disharmony. However, the parents have already taken a positive step in dealing with these feelings by choosing to give the child a religious identity – in this case, Judaism. In honoring this commitment, parents not only preserve the best of Judaism, but, at the same time, enable the child to learn about and respect the best of the Christian family's religion without its taking way from a Jewish identity. Such clarification of the differences present in an intermarriage prevents the denigration of either religion by reducing their traditions to mere superficial celebrations by everyone."

WHAT MAY BE THE LONG TERM EFFECTS ON OUR MARRIAGE?

"I don't know. Statistics about the long term success of intermarriages are not yet available. What are you particularly concerned about?" Then: "What do you think could be done to prevent any negative effect on your marriage?"

HOW CAN A PARTNER MAINTAIN HIS OR HER OWN RELIGIOUS IDENTITY IF IT IS NOT THE DOMINANT RELIGION OF THE HOUSEHOLD?

"That's a good question. First of all, if there is a strong commitment on the part of that partner, it can be done successfully. It's important to remember that although your primary focus is on each other right now, your families and friends hopefully will remain important parts of your lives. Holiday celebrations and religious experience can be shared with parents, other relatives, or friends. Let me give you an example: There is no reason why an intermarried couple who has agreed to have a Jewish home can't go with their children to Grandma Maureen's for Christmas. I think it's important to underline that we will always share families, memories, and some very strong emotional ties to our pasts."

SO WON'T ANY AGREEMENTS WE MAKE NOW BE USELESS SINCE OUR FEELINGS WILL CHANGE ANYWAY?

"There is something that is much more important than any decision you make now: the process of learning to discuss these issues in a way that is healthy and productive for your relationship. Much of what you have been doing in this group has been learning how to talk about religion with each other and with your families. Those are invaluable skills that will stay with you to help keep the lines of communication open every step of the way. You'll have the basic skills you need to deal with changes as they arise."

HOW IMPORTANT – REALLY – IS ALL THE OUTER STUFF ABOUT RELIGION? WHAT ABOUT THE REAL SPIRITUAL LOVING CONNECTION WE HAVE? AM I MAKING A BIG DEAL ABOUT NOTHING?

"Of course, the loving bond that you have with your partner is important, whether it is defined in spiritual terms or not. It is the basic ingredient of a good, healthy relationship. The importance of the 'outer' stuff about religion is what you need to determine for yourself. You must feel it has some importance or you wouldn't be here. This really is the topic of some of the early sessions of the program: what does it mean to me to be Jewish/Christian? To those who care deeply about and are committed to their religion, religious identity is not 'outer stuff'."

IV.   PARENTS AND FAMILY

HOW CAN I DEAL WITH MY PARENTS' DISCOMFORT WITH CHANGING EXPECTATIONS FOR ME? SPECIFICALLY, HOW CAN I HANDLE THEIR DISAPPOINTMENT, EVEN ANGER?

"It is important to place this discussion in the context of the normal process of separation between parents and children that occurs with a marriage. How would your parents respond if you married a Jew with little education, or one who was too 'unacceptable' to them in some way, etc. (Is anyone good enough for their baby)? Some of these feelings may be hung on the convenient peg of intermarriage. Some parents may go through a mourning period as they give up their personal dream of your future. The process of separation takes time for them as it does for you; it does not happen all at once during the wedding ceremony. Understanding, reassurance of your love for them and time all help this process along." (It might be helpful to role-play a parent-child discussion so that group members can model for each other).

WILL MY SPOUSE'S PARENTS ACCEPT JEWISH GRANDCHILDREN?

"There is, of course, no clearcut response to this question. People are different and respond to the situations they are presented with in different ways. Grandmother and grandfather may respond in different ways. There may be a religious issue involved, such as a fundamentalist Christian grandparent fearing their grandchild will not be saved. On the other hand, this is often an interpersonal issue. A parent may fear that the grandchild will be different in some way, will not love him or her as fully, or the parents may feel betrayed. Many parents need some *time* to adjust to changed expectations and to experience the love that can grow between them and their grandchildren. Perhaps the best indicator of your in-laws' response to having Jewish grandchildren will be their response to other challenges in the past."

I HAVE TROUBLE DEALING WITH THE FACT THAT EVERYONE (IN-LAWS, MY PARENTS, FIANCE) CANNOT BE HAPPY WITH THE ULTIMATE DECISIONS? HOW DO OTHERS DEAL WITH THIS?

(The maturity of each participant will influence his or her response to this question, a more mature person feeling that personal integrity would carry more weight in decision-making than the happiness of others). "How do you define 'happiness?'" Describe various levels of acceptance and your comfort in living with a higher or lower level of parental acceptance. Whose happiness is most important to you—yours, your partner's, your parents, your in-laws? Couples who are already married may already have confronted this issue. How did they cope?

I WOULD LIKE TO DISCUSS HOW PARTICIPANTS' PARENTS HAVE REACTED TO THEIR SITUATIONS AND HOW IMPORTANT OR UNIMPORTANT DEALING WITH THIS REACTION IS IN THE ULTIMATE DECISIONS THEY MAKE.

(The Mary and Herb Kushner scenario, which is included in Chapter 4, "Baptism or Bris?" would be very useful in focusing attention on the paralyzing effect of opposite pulls from two sets of parents).

"The couples themselves must make the ultimate decisions for their family, and they must be able to live with the consequent feelings of their parents. What is meant by 'ultimate decisions?' This most likely refers to decisions relating to childrearing. It might be important to note at some point that, as important as it is to make decisions about childrearing, such decisions are not written in stone. They can be changed if they become unworkable. Changing the idea of 'ultimate decisions' to the idea of the process of decision-making may alleviate some of the anxiety surrounding these issues."

V.   CHILDREN

DO PEOPLE'S RELIGIOUS VIEWS BECOME STRONGER ONCE THEY ARE MARRIED AND HAVE CHILDREN?

"Yes, in our experience, they often do become stronger. Religion isn't static; it changes in relation to changes we experience throughout our lives. You probably don't feel the same way now about your religion as you did as a child. Many of us don't realize this, and we are caught off guard by the intensity of religious feelings raised by the birth of a child, for instance, when we never felt those feelings before."

IF YOU ARE A JEW AND YOUR SPOUSE ISN'T AND EACH ACCEPTS THE OTHER'S RELIGION, THEN HOW DO YOU DECIDE WHICH RELIGION TO CHOOSE FOR YOUR CHILDREN?

IF YOU CHOOSE TO RAISE YOUR CHILDREN AS JEWS, HOW DO YOU EXPLAIN TO THEM THAT THEIR MOTHER/FATHER BELONGS TO A DIFFERENT FAITH?

"Children in an intermarriage will have a religious identity if parents agree to make a choice – a decision made difficult when the parents themselves come from two different religious backgrounds. By participating in this program, they are taking important first steps toward a decision.

Partners must first explore in depth what their own religious identities mean to them and what each believes is important in nurturing someone else's religious identity. With this honest evaluation, parents can begin to explain to children why a choice is necessary, why one parent feels the need to remain who he or she is and thus provide a basis for sensitivity to the parent whose religion was not chosen."

IF YOU DECIDE TO RAISE YOUR CHILDREN ACCORDING TO YOUR SPOUSE'S RELIGION:

    A. HOW DO YOU DEAL WITH YOUR FEELINGS?

    B. HOW DO YOU RECONCILE NOT BEING ABLE TO PRACTICE YOUR RELIGION WITH YOUR CHILDREN?

    C. HOW DO YOU PREVENT YOURSELF FROM BECOMING AN OUTSIDER TO YOUR CHILDREN AND YOUR SPOUSE?

"If one spouse decides to raise the children in the other spouse's religion, it is crucial that feelings are dealt with openly and honestly on an ongoing basis. Understand that feelings change in response to life experiences and situations. By keeping in touch with how you feel and communicating those feelings with a loving spouse and family, you enable others to be sensitive to you and to respond to your needs in a supportive way.

You can reconcile your choice to honor a commitment to raise children in a religion different from your own by being respected and supported in your decision to practice your religion privately in a way you feel comfortable.

If you are free to express who you are in a way that does not undermine your commitment to your children, you can return that respect by helping your children celebrate who they are in the context of a supportive family united by a shared commitment."

HOW DOES ONE INSTILL JEWISH IDENTITY, VALUES, HISTORY IN CHILDREN WHILE MAINTAINING A FAMILY UNIT WHICH DOES NOT EXCLUDE THE NON-JEWISH PARTNER?

"When two religions are practiced in the home, and the choice has been made to raise Jewish children, it is still possible to maintain a family unit without excluding the non-Jewish partner as long as each spouse in respectful and sensitive to the needs of the other.

The non-Jewish partner must be willing to honor a Jewish commitment for the children by learning what is important in shaping a Jewish identity for the children and subsequently participating in the process of education and celebration needed to fulfill that goal.

Similarly, the Jewish partner must be willing to respect and support the non-Jewish spouse's religious choice; the children should be taught to respect this choice. Great sensitivity must be exercised by the Jewish family members to include and encourage participation by the non-Jewish spouse and to recognize feelings of loss and pain that the non-Jew may experience at different times throughout the relationship as a result of having a separate religious identity."

IS IT POSSIBLE TO RAISE CHILDREN WITH TWO RELIGIONS:

"Children need and want to feel a sense of belonging, to have an identity as a member of a family, group, or community. They ask questions of 'who am I' and form that identity by taking clues from their parents and peers.

In the process of developing an identity, children use parents as role models and are concerned first about being like 'Mommy' and 'Daddy,' and then later search for an identity as a belonging member of a group or community.

In our pluralistic American society, religions are often seen as variations of a common religious theme. Yet, by definition they represent very different commitments and understanding of fundamental truths.

Thus, although children may learn from each parent what his or her religion means and represents for him or her, unless a choice is made, the children cannot become full members of either religion – an essential part of forming one's own identity."

IS IT A PROBLEM FOR CHILDREN TO HAVE PARENTS PRACTICING TWO DIFFERENT RELIGIONS IN THE HOUSEHOLD?

"Although an underlying awareness of difference exists when parents practice two religions in the home, a problem for children would manifest itself only if both parents were not comfortable with that possibility. A problem exists when parents are incapable of communicating truthfully with children about these very differences.

It is important for parents to make a choice for the children's religious identity and subsequently work out a way of being sensitive and supportive of the parent whose religious identity was not chosen. In this way, rather than blur the differences present in the home, parents can deal with feelings of loss and lessen any jealousy or competition that would undermine mutual respect.

Such a decision could then be communicated with other family members and friends in such a way as to elicit understanding and support to pave the way for relationships sensitive to the unique situation of the practice to two religions in the home."

VI.   COMMUNITY AND ACCEPTANCE

HOW WILL WE BE VIEWED BY THE COMMUNITY AT LARGE?

"In North America today there are many intermarried families and communities in which to live. People with prejudicial attitudes may be found anywhere. Most intermarried families have nevertheless found a comfortable community for themselves. A local Reform congregation may be a good place to start."

HOW CAN I AS A JEWISH PARENT IN AN INTERMARRIAGE BE PART OF THE JEWISH COMMUNITY?

"Jewish partners in intermarriage are accepted in Reform congregations with no restrictions at all. Some Conservative and Orthodox congregations might place certain restrictions on ritual participation or leadership positions for an intermarried Jew. Although you may encounter individuals in communal organizations who have negative attitudes toward intermarriage, you will generally be welcomed warmly as someone willing to work toward organizational goals."

WILL MY SPOUSE, A CHRISTIAN, BE ACCEPTED *WITHOUT* CONVERSION IN A SYNAGOGUE, IF WE DECIDE TO JOIN AS A FAMILY RAISING A JEWISH CHILD?

"Your spouse will be accepted in all Reform congregations. He or she will be welcome to participate in worship services and in many other aspects of temple life – choir, adult education, temple committees, etc. It is important to ask at the temple you are considering joining about its particular membership policy. Many temples do not permit non-Jews to hold leadership positions in the congregation or to participate on the *bimah* in certain rituals. In general, however, non-Jewish family members are welcomed in Reform congregations.and their participation is encouraged."

ADDITIONAL QUESTIONS FROM INTERFAITH DISCUSSION GROUPS

RELIGIOUS IDENTITY

• Must a choice be made for one household religion?

• Will my partner understand how important it is to me to maintain my roots and identity?

• How do I deal with my feelings about giving up part of my heritage?

• How can one of us maintain our religious identity if it is not the dominant religion of the household?

• How can the non-Jewish partner actively help to raise Jewish children without his/her converting or feeling diminished?

• I would like to be able to articulate more clearly for myself and for my partner what my "Jewishness" is.

• Will I feel pressured to convert?

• What compromises should we make? Should we agree to "equal time" for each other's religious beliefs?

• How do I participate comfortably in religious and traditional services?

• Is it harder for a person actively practicing a religion to convert to another, as opposed to a person with no religion?

• How do you explain why you are devoted to a religion even though you do not know very much about it?

• Can a convert really know about being Jewish? Can that person pass on a feeling of being Jewish?

• What will happen in our relationship if one or both of us becomes more committed to his/her religion?

• How have our values and belief systems been influenced by our religious upbringing? Are there big differences between a Catholic and Jewish upbringing?

FAMILY AND FRIENDS

• How can we handle the holidays: Christmas/ Hannukah; Easter/ Passover?

• How can I deal with my parents' disappointment and pain?

• Will I feel comfortable and an equal member among other Jewish families in a Temple?

• Do my friends accept my Jewish partner?

• How do you split up the holidays that fall at the same time?

• How do we establish common ground between in-laws who come from different religious backgrounds?

• How can I feel that I'm not overshadowing my partner with my religion, because his family is so far away and mine is here to help me celebrate my holidays?

• How will we manage the wedding without offending anyone's family?

• How do we bridge the generation gap between our experience and that of our parents regarding intermarriage and bigotry, etc.?

• Why do my parents bring up the Holocaust when discussing intermarriage?

• What can I do with pressure from the in-laws?

• How do we respond to our parents' notion that our interfaith marriage represents a failure on their part?

• How can we find a community as an interfaith couple? Who will be our friends?

CHILDREARING

• Please discuss specifically how to bring up Jewish children with a non-Jewish, non-converted spouse.

• What do I do if my partner feels resentment towards the idea of raising the children Jewish?

• Why is it okay for me to love my Catholic partner, yet it is not okay for me to raise my child Catholic?

• Is there any way of raising a child in a Jewish household without denying the religion of the non-Jewish partner? How will this affect my child?

• How do we present the "other" religion to the children?

• What would my role be in the children's religious education and the family structure? How active and supportive a role would I need to take? How do I explain the contradiction in belief and action on my part if I observe (or if they participate in) Christian holidays?

• Can we raise our children in two religions?

• If we have a Jewish household, will it confuse the children to have a Christmas tree?

• How will we decide what religion to raise our children?

• Are there any studies on children who were raised with more than one religion? Do they usually select one religion over another?

• How do children of interfaith couples define themselves? What does "half and half" mean?

• Will I feel like an outsider in my own family if my spouse and children practice another religion?

• How can I share my childhood experiences with my child if we do not celebrate my holidays?

• How do you raise a child as a Jew and still help him or her understand Christianity?

• How is a child accepted into the Jewish community if he or she is not born of a Jewish mother? What happens if the mother converts after the child is born?

• How does an interfaith couple create a true sense of family?

• If my religion prevails in our home, how will my partner feel? How can I help my partner not to feel left out?

This article is reprinted by permission of the author, Esther Perel, and Egone Mayer, editor of the Journal of Jewish Communal Service, volume 66, number 3.

ETHNOCULTURAL FACTORS IN MARITAL COMMUNICATION AMONG INTERMARRIED COUPLES

ESTHER PEREL

Intermarriage can be seen as the victory of love over tradition. Yet, the persistence of each partner's attachments to his or her cultural and religious background and its meaning and symbols influence the marriage. It is the drawing out of these meanings and attachments through marital therapy that can help the couple achieve a deeper intimacy and harmony.

Dealing with differences is the key theme when approaching couples of mixed ethnocultural heritage. To be sure, dealing with differences is a central issue in the lives of all couples, but with the mixed couple the domain of difference expands to include cultural and religious differences. These provide the backdrop against which couples' issues of identity, commitment, intimacy, and separation from their family of origin are played out. Since the core of one's ethnic and religious experience originates in the family, often underlying the manifest differences is an intense web of emotions and invisible loyalties.

Partners' very differences may be the basis of their initial attraction to one another. Alternatively, couples may downplay their differences and emphasize their similarities. Where some couples see their differences as a contributing factor to the success of their relationship, others see them as being the cause of its downfall.

Often the question is: how can the persistence and impact of culture and religion be acknowledged, when intermarriage is seen as a victory of love over tradition, as an overcoming of cultural barriers?

This article describes some of the challenges of marital communication faced by intermarried couples and the role that marital therapy can play in enhancing the communications skills of such couples. The couples used as examples are composites drawn from the private practice of the author.

For couples who come for marital therapy, it is the drawing out of these differences—speaking the unspoken—that can help them come together as a couple and achieve a deeper intimacy. In this process, working out their sense of cultural identity is part of differentiating from their family of origin.

This article follows a progression fairly similar to the one that occurs in work with couples in general marital therapy. Many intermarried couples come to treatment presenting problems that are explicitly related to their cultural conflicts. Treatment with these couples involves (1) helping them understand the meaning of this conflict in the context of the relationship by uncovering the underlying emotional and interpersonal processes, (2) helping each partner clarify the meaning and importance of his or her ethnic and religious identity, and (3) facilitating their mutual exploration and negotiation of their differences.

PRESENTING PROBLEMS

The couples discussed here present problems specifically related to Jewish-Gentile interethnic conflict. However, many of the issues raised here are relevant to other ethnic configurations. Among the issues most often presented are those concerning

Presented at the Paul Cowan Memorial Conference on Intermarriage, Conversion and Outreach at the City University of New York, October 24, 1989.

life-cycle transitions, relations with their families of origin, religious practice, celebration of holidays, and child rearing.

Often, couples seek help when they have reached a transition point in their relationship and/or are faced with the need to make a major commitment.

> We've been going out for 5 years, but we never talked about marriage. Then we would have had to talk about the religion thing. For 4 years this has never been an issue, but now, when marriage comes up we suddenly become fierce representatives of our religions, which we thought we had long abandoned.

> I think the reason we haven't had children in our 7 years of marriage is that he wants his children to be Jewish and I want mine to be Catholic, so we just avoid the issue.

Other sources of discord are disagreements around religious practices, holiday celebrations, and child rearing. Typically, these concerns emerge periodically, corresponding to the religious calendar. They inevitably raise questions of how the partners in an intermarriage will negotiate their respective traditions within the family framework.

> I agreed to raise our children as Jews, but I really want to share Christmas with them and I want my wife to accept that. For me Christmas is a time for family reunion; for her it's the domination of the "cross" and the Christian world.

Parental opposition to or interference in the relationship is regularly cited as a cause of conflict.

> For 3 years my mother has refused to see my girlfriend because she's not Jewish, and every time I go to my parents' home to visit, my girlfriend and I get into a big fight.

What all the couples have in common is their difficulty communicating their ethnic and religious predicament, often because it has become the symptom around which other issues in the relationship have become crystallized.

CLARIFYING THE EMOTIONAL AND INTERPERSONAL CONTEXT

In working with interfaith couples it is essential to distinguish between the content of the cultural material that is presented and the emotional dynamics surrounding it. Often, the process of therapy necessitates dealing with the latter before addressing the content itself. In other words, it is not initially the content of differences that is central but rather the emotional and interpersonal context in which they occur.

Asking these questions during the initial phase of treatment will serve as a guide for future work and provide a better understanding of the problem and the pattern of transactions around it.

- What function does the problem serve in this relationship?
- Have the differences in the partner's ethnic and religious background been a source of chronic tension and anxiety since the beginning of their relationship?
- Does the couple communicate about the conflict openly, or do they hold secrets from each other, which erode their communication?
- Have they avoided dealing with their differences in order to maintain harmony? And if so, does this avoidance prevent them from coming together?
- Do they experience their being together as trespassing a group or family taboo? To what extent does this prevent them from committing to each other?
- How disruptive is the choice of the partner to the family's organization, and who in the family has the strongest reaction to that choice?
- Does the couple feel overwhelmed and helpless in the face of the sudden and unexpected eruption of visceral reactions to dimly understood religious feelings?

The trigger that causes couples to face their ethnic and religious differences can go off from the very moment of the en-

30 / *Jewish Intermarriage, Conversion and Outreach*

counter with "the other." Being faced with the differentness leads them to look at themselves in a different light. The trigger may also be life-cycle transitions—marriage, the birth of a child, or the death of a loved one.

The stress of dealing with the developmental crisis is compounded by the fact that it is usually during these transition times that we seek the familiarity of our cultural and religious traditions as frames of reference to guide us through the changes. Partners in a state of transition run into difficulty as they suddenly come up against their different interpretations, symbols, and rituals for managing shared life events. Long-dormant ethnic and religious feelings may explode at these critical moments in the relationship when one or both partners experience a reawakening of their cultural identity.

New couples in particular need the confidence to talk openly about their differences. They may fear that their cultural and religious differences will threaten their relationship. Often, new couples feel caught between remaining silent to ensure togetherness, yet at the same time desiring greater self-revelation, which will inevitably lead to the uncovering of tribal affinities and spiritual feelings.

> When we first met, religion didn't enter into our relationship. I told her early on that I was Jewish but that was it. I didn't want to expand on the issue too soon. But it's a difficult situation. I didn't want to wait too long once I saw we were getting serious, but I also wanted to be more sure about us as a couple first. After a few months, the more happy I was with her, the more anxious I became. So I finally told her that being Jewish was something very important for me and that I wanted to have a Jewish family.

To assess the latent emotional material underlying the manifest problem, it is useful to listen to how couples define their predicament and the language they use. The more condensed the language, the more undifferentiated the material, i.e., "this religion thing" or "the religion issue." Such objective-sounding phrases about matters that touch on one's emotional life are usually an indication of unspecified, unresolved complex issues in the life of an individual or couple. It is then the task of the therapist to probe the meaning of these phrases and expand the client's definition of the problem.

Otherwise very articulate individuals often find themselves at a loss for words when trying to communicate their cultural attachments to each other. It is as if this is a part of themselves that has remained rooted in childhood and not matured. Perhaps, one reason for this inarticulateness is that for many individuals, religious education ended at age 12, a crucial age of identity development. Consequently, they may lack a cognitive framework and vocabulary to understand and describe their powerful emotions.

Interfaith couples generally focus on the religious aspects of their differences and overlook the cultural ones. Yet, the Jewish-Gentile intermarriage also brings to light the meeting of two cultures in which "each affects, transforms, as well as illuminates the other" (Crohn, 1986, p. 20). Each spouse is the bearer of a world view that imbues such notions as gender roles, food, affection, child rearing, money, and health with a particular system of beliefs, norms, and behaviors.

Particularly important are the value differences between the two cultures with respect to attitudes toward marriage, i.e., the place of marriage in the family system and the nature of the boundaries around the married couple (McGill, 1983), gender roles and power distribution, response to stress and conflict, patterns of emotional expressiveness and communication (McGoldrick & Preto, 1984), and the meaning of autonomy and dependency.

In their initial description of religion, couples tend to focus primarily on its formalistic, ritualistic, and institutional aspects. Religious difference quickly becomes a church-synagogue dichotomy, a Christmas-Chanukah split, a me-you battle. When couples become thus polarized around their differences, the intensity and reactivity generated prevent them from dealing with any other issue in the relationship. They remain stuck around the all-consuming preoccupation of religious difference.

> We really get along very well—this is the only thing we can't deal with. It gets so emotional and explosive sometimes. It's as if we've gathered all our disagreements around this issue.

In polarized couples, there is an "all or nothing" quality to their transactions. Each thinks the solution to their problem as a couple lies in the other person changing. They exert enormous pressure on each other to give in. Religious beliefs and cultural attachments become the arsenal of each partner caught in a system of mutual repression. Yet, by defocusing the cultural issue and working on the emotional processes that produce the extreme reactions, one can affect the rigidity and intensity in the couple (Friedman, 1982).

The following are examples of a variety of typical configurations.

> Mike and Susan have decided to get married. They have chosen to have a Jewish home and to raise their children in the Jewish faith. They have spoken about the possibility of Susan converting to Judaism. Mike insists on Susan converting before the wedding so that "they can be defined as a Jewish family from the start." Susan maintains that she has agreed to raise her children as Jews and that, if she were to consider conversion, she would want to do it when she felt ready. Mike does not trust Susan to follow through on her commitment. Susan feels that he is pressuring her and that he does not trust her. At this point they have called off the wedding and have come to seek help. When asked about how things would be if Susan were to make the same request of Mike to convert, the couple acknowledges that the relationship would end. The secret knowledge that they both have is the fact that Mike has the power to break off the relationship. Issues of power and trust on both sides are being played out around a religious conflict. Susan

feels coerced and Mike fears her betrayal. The couple was able to work out its religious dilemma by first addressing the interpersonal dynamics that activated the conflict and threatened the relationship.

> John and Debbie have been dating for 3 years. John comes from a white, Anglo-Saxon family, which has been in the United States for seven generations. His family is very proud of their uninterrupted legacy. His father has even written a book about the topic. John was raised in the Episcopalian faith, and religion played an important role in his family until his parents divorced. Today John feels very disconnected from his family and his past.
>
> Debbie comes from a second-generation Jewish family that immigrated to the United States after World War II. Debbie carries the name of her maternal grandmother who perished in the Holocaust. Although they are talking about marriage in the coming year, Debbie finds herself incapable of introducing John to her parents.
>
> The couple initially sought help in dealing with their families and having both sets of relatives attend their wedding. They are caught up in a battle and are experiencing increasing tension in the relationship.
>
> In trying to sort out what is important to her with respect to her background and what she would like to maintain, Debbie finds herself unable to distinguish between her feelings and those of her parents. Debbie is an only child, and for her, marrying out is a betrayal of her survivor parents. Feelings of guilt abound. John feels that she continuously puts her parents ahead of him. Cultural issues and separation difficulties in the family of origin blend here, and loyalty for the group is intertwined with loyalty to the family. Implicit in her references to intermarriage as a threat to the survival of the Jewish people is the fear that intermarriage is a threat to the survival of Debbie's family structure.
>
> The initial focus of treatment is on expanding the couple's definition of the problem: enabling them to move beyond those condensed statements of their problem that obscure personal meaning. Next, working through the family of origin issues and helping Debbie separate from her family are pre-

32 / *Jewish Intermarriage, Conversion and Outreach*

liminary steps that must be taken before she can clarify her feelings about her Jewish identity. This clarification requires dealing with the loyalties that undermine the couple and create a clear boundary around them. John can help Debbie in separating from her family. Debbie can help John reconnect with his. As the couple solidifies, they can begin to negotiate and make cultural choices for their marriage.

In the interfaith couple, culture and religion provide a ground on which the issues of autonomy and togetherness are being negotiated.

My religion is part of who I am. I can't separate one from the other. It's important for me not to lose that part.

We want to have one marriage and one religion in the home. Otherwise it's confusing for the children, and since mine isn't as important to me as hers, I don't feel I would be losing something important.

We wanted our kids to be exposed to both traditions. We didn't want to choose one over the other. But now if he takes the kids to church, I feel I have to take them to synagogue.

Religious conversion is a central issue in a significant minority of Jewish-Gentile intermarriages. It can happen that one partner (usually the Gentile partner) experiences a gradual shift of allegiance and a change in religious beliefs, thereby incorporating a new world view. This process is similar to a resident alien who, after years of residing in a foreign country, sharing its customs, and identifying with its cultural heroes and institutions, decides to adopt the nationality of that country. So it is that cultural content impresses itself in one's life.

This type of conversion is quite different from a conversion that takes place in an atmosphere of pressure, coercion, and anxiety. The latter conversion is more related to certain unstated needs for emotional togetherness than to religious beliefs or acculturation (Friedman, 1973).

He wants me to convert first and then he'll introduce me to his parents. It feels like this conversion has little to do with Judaism, and more with his expecting me to smooth things over between him and his father.

In this example, conversion is related to loyalty and subversion and not to philosophical orientation. In such situations, conversion is not an existential process but rather an interpersonal transaction intended to help the Jewish partner maintain his emotional position in his family of origin.

There is also a kind of cultural complementarity around autonomy and togetherness that takes place in Jewish-Gentile marriages. The Jewish partner, who often comes from a family that emphasizes cohesion and togetherness, is attracted to the Gentile partner, particularly one from an Anglo-Saxon background, whose family style encourages autonomy and independence. Reciprocally, the Gentile partner is attracted to what he or she perceives as the warmth and togetherness of the Jewish family. Seen in this light, the cross-cultural marriage is one in which partners are often attracted to the very cultural and familial traits that the other is trying to escape (Crohn, 1986). Ironically the other's family style often remains alien, and the very traits that initially attract become the source of tension later, especially in times of stress. Closeness then can feel intrusive and independence perceived as distance.

To uncover the ethnic and religious dynamics in the couple is to continuously sort out the content of the cultural material from the emotional processes that surround it. Only when the partners become more differentiated from their families can they also achieve "ethnic individuation," thereby enabling them to clarify the meaning and importance of their ethnic and religious identity.

MEANING AND IMPORTANCE OF ETHNIC AND RELIGIOUS IDENTITY

Just as it is important to sort out the cultural material from the emotional processes that affect it, it is also important to identify and work with the identity issues raised in an intermarriage.

Ethnic identity is based on a continuous process of self-definition in relation to one's group. The major feature of the relationship between the individual and the group is the sense of belonging and historical continuity, which relies on the assumption of similarity and interdependence (Herman, 1974). How important the sense of belonging to an ethnic group is for one's overall self-identity varies from person to person. The core of one's ethnic and religious experience is located in the family. Thus, one's earliest associations and memories of one's culture concern images of the family and identification with one's parents. It is apparent then that primary family issues are often expressed in conflicts over ethnic identity.

Culture is an important determinant of family life, but conversely, families choose from their culture those customs and beliefs that support the family's relational style (Friedman, 1982). In families in which the emotional intensity is particularly high, there is a tendency to confuse feelings about one's ethnicity with feelings about one's family. A kind of blending follows in which undesired traits in the family are attributed to the culture.

Intermarriage presents a whole range of transactions around one's ethnicity. These vary, depending on how central or peripheral ethnicity is to the individual's life and personality. For some, marrying outside their faith or ethnic group can represent an escape from their ethnic background. For others it is a vehicle for separation from their families of origin; they can compensate or change what is disliked in the family and perceived as culturally bound. For others, intermarriage holds out an opportunity to readjust the undesired characteristics that they attribute to their ethnic background by associating with another cultural group (McGoldrick & Preto, 1984). In this way intermarriage may be seen as an attempt to establish complementarity via culture. Paradoxically, it sometimes offers the individual an opportunity to reaffirm his or her ethnic identity and to make creative personal changes. Intermarriage highlights the discontinuity with one's past and cultural roots. It can disrupt family patterns and connections, yet its very diversity also opens the system to new patterns, connections, and creative changes (McGoldrick & Preto, 1984).

Intermarriage challenges one's ethnic and religious identity. It forces both partners to clarify the meaning and importance of their respective backgrounds. It compels an understanding of their feelings about their ethnic identity and its relation to their overall sense of self, as well as confrontation with their internalized negative stereotypes and ethnic ambivalences. It calls forth an examination of their prejudices and bigoted thinking, as well as the attractions and pulls toward the partner's background. It requires that the partners differentiate from their parents with respect to their ethnic and religious identities and achieve a kind of ethnic individuation that allows them to make a broader range of independent and mature choices.

It is in the meeting with the "other" that one is brought to examine one's self.

To meet Don was a real eye-opener for me. I grew up in an Orthodox home and community and went to an Orthodox school. Until I went to college I never knew anyone but Jews. I knew there was a whole world out there and I thought that in order to enter it I had to shed my Jewishness. Being with Don has opened the door of America for me. I learned about his religion and realized that Christians are not all out there to hunt after the Jews. In a strange way the world has become a safer place for me. I can be a Jew in a world with non-Jews. I want to maintain my Jewishness and have a Jewish family, but not the way it was when I grew up and I also want there to be room for Don's heritage. I don't know how we will do that.

Members of any ethnic group experience cultural conflict when they attempt to mediate between the values of their traditional culture and those of the dominant

34 / *Jewish Intermarriage, Conversion and Outreach*

culture. Thus, ambivalence is a natural emotional condition for most members of any minority. In the mixed couple, one partner can bring the other to confront his or her ethnic ambivalence.

> I grew up in a Catholic family and went to Catholic school for 12 years. I never liked it. It was dogmatic and no questions allowed. I knew I wanted a spiritual place, but I didn't feel I belonged in church. When I met Dan he was fairly disconnected from his Jewishness. On the other hand, I became very interested in Judaism. I kept wanting him to take me to synagogue and to show me the rituals. I started to take classes and learn about Judaism, and Dan seemed bothered by it. In a way he slowly became interested in his background through me. I knew he felt more strongly about his Jewishness than he admitted. I wanted to belong to his group, which he was ambivalent about.

Jews, for whom Jewishness is a powerful sentimental attachment to the past, who have a strong but unintegrated feeling of being Jewish, often feel that their Jewishness, precisely because it is so unintegrated, could easily be taken away from them. It lacks an active expression in their lives and tends to express itself as a deep sense of vulnerability (Wasserman, 1988). Their sense of Jewishness is a strong, but passive and often unarticulated group loyalty, which is unbalanced by the situation of intermarriage. Intermarriage raises both the specter of betrayal of the group and its history and the fear of loss.

The reaction of Steve, in the following vignette, stems more from the fear of being overwhelmed by Tracy's "gentileness." In his confusion, Steve is pressuring Tracy to commit herself to a Jewish way of life in an attempt to maintain his fragile sense of Jewishness.

> *Steve:* I feel very strongly about being Jewish. I can't explain it. I am not religious, but I do want to raise my children Jewish.

> *Tracy:* Why should I give up my Christian beliefs and practices when you don't follow

your religion? I have a feeling that Judaism is being forced upon me with no respect for my own cultural beliefs and how important my heritage is to me. In your desire to have a Jewish home, you are not ready to accept any other influence. Why is the non-Jewish partner supposed to bend completely?

> *Steve:* I know it does not make sense to you. Why this gut reaction, "carry on the religion," when I don't even believe in God? But I feel very strongly about the history of my people and there is a part of me that feels like I would be abandoning the dead.

In his ambivalence, Steve transmits a number of mixed messages. Although he wants to raise his children Jewishly, he does not really want Tracy to convert and become like him.

> Be like me but not too much. Be acceptable to my parents but remain acceptable to me. Convert, but I don't want you to become too Jewish.

She is willing to consider conversion, but he maintains that he is not religious and that being Jewish is a feeling that cannot be acquired through conversion. Yet, he wants her to alleviate his guilt and puts her in charge of his ethnic continuity. Her feeling of resentment stems from the one-sided commitment to have a dominant religion in the family, which is his and for which he does not take responsibility.

In such situations, the Gentile partner often becomes resentful and fearful of the pressure, and the issue becomes whether to submit or rebel, rather than to examine feelings about his or her own background and about Judaism.

To create change in such an entangled situation, it is necessary to shift the focus from changing the other to defining oneself. This can be achieved by engaging in a guided exploration of each partner's identity and helping them articulate this to their partner. When each partner becomes more secure in him- or herself, the

her becomes less threatening. With this
duction in anxiety, the partners can
come creative in their negotiation of the
ltural fabric of their family and the future
entity of their children.

Jewish identity is both an ethnic and
ligious identity. For Jews who are not
ligious, it is often difficult to explain the
otion of peoplehood and its emotional
mplications. Yet, their conflict often
enters around the sense of betraying their
eople. In contrast, the Gentile partner
ees Judaism solely as a religion. The Gen-
ile partner often fears jeopardizing the soul
of the child if the child is not baptized.

Children often represent a blank screen
against which the partners can project
their ethnic and religious differences that
they are loath to confront within themselves. Because children symbolize the
continuity of the family, its values, and
traditions, they bring into focus the
differences of the partners' background—
the challenge of transforming two cultures
into one.

In the intermarried family, children
bring to the fore a host of questions.

> I don't know why after not caring about my
> Jewishness for years, I suddenly want to pass
> my heritage onto my children.

> If the children are brought up with the
> same religion as the mother and the father
> remains a different religion, how does the
> father maintain his religious independence
> but also become a vital part of that aspect
> of our family life?

> If you say we'll teach the kids about both
> religions, that's pretending religions are
> academic, not emotional. If you want your
> child to share your convictions but not
> negate your partner's, how do you educate
> your kids?

> I am concerned that the children will deny
> my values because I am not Jewish.

In particular, holidays reawaken one's
connectedness to rituals and childhood
memories. Religion, its meaning, and
linkages to the family become especially
significant at holidays. The so-called
December dilemma is a focal point in the
Jewish-Gentile couple. More than any
other time, it brings into play the differences between Gentile and Jew, majority
and minority, and places an individual
relationship into a larger historical context.

> I am Christian but always considered myself
> an atheist. David is Jewish and also con-
> siders himself an atheist. Religion is really
> not an issue in our life. But when Christmas
> comes, I feel like I am standing on the side-
> lines. I want to participate in the holiday
> with my partner, but am unable to because
> he suddenly becomes Jewish at Christmas.
> He opposes any symbols of my Christianity,
> even though for me it is not religion, but
> tradition, family, and a feeling of belong-
> ing. I not only feel an alienation from my
> family, but I feel very distanced from
> David. I've become a minority in my own
> tradition.

As partners become clearer and more
secure in who they are they can be clearer
about if and how to explore and negotiate
the two worlds to create one of their own.

EXPLORING AND NEGOTIATING DIFFERENCE

Religion and culture are all-encompassing
phenomena. They comprise the intellectual and the emotional, the conscious and
the unconscious, the irrational, the visceral,
and the tribal. Their experience is syn-
thetic—at once physical and sensual, taste,
and smell. Once the partners have become
clear and more secure in their own identities, it is then the task of the therapist to
help the couple explore and negotiate
their two worlds and create their own
unique one for their family. Or else they
may decide to go their separate ways.

In the mutual exploration, the partners
become anthropologists of each other's
cultures and archaeologists of their own
history. A number of structured exercises
enable the couple to look at their childhood memories associated with their ethnic

and religious upbringing. Such exercises draw out the ethnic identity lifeline of the family, patterns of communication around religion, forms of affiliation and observance, and the ebb and flow of ethnic involvement.

In doing the exercises the partners compare and contrast the parental messages they received about their own group and its religion, as well as about their partner's group and religion. They also examine the people and events that strongly influenced their ethnic identity. They discuss their views and experiences of the restrictions and supports they have found in their respective traditions. They establish the commonalities in their values that will serve as a foundation for creating a new world for their family, allowing them to bridge their differences. It is this simultaneous process of deconstruction and conservation in dealing with the past that underlies the potential for change.

The couple negotiates choices and strategies for such issues as planning the wedding, determining the extent of involvement with their families, celebrating holidays, planning their children's religious upbringing, or deciding whether to affiliate formally with any religion. Three main strategies emerge—conversion, integration, and rejection. In the first the couple responds to the differences by having one partner convert to the other's religion. In the second the couple creates their own blending of what they have chosen as important from their backgrounds. In the third, they relinquish any involvement with tradition and even reject all forms of ethnic and religious group identification (Mayer, 1985).

Most common among intermarried couples is the integrationist approach in which observance, ritual, and celebration enhance the richness and pleasure of family life. More than a blending, it is often the recognition of continuity, where each one grants limited territorial rights for their respective heritages in a jointly shared home (Mayer, 1985).

Ours is an open society in which we enjoy wide exposure to members of other groups in school, at work, and with friends. We are at the end of a long process in which the marital pact has been stripped of the old rules of alliance and is legitimized by the feeling of love. Although the wedding is a public event, a marriage is made at the initiative of individuals and is a private affair at the center of which lies the notion of intimacy. In the modern ideology of intimacy, the spouses stand in the center of the marriage, replacing the extended family and culture. Society has chosen Romeo and Juliet over the Montagues and the Capulets.

Intermarriage points to the continuous dialectic between distinctiveness and similarity. It poses the question of how to reconcile mutual love with the love for one's tradition. Expectations of mutual self-revelation lead to the disclosure of ethnic and religious differences. Yet in our embrace of the victory of love over tradition, we have come to overlook the persistence of meaning, symbols, and attachments to our ancestral heritage. The integration of these divergent forces is a crucial task of the intermarried couple as well as of family therapy as it enhances the capacity of these couples for more effective communication and greater intimacy.

REFERENCES

Bowen, M. (1978). *Family therapy in clinical practice*. New York: Jason Aronson.

Carter E. A., & McGoldrick, M. (Eds). (1982). *The family life cycle: A framework for family therapy*. New York: Gardner.

Cowan, P. & R. (1987). *Mixed blessings: Marriage between Jews and Christians*. New York: Doubleday.

Crohn, J. (1986). *Ethnic identity and marital conflict: Jews, Italians, and WASPs*. New York: American Jewish Committee.

Friedman, E. H. (1973, May). Conversion, love and togetherness. *Reconstructionist, 39,* 4.

Friedman, E. H. (1982). The myth of the shiksa: A study in cultural camouflage. In M. McGoldrick, et al. (Eds.). *Ethnicity and family therapy*. New York: Guilford.

Ethnocultural Factors / 37

Herman, S. (1974, November). *The components of Jewish identity: A psychological analysis.* Working paper prepared for the American Jewish Committee Colloquium on Jewish Education and Jewish Identity, New York.

Kelman, H. (1974, November). *The place of Jewish identity in the development of personal identity.* Working paper prepared for the AJC Colloquium on Jewish Education and Jewish Identity, New York.

Klein, J. (1980). *Jewish identity and self-esteem: Healing wounds through ethnotherapy.* New York: American Jewish Committee.

Mayer, E. (1985). *Love and tradition: Marriage between Jews and Christians.* New York: Plenum Publishing Company.

McGill, D., & Pearce, J. K. (1982). British families. In M. McGoldrick, et al. (Eds.). *Ethnicity and family therapy.* New York: Guilford.

McGoldrick, M., & Preto, N. G., (1984). Ethnic intermarriage: Implications for therapy. *Family Process, 37*(3), 347–364.

Minuchin, S., & Fishman, C. (1981). *Family therapy techniques.* Cambridge, MA: Harvard University Press.

Weidman Schneider, S. (1989). *Intermarriage. The challenge of living with differences between Christians and Jews.* New York: Free Press.

Wasserman, M. (1988, Fall). Outreach to interfaith couples: Two conceptual models. *Conservative Judaism, 41,* 1.

INTERMARRIAGE IN CONTEXT

A note to facilitators:

The diagram on the previous page is a teaching tool that will be helpful in explaining the notion that couples do not exist in a vacuum, despite their love, commitment, and resolve to find solutions to problems that arise. It may be photo copied for distribution as a handout or redrawn on a blackboard or large pad.

To explain the diagram, begin at the inner circle (couple) and move outward. A couple's immediate social context begins with their families and grows broader to include friends and community. The "broader national/world community" circle is especially important for Jews, and provides an opportunity to explain the concept of K'lal Yisrael and Jewish peoplehood. The outermost circle of philosophical issues reflects some of the primary concepts that arise in relation to intermarriage and the concern that future generations will have a greatly reduced Jewish population.

You will note that "Non-Jewish religious/existential/philosophical issues" are not specified. They have been omitted because we cannot assume that we can speak for non-Jews. Ask your group if they believe that there are similar issues for non-Jews which affect the issue of intermarriage. Are they the same for all non-Jews? Are they related to religion? Culture? Majority/minority status? What are they (be specific)? Are there other Jewish issues that the group would add?

Invite participants to personalize the diagram. How do they relate currently to each circle? Do they expect that this will always be the case? Do they relate differently from their partner? Does their partner understand their own context fully? What parts of the diagram would they change?

INTERMARRIAGE IN CONTEXT

JEWISH

RELIGIOUS/EXISTENTIAL/PHILOSOPHICAL ISSUES
(which include: GOD, Who is a Jew, Holocaust
the connectedness of generations—L'Dor Vador, etc.)

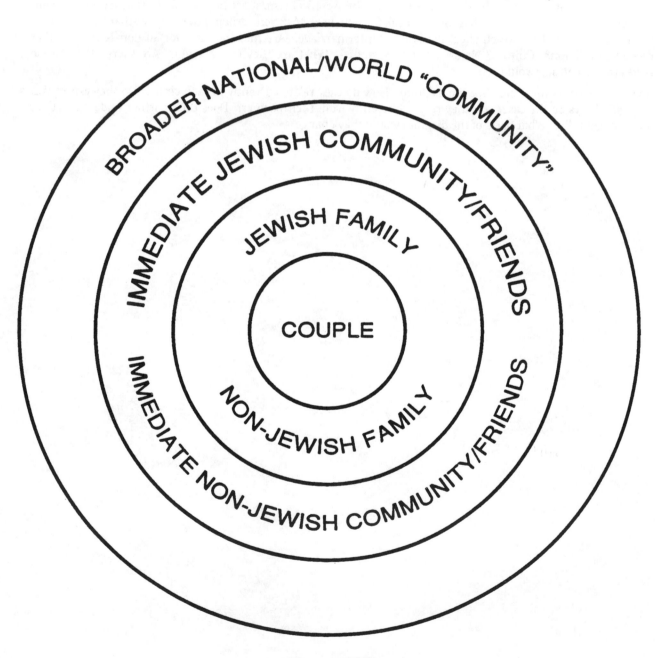

BROADER NATIONAL/WORLD "COMMUNITY"

IMMEDIATE JEWISH COMMUNITY/FRIENDS

JEWISH FAMILY

COUPLE

NON-JEWISH FAMILY

IMMEDIATE NON-JEWISH COMMUNITY/FRIENDS

NON-JEWISH

RELIGIOUS/EXISTENTIAL/PHILOSOPHICAL ISSUES

APPENDIX B:

SELECTED BIBLIOGRAPHY

Note to facilitators: The following suggested resources are only a sampling of the various publications that are available. We have selected materials which are easily accessible and provide the basic background information needed for the discussions that may take place as you work with interfaith couples.

BASIC JUDAISM

Bial, Morrison D. *Liberal Judaism at Home: The Practices of Modern Reform Judaism.* Revised edition. Union of American Hebrew Congregations, 1971.

Kertzer, Morris. *What Is a Jew?.* Collier, 1973.

Knobel, Peter, ed. *Gates of the Seasons.* Central Conference of American Rabbis, 1983..

Kukoff, Lydia and Stephen J.Einstein. *Every Person's Guide to Judaism.* Union of American Hebrew Congregations, 1989.

Maslin, Simeon J., ed. *Gates of Mitzvah.* Central Conference of American Rabbis, 1979.

Steinberg, Milton. *Basic Judaism.* Harcourt Brace Jovanovich, 1947.

Syme, Daniel B. *The Jewish Home.* Union of American Hebrew Congregations, 1988.

Telushkin, Joseph. *Jewish Literacy: The Most Important Things to Know About The Jewish Religion, Its People and Its History.* Morrow, 1991.

CHILDREARING

Bial, Morrison D. *Your Jewish Child.* Union of American Hebrew Congregations, 1978.

Diamant, Anita and Howard Cooper. *Living a Jewish Life: A Guide for Starting, Learning, Celebrating, and Parenting.* Harper Perennial, 1991.

Kushner, Harold. *When Children Ask About God.* Reconstructionist Press, 1971.

Reuben, Steven Carr. *Raising Jewish Children in a Contemporary World*, Prima, 1992.

CHRISTIANITY AND JUDASISM

Goldberg, Michael. *Jews and Christians: Getting Our Stories Straight.* Abingdon Press, 1985.

Jacob, Walter. *Christianity Through Jewish Eyes – The Quest for Common Ground.* KTAV, 1979.

Sandmel, Samuel. *We Jews and Jesus.* Oxford University Press, 1973.

Silver, Abba Hillel. *Where Judaism Differs.* Collier Books, 1987.

Weiss-Rosmarin, Trude. *Judaism and Christianity: The Differences.* Jonathan David, 1965.

CONVERSION AND INTERMARRIAGE

Belin, David. *Why Choose Judaism: New Dimensions of Jewish Outreach.* Union of American Hebrew Congregations, 1984.

Compass: New Directions in Jewish Education. "Interfaith Marriages." Union of American Hebrew Congregations, 1985.

Cowan, Paul with Rachel Cowan. *Mixed Blessings: Marriage Between Jews and Christians.* Doubleday, 1987.

Friedman, Edwin H. "The Myth of the Shiksa" in *Ethnicity and Family Therapy.* Guilford Press, 1982.

Goodman-Malamuth, Leslie and Robin Margolis. *Between Two Worlds: Choices for Grown Children of Jewish-*

Christian Intermarriage. Pocket Books, 1992.

Jacobs, Sidney and Betty. *122 Clues For Jews Whose Children Intermarry.* Jacobs Ladder Publications, 1988.

Kukoff, Lydia. *Choosing Judaism.* Union of American Hebrew Congregations, 1981.

Mayer, Egon. *Love and Tradition: Marriage Between Jews and Christians.* Plenum Press, 1985.

Mayer, Egon and Amy Avgar. *Conversion Among the Intermarried: Choosing to Become Jewish.* American Jewish Committee, 1987.

Petsonk, Judy and Jim Remsen. *The Intermarriage Handbook: A Guide for Jews and Christians.* William Morrow, 1988.

Reuben, Steven Carr. *A Guide to Interfaith Marriage: But How Will You Raise Your Children.* Pocket Books, 1987.

Sandmel, Samuel. *When A Jew and Christian Marry.* Fortress Press, 1977.

GENERAL REFERENCES - Counseling:

Egon, Girard. *Skilled Helper.* Brooks Cole Publishers, 1975.

Hackney, Harold and Sherilyn Nye. *Counseling Strategies and Objectives.* Prentice-Hall

Peterson, C.W. *Relationship Counseling and Psychotherapy.* Harper and Row.

GENERAL REFERENCES - Jewish:

Encyclopedia Judaica (selected subject headings).

Freehof, Solomon B., ed. *Today's Reform Responsa.* Hebrew Union College Press, 1990.

Jacobs, L. *The Book of Jewish Belief.* Behrman House,

Keeping Posted, available from the Department of Education, Union of American Hebrew Congregations, New York.

America:
"1873, 1973, 2073: A Glimpse into the Jewish Community"
"A Century of German Jewish Immigration"
"The Golden Land (Eastern European Immigration)"

Concepts:
"Tzedakah"
"Jewish Symbols"
"Who Is A Jew?"

Ethics, Law and Issues:
"Jewish Law"
"A Time to be Born...A Time to Die"
"Why Do the Innocent Suffer?"

Holocaust:
"Aspects of the Holocaust"
"Righteous Gentiles"

Israel and Zionism:
"Zionism" Jerusalem: Why are the Nations in an Uproar? (The importance of Jerusalem)"
"The Covenant (The people, the land)"
"Israel-Diaspora"

Jewish Movements:
"The Chasid"
"What is Reform?"
"Orthodox Judaism"

"Conservative Judaism"
"Reconstructionist Judaism"
"The Sephardim"

Judaism and Christianity:
"The Messiah Idea, False Messiah, Modern Pied Pipers"
"Judaism and Christianity: Parting of the Ways"
"A Missionary Faith? (Shall Jews seek converts?)"

Love, Marriage, Family:
"The Jewish Family: Continuity and Change"
"Love, Marriage, Intermarriage"
"Peace in the Home"

Traditional Texts and Holidays:
"The Hebrew Bible"
"About Prayer and Prayerbooks"
"The Mishnah"
"Passover Haggadah"
"Roots of Chanukah"
"Midrash (Folk tales and folklore)"
"The Sabbath"
"Understanding the Bible"
"The Harvest Festivals"

Theology and Mysticism:
"Jewish View of God"
"Jewish Mysticism"

Klein, Isaac. *A Guide to Jewish Religious Practices.* Jewish Theological Seminary, 1979.

Latner, Helen. *The Book of Modern Jewish Etiquette.* Schocken Books, 1981

Questions and Reform Jewish Answers. CCAR Press, 1992.

Samuel, Edith. *Your Jewish Lexicon.* Union of American Hebrew Congregations, 1982.

HISTORY

Bamberger, Bernard J. *The Story of Judaism.* Schocken, 1964.

Dimont, Max I. *Jews, God and History.* Signet, 1962.

Margolis, Max L. and Alexander Marx. *A History of the Jewish People.* Atheneum, 1977.

Roth, Cecil. *A History of the Jews: From the Earliest Times Through the Six Day War.* Revised edition. Schocken, 1964.

Sacher, Howard M. *The Course of Modern Jewish History.* Dell, 1977.

Seltzer, Robert M. *Jewish People, Jewish Thought: The Jewish Experience in History.* Macmillan, 1980.

HOLIDAYS, FESTIVALS AND THE SABBATH

Come, Let Us Welcome Shabbat. Union of American Hebrew Congregations, 1989.

Gates of Shabbat. Central Conference of American Rabbis, 1991.

Knobel, Peter, ed. *Gates of the Seasons.* Central Conference of American Rabbis, 1983.

Seigel, Richard, Michael Strassfeld and Sharon Strassfeld. *The Jewish Catalogue, Volume I.* Jewish Publications Society, 1973.

Syme, Daniel B. *The Jewish Home.* Union of American Hebrew Congregations, 1988.

HOLOCAUST

Altshuler, David A. A young reader's version of *Hitler's War Against the Jews:* 1935-1945. by Lucy S. Dawidowicz. Behrman House.

Spiegelman, Art. *Maus II: And Here My Troubles Began.* Pantheon Books, 1991.

Wiesel, Elie. *Night.* Avon, 1972.

ISRAEL

Hertzberg, Arthur, ed. *The Zionist Idea.* Atheneum, 1959.

Sachar, Howard M. *A History of Israel: From the Rise of Zionism to Our Time.* Knopf, 1979.

THEOLOGY

Borowitz, Eugene. *Liberal Judaism.* Union of American Hebrew Congregations, 1984.

Schulweis, Harold. *In God's Mirror.* KTAV, 1990.

Syme, Daniel B. and Rifat Sonsino. *Finding God.* Union of American Hebrew Congregations, 1986.

UAHC OUTREACH PUBLICATIONS

Commission on Reform Jewish Outreach. *Defining the Role of The Non-Jew In The Synagogue: A Resource for Congregations.* Union of American Hebrew Congregations, 1989.

____ . *Jewish Parents of Intgermarried Couples: A Guide for Facilitators.* Union of American Hebrew Congregations, 1987.

___. *Outreach And The Changing Reform Jewish Community: Creating an Agenda for Our Future.* Union of American Hebrew Congregations, 1989.

____. *Reaching Adolescents: Interdating, Intermarriage, and Jewish Identity.* Union of American Hebrew Congregations, 1990.

___. *Reform Jewish Outreach: The Idea Book.* Union of American Hebrew Congregations, 1988.

___. *To See The World Through Jewish Eyes: Guidelines for Outreach Education.* Union of American Hebrew Congregations, 1986.

___. *Working With Interfaith Couples: A Guide for Facilitators.* Union of American Hebrew Congregations, 1992.

Einstein, Stephen J. and Lydia Kukoff. *Every Person's Guide to Judaism.* Union of American Hebrew Congregations, 1989.

____. *Introduction To Judaism: A Course Outline and Student's Resource Book.* Union of American Hebrew Congregations, 1983.

Seltzer, Sandford. *Jews And Non-Jews: Falling in Love.* Union of American Hebrew Congregations, 1976.

___. *Jews And Non-Jews: Getting Married.* Union of American Hebrew Congregations, 1984.

Pamphlets (Available from your Regional Outreach Coordinator.)

Belin, David. *What Judaism Offers For You: A Reform Perspective.* Union of American Hebrew Congregations, 1991.

Inviting Someone You Love to Become a Jew. Union of American Hebrew Congregations, 1991.

What Is Reform Jewish Outreach? Union of American Hebrew Congregations, 1991.

Films

Choosing Judaism: Some Personal Perspectives (A Videocassete). Union of American Congregations TV and Film Institute.

Intermarriage: When Love Meets Tradition/This Great Difference. Direct Cinema Ltd., P.O. Box 69799, Los Angeles, CA 90069.

Discussion Guide for the above film available through the National Outreach Office, Union of American Hebrew Congregations.

JEWISH PERIODICALS

Reform Judaism
quarterly magazine
Union of American Hebrew Congregations
838 Fifth Avenue, New York, NY 10021
(212) 249-0100

Moment
a bimonthly magazine
Subscription Services: P.O. Box 7028, Red Oak, IA 51591
1-800-777-1005

Sh'ma
a bi-weekly journal
Box 567, Port Washington, NY 11050
FAX: 516-767-9315

APPENDIX C:

WHAT IS REFORM JEWISH OUTREACH?

WHAT IS REFORM JEWISH OUTREACH?

Reform Jewish Outreach is a program which aims to:

• Welcome those who seek to investigate Judaism;

• Integrate Jews-by-Choice fully into the Jewish Community;

• Encourage intermarried couples to affiliate with a congregation and to meet the needs of those already in the congregation. Outreach seeks to enable intermarried couples to explore, study and understand Judaism, thereby providing an atmosphere of support in which a comfortable relationship with Judaism can be fostered;

• Educate and sensitize the Jewish community to be receptive to new Jews-by-Choice and intermarried couples;

• Encourage people to make Jewish choices in their lives through special discussion groups, community support, adult education and availability of Jewish resources;

• Assist young people in strengthening their Jewish identity and in examining the implications of interdating and intermarriage for themselves.

WHAT IS THE HISTORY OF THE OUTREACH PROGRAM?

On December 2, 1978, Rabbi Alexander Schindler, President of the Union of American Hebrew Congregations, called upon the Board of Trustees to establish a program of Outreach which would develop responses to the needs of individuals converting to Judaism, intermarried couples, children of intermarriages and those interested in learning about Judaism. The UAHC Trustees unanimously adopted a resolution calling for the study and development of a program of Reform Jewish Outreach and endorsed the creation of a Joint Task Force with the Central Conference of American Rabbis. David Belin was named Chairperson and Rabbi Max Shapiro Co-Chairperson, followed by Rabbi Sheldon Zimmerman. This Task Force presented a report to the 1981 UAHC General Assembly, which then adopted five resolutions calling for a comprehensive program of Reform Jewish Outreach.

(For a detailed report of the Task Force, see "A Summary of the Report of the UAHC/CCAR Joint Task Force on Reform Jewish Outreach," August 1981.)

In 1983, the Task Force became a Joint UAHC/CCAR Commission on Reform Jewish Outreach with a mandate to develop programming, resources and materials for the various Outreach target populations. Lydia Kukoff was named Commission Director, David Belin continued as Chairperson, and Rabbi Steven Foster was named Co-Chairperson. In 1988, Mel Merians was named Chairperson, and Rabbi Leslie Gutterman was named Co-Chairperson. In 1991, Harris Gilbert was named Chairperson, Dru Greenwood was named Director and Rabbi Leslie Gutterman continued as Co-Chairperson.

WHERE IS OUTREACH TODAY?

The program has expanded and currently includes programming for:

• Jews-by-Choice

• Those interested in choosing Judaism

• Intermarried couples and couples contemplating intermarriage

• Children of intermarried couples

• Parents of intermarried couples

• Jewish youth on interdating, intermarriage and Jewish identity

• Inreach to born Jews on issues relating to Jewish identity, attitudes toward the changing Jewish Community, and policy for defining the role of non-Jews in the synagogue.

The goals of Outreach are implemented on many levels. The national UAHC/CCAR Commission on Reform Jewish Outreach meets annually and its Executive Committee meets three times a year to evaluate progress and set policy. Each UAHC Region has a Regional Outreach Committee whose members work closely with the regional Outreach Coordinator to increase awareness of Outreach and disseminate a broad range of programs throughout the region. The Regional Chair and Co-chair sit on the national Commission. In addition, many congregations have Outreach Committees whose task it is to plan and carry out a variety of Outreach programs tailored to meet local needs.

The Outreach Staff currently includes the Director, Dru Greenwood, and Outreach Coordinators in every UAHC region. Coordinators staff the Regional Outreach Committee and serve as resources for congregations in their region, working closely with professional staff and Outreach committees to design and implement an Outreach program suitable for each congregation. Coordinators also administer regional and sub-regional programs such as Introduction to Judaism, " Times and Seasons", and various follow-up programs for intermarried couples and Jews-by-Choice.

WHAT PROGRAMS DOES OUTREACH OFFER FOR THOSE CONTEMPLATING CONVERSION TO JUDAISM AS WELL AS FOR THOSE WHO ARE INTERESTED IN LEARNING MORE ABOUT JUDAISM?

Introduction to Judaism classes are offered on both the community and congregational levels. The main focus of the class is basic Judaism, including holidays, life cycle events, history, theology and Hebrew. Students learn what it means to live a Jewish life and how to begin to practice Judaism. This program may include a psycho-social component which deals with the personal implications of choosing Judaism. A basic curriculum, as well as material on conversion, may be found in the *Introduction to Judaism* Resource Book and Teacher's Guide, available from the UAHC Press.

Post-introduction programs and various workshops and discussion groups are also offered. One of our hopes is that participants in these groups will integrate fully into temple life and take advantage of the many educational, social and worship opportunities in their own temples. Some congregations offer a series of programs designed to help new Jews-by-Choice become integrated into the Jewish community. The Programs often include discussion groups, workshops, study sessions and Shabbatonim. Program ideas may be found in *The Idea Book*, available from the UAHC Press.

WHAT PROGRAMS DOES OUTREACH OFFER FOR INTERMARRIED COUPLES AND COUPLES CONTEMPLATING INTERMARRIAGE?

Many congregations offer a variety of programs for affiliated and/or unaffiliated intermarried couples and their children.

"Times and Seasons: A Jewish Perspective for Intermarried Couples" is one program which was created in response to the needs of the intermarried, to serve as the critical first step taken by unaffiliated intermarried couples seeking to explore Judaism in the context of differences in their backgrounds.

This eight-week discussion group, like other programs for interfaith couples is designed to clarify the Jewish partner's feelings about Judaism and to provide the non-Jewish partner with a greater understanding of Judaism and the Jewish community. Relevant personal issues discussed include: religious involvement while growing up, the religious and cultural differences each partner confronts in the relationship with each other and with extended family, holiday celebrations, and each couple's concerns about the religious upbringing of their children.

Although the programs are offered from a Jewish perspective, there is no attempt to convert the non-Jewish partner. The programs, however, do help participants to articulate the differences between Judaism and Christianity. We believe that understanding these differences will allow fuller communication between partners and a more secure base for decision-making for the couple. Facilitators have been trained by Outreach staff to lead these groups. A complete guide to the programs for interfaith couples, *Working With Interfaith Couples: A Jewish Perspective: A Guide for Facilitators,* is available from the UAHC Press.

WHAT PROGRAM HAS OUTREACH CREATED TO ASSIST RELIGIOUS SCHOOL TEACHERS, CANTORS, AND RABBIS IN DEVELOPING A SENSITIVITY TO THE NEEDS OF CHILDREN WHO HAVE NON-JEWISH RELATIVES?

The William and Frances Schuster *Guidelines for Outreach Education* reflect the cooperative effort of the UAHC Department of Religious Education and the Joint Commission on Outreach. The Guidelines contain three basic sections:

1) A statement of background and goals;

2) A faculty workshop to:

•Provide background information about Reform Jewish Outreach,

•Articulate some of the needs of children who have non-Jewish relatives,

•Help congregational and professional leadership clarify their feelings regarding Outreach-related issues and policies,

•Explore scenarios and strategies for dealing with various related situations which arise in the classroom;

3) A suggested approach to dealing with Outreach-related issues through the religious school curriculum.

Currently, the regional Outreach staff and the Department for Religious Education staff are available to assist with the faculty workshop.

WHAT PROGRAMS DOES OUTREACH OFFER FOR THE JEWISH PARENTS OF INTERMARRIED COUPLES?

Jewish parents of intermarried couples or couples contemplating intermarriage are one of the most accessible Outreach populations. Yet these parents often report feeling isolated within the very community that they have been a part of for so long.

The goals of the discussion groups for parents are:

• To provide participants with a non-judgmental, supportive setting in which they can meet with others sharing similar concerns;

• To provide participants with an opportunity to discuss the impact of their child's interfaith relationship on their family and to develop constructive responses to various family dilemmas that arise;

• To communicate the philosophy and objectives of Reform Jewish Outreach;

• To acquaint participants with existing Outreach programs in their own community;

• To provide participants with the clear message that the Reform Jewish community seeks to continue to reach out to them, their children and their grandchildren.

These groups are led by trained facilitators, many of whom have been trained at regional Outreach training sessions. A complete guide to the program, *Jewish Parents of Intermarried Couples: A Guide for Facilitators,* is available from the UAHC Press.

WHAT PROGRAMS DOES OUTREACH OFFER FOR REFORM JEWISH YOUTH?

One of our goals is to assist young people in examining the implications of interdating and intermarriage for themselves as well as for the future of the Jewish people. We encourage our youth to explore and strengthen their Jewish identity so that they will be advocates for Judaism in all their relationships.

A number of programs have been created for use in a variety of settings. Several of them are highlighted in *The Idea Book* and *Reaching Adolescents: Interdating, Intermarriage and Jewish Identity,* available from the UAHC Press.

HOW IS OUTREACH INVOLVED IN INREACH?

The ultimate goal of the Outreach program is to strengthen Judaism by helping individuals build their personal connectedness to Reform Judaism. We seek to assist born Jews and Jews-by-Choice in developing and enhancing their Jewish identity. The success of Outreach is dependent upon our ability to strengthen the bonds between members of the Jewish community and those who have chosen to associate with the community. These bonds are strengthened when every individual has a clear sense of his or her religious and ethnic identity. Outreach is not only about conversion and intermarriage. It is about being Jewish. Outreach enables us to look inward at who we are as Reform Jews and outward toward our changing community. Awareness of each enriches the other.

A valuable resource which enables congregations to explore the relationship between Outreach and Inreach is *Outreach and the Changing Reform Jewish Community: Creating An Agenda for Our Future—A Program Guide,* available from the UAHC Press.

HOW DOES OUTREACH PREPARE CLERGY, EDUCATORS, MENTAL HEALTH PROFESSIONALS AND LAY LEADERS TO WORK WITH THE VARIOUS OUTREACH POPULATIONS?

Facilitator training sessions for interfaith couples' groups and groups for the Jewish parents of intermarried couples are held on a regional basis. During the past few years, professional development courses have been offered through the Hebrew Union College-Jewish Institute of Religion in New York to prepare clergy for meeting the changing needs of the Jewish community. HUC-JIR students also participate in special one-day seminars. An intensive one-week Outreach internship, hosted by Temple Emanuel in Denver, Colorado provides students with an opportunity to experience and learn about the implementation of Outreach programs on a congregational level.

Defining the Role of the Non-Jew in the Synagogue: A Resource for Congregations (available from the UAHC Press) provides a framework for congregations to explore issues relating to membership, governance and ritual participation of non-Jews. Our goal is to preserve the integrity of Judaism while remaining open and sensitive to non-Jews who have made a commitment to raising children as Jews.

The Commission on Outreach offers on a regular basis workshops and presentations at various professional conferences, e.g. Central Conference of American Rabbis (CCAR), American Conference of Cantors (ACC), Coalition for the Advancement of Jewish Education (CAJE), and the American Psychological Association (APA). We also work closely with the CCAR Committee on Gerut.

APPENDIX D:

REFORM JEWISH OUTREACH STAFF

Dru Greenwood, Director

Rabbi Renni Altman, Task Force on the Unaffiliated

838 Fifth Avenue
New York, NY 10021-7064
(212) 249-0100

REGIONAL COORDINATORS

Canadian Council
Jessie Caryll
1520 Steeles Ave. West, Suite 113
Concord, Ontario
Canada L4K 2P7
(416) 660-4666

Great Lakes Council/
Chicago Federation
Mimi Dunitz
100 W. Monroe St., Suite 312
Chicago, IL 60603
(312) 782-1477

Mid-Atlantic Council
Elizabeth (Robin) Farquhar
2027 Massachusetts Ave. NW
Washington, D.C. 20036
(202) 232-4242

Midwest Council
Marsha Luhrs
10425 Old Olive St. Road, Suite 205
St. Louis, MO 63141
(314) 997-7566

New Jersey/West
Hudson Valley Council
Kathryn Kahn
1 Kalisa Way, Suite 104
Paramus, NJ 07652
(201) 599-0080

New York Federation
of Reform Synagogues
Ellyn Geller
838 Fifth Avenue
New York, NY 10021
(212) 249-0100

Northeast Council
Paula Brody
1330 Beacon St.
Suite 355
Brookline, MA 02146
(617) 277-1655

Northeast Lakes Council/
Detroit Federation
Nancy Gad-Harf
25550 Chagrin Blvd.
Suite 108
Beachwood, OH 44122
(216) 831-6722

Northern California Council/
Pacific Northwest Council
Linda Walker
703 Market St.
Suite 1300
San Francisco, CA 94103
(415) 392-7080

Pacific Southwest Council
Arlene Chernow
6300 Wilshire Blvd.
Suite 1475
Los Angeles, CA 90048
(213) 653-9962

Pennsylvania Council/
Philadelphia Federation
Linda Steigman
2111 Architects Building
117 S. 17th St.
Philadelphia, PA 19103
(215) 563-8183

Southeast Council/
Southeast Florida Federation
Rabbi Rachel Hertzman
Doral Executive Office Park
3785 N.W. 82nd Avenue, Suite 210
Miami, FL 33166
(305) 592-4792

Southwest Council
Debby Stein
12700 Hillcrest Road
Suite 270
Dallas, TX 75230
(214) 960-6641